COST MANAGEMENT

COST MANAGEMENT

[For Hospitality Industry and Other Service Business Sectors]

M.N. Ahmed

ANMOL PUBLICATIONS PVT. LTD.

NEW DELHI - 110 002 (INDIA)

ANMOL PUBLICATIONS PVT. LTD.
4374/4B, Ansari Road, Daryaganj
New Delhi - 110 002
Ph.: 23261597, 23278000
Visit us at: www.anmolpublications.com

Cost Management

First Published, 2005

ISBN 81-261-2323-0

PRINTED IN INDIA

Published by J.L. Kumar for Anmol Publications Pvt. Ltd., New Delhi - 110 002 and Printed at Mehra Offset Press, Delhi.

Contents

Preface

Tourism and Hotel Industry are the two significant sectors of modern day economy and are complimentary to each other. The new world order has turned the whole mankind into one family or society. Today's world is a global village, where distances have no meaning. Although, tourism and travelling are the two phenomena, as old as the civilized world, yet, tourism evolved into a regular and well-organised industry, during the last century only.

Hotel industry is part and parcel of tourism sector. The tourists are honoured guests and the hotels offer them the demanded hospitality. Hence, the two form a correlated industrial sector, which is growing and flourishing fast, with promises for future.

Extension of education and expansion of knowledge have created a new anxiety, among the members of the new generation, regarding the above said two areas. In fact, the two sectors offer high profile career avenues and good opportunities for aspirants and job-seekers. However, like other disciplines, Tourism and Hotel Management also require proper training for professionals. Hence, a large room for exhaustive and exclusive books on the subject, is there.

This series of comprehensive books has been outlined within the parameters of the syllabi of various universities and institutes, in a broad-based manner, in order to cover all streams of the discipline and for the benefit of students at graduate and post-graduate levels.

The undersigned is confident of a due recognition and proper acknowledgement from concerned circles. Further expectation is that this series of useful books would prove to be practically helpful to the professionals and students equally.

— Editor

1

Introduction

All companies manufacture products, for which cost can be calculated and inventories are valued. Many companies do not manufacture products. They offer services instead of manufacturing tangible products, with no inventories.

Meaning of Service Business : A service business is one, that produces an output, that is not tangible or physical in nature. Many companies come under this category. For exampie, hotel Industry, banking and insurance companies, computer software companies, engineering companies and companies working under architecture, accounting, legal, consulting and communication fields come under this category. In these companies output is provided in the form of advice or information. The concept can be extended further to include such industries, as transportation, utilities, recreation and medical services. In these cases also, services provided in non-physical in nature but requires significant investment in fixed assets. A good example is of Walt Disney World, who provided a services *(i.e.,* recreation or amusement) and invested multibillion dollars in fixed assets to do so. Similarly a firm of chartered accountants, renders services. It requires smaller capital investment but it invests considerably in recruitment, training and retention of employees to provide various services.

The entities working under service sector may provide different types of services and capital investment in different companies may also differ considerably. But one thing is typically common in all service sector companies from a cost accounting perspective—there is no tangible unit of production to measure. There is no physical entity, that can be called work-in-progress or finished goods. In these companies there is no problem of valuation of inventories. This singular difference may call for entirely different approach to cost accounting.

Service business have essentially ignored the key role that cost accounting can play in their operations. Some of the facts are as follows :

Normally attempt is made to determine the variable cost in a service business. Instead all costs are considered fixed. This results in an income statement with no cost of goods sold. Instead there is a revenue line against which all costs are offset, assuming these costs to be fixed. It is noticed that there is no attempt to divide revenues and cost into profit centres. In some cases income statement is made to carefully itemise all types of revenues but cost is offset as lump-sum like fixed costs. Since there is no cost of goods sold, the managers of a service company assume that the break-even point at which zero profits are earned is identical to the points at which all costs equal revenues.

This concept ignores the key issue that some additional cost must be incurred in order to generates additional sales, which increases break-even point. It is often different in services business to ascertain exactly what price to charge for a service. Therefore, it leads to a situation, where many service businesses charge whatever their competitors charge or what they are forced to charge by regulatory mandate. Since there was no emphasis on traces, responsibility accounting was overemphasized. This involves careful tracing of all costs for a specific department, comparing its results to a budget and reporting any variances back to management team.

The above mentioned discussion makes it clear that service companies are not being served well by traditional cost accounting systems. They do not know cost of providing services. They are not in a position to identify the key factors, that would allow them to better manage their business.

Following points should be particularly taken case of by managers of service organisations to bring about cost accounting improvements: It is crucial to direct efforts towards determination of all variable costs incurred whenever a service-related activity is completed. Efforts should be made to organise the cost collection and cost assignment in such a manner that it should be possible to calculate the cost of individual service jobs. Job costing should be used, where jobs require unique output. For example, banking industry for equity placement or a specific audit carried out for a particular objective. Time cards should be kept to record all time spent in working on these jobs, which is then costed summarised by jobs. There are certain situations involving high service transaction volumes where process costing can be used to determine the cost of specific, activities. Examples of this are processing of checks by a bank and the processing of insurance claim forms by an insurance company. The cost accounting staff should keep proper information (data) to facilitate cost-volume-profit analyses for each activity. They should also identify profit centres, to which fixed costs can be assigned with certainty. Managers should collect variable cost and fixed cost by activity and this information can be used to adjust pricing levels, allocate capital, and measure revenue profit centre performance. Pricing for services is frequently driven by rates charged by competitors than by internal costs. In many cases, free services are provided to customers for competition without realisation of about the cost of these services. For example, banking services, for many years included free services related to automated teller machines. Recently some banks have carried out costing services to find out the cost of these functions and now some banks are attempting to pass cost of these services to customers to the outrage of those customers, who have grown accustomed to obtaining these services at no cost. For this purpose, it is necessary to calculate determine capital relating to different activities. For the purpose it is necessary to determine, whether capital should be withdrawn from other service areas. Determine managers' performance based on profitability of service activity under his/her control. It always happens that in some costs, will be incurred during the accounting period for which billing will not occur at a later period. These costs, are service version of capital work-in-progress and should be capitalised during the period. When all the relevant data have been collected and progressed, it is necessary to determine the timing and the details, of reports, to be generated. Speed in generating, the report is vital for good result.

It is possible that all points mentioned above will not be applicable in each case of service costing. However, bottom line is to collect variable cost of each activity so that managers can properly price the activity.

It is often observed that service firms typically charge off all costs to current period. In many cases there are jobs being carried on at the end of accounting period which will still last for many months. The result is distorted profit in both the related accounting periods. In one accounting period cost will be booked with no matching revenue and in the following year, some cost will not be booked for the revenue booked in that year. This problem is very common in auditing, architectural design, consulting and engineering firms. The best remedy for this problem is to capitalise the cost in inventory account under the headings "Jobs work-in-process", and release expenses from this account as matching revenues are billed out. For this purpose, it is necessary that date and time relating to jobs should be properly compiled.

The main requirement for this purpose is that a time tracking system must be in place so that accounting staff can verify how many hours have been worked, that have not been billed. This approach will be particularly useful in companies where levels of profitability constantly change from period to period, because large quantities of unbilled costs, are charged to expenses.

A service company may also suffer from quality-related problems like manufacturing firm. A clear example will be incorrectly processed insurance claim. It must be retrieved from a storage data examined and corrected. Therefore, the working people should have a good knowledge of what type of quality cost it incurs. Typical quality costs are: (i) Appraisal costs, (ii) Prevention costs, (iii) Internal failure costs, and (iv) External failure costs.

In service environment, there is no tangible product and cause of quality problem is traced to the chief source employees. Cost accountant helps in tracking down the causes of specific quality issues. In service environment special attention should be directed towards recruiting best possible employees and retention of those who produce high quality of work.

Even in service environment due attention should be given to preparation of budget. A revenue budget is developed around the major services that the firm provides. For example, in an audit, first major services can be audit, consulting and tax. The professional labour hours to be worked in each area are budgeted based on firm's knowledge of time spent on continuing clients in the past, expected new business and expected mix of audit, consulting and tax work. Billing rates reflect the firm's best estimate of what it will charge for the various categories of professional labour.

2

Development and Growth

Accounting plays a critical role in the efficient use of a firm's resources. Decision-makers operate in a dynamic and complex business environment. Therefore, their information needs change with the changing environment and accounting must adapt to satisfy these changing needs. The importance of financial information has always been recognized but in the light of present business scenario, such information has become a resource parallel in importance to factors of production. As business organisations have begun to recognize this vital resource and their dependence on it, they have also begun to realize that a system for managing this resource is essential. This is perhaps the basic reason for business students to possess some knowledge about accounting.

Modern accounting as a dynamic and growing field has to monitor and analyse the rapidly changing business environment. It has to serve as a vehicle for communicating the essential data about the financial activities of a business to its management for making decisions. At the same time, management must possess a fair knowledge of tools and techniques that it can use for analysing and interpreting the available information in order to accomplish managerial objectives Both these essential elements of modern business financial information and analytical techniques are covered by Management Accounting as it involves the study of accounting information and techniques that managers use in analysing such information.

The Concept

Accounting involves the collection, recording, classification and presentation of financial data for the benefit of management and outside agencies such as shareholders, bankers, creditors and government.

Smith and Ashburne describe it as,, "Accounting is the science of recording and classifying business transactions and events, primarily of a financial character, and the art of making significant summaries, analysis and interpretation of those transactions and events and communicating the result to persons who must make decisions or form judgements." This definition emphasises financial reporting and decision-making aspect of accounting.

The word accounting can be classified into three categories, which are : I. Financial Accounting, II. Cost Accounting, and III. Management Accounting.

Financial Accounting

Financial Accounting may be defined as the science and art of recording and classifying business transactions and preparing summaries of the same for determining year and profit or loss and the financial position of the concern. It is that part of accounting which is employed to communicate the financial information of a business unit.

According to *American Institute of Certified Public Accounts*, "Accounting is the art of recording, classifying and summarising in a significant manner and in terms of money, transactions and events, which are impart at least, of a financial character and interpreting the result thereof."

The analysis of the above definition brings the following points to light :

(i) It is the art of recording and classifying business transactions and events in a systematic manner,

(ii) Transactions to we recorded in monetary terms,

(iii) Summarizing, analysing and interpreting the result of accounting infor-mation, and

(iv) Communicating and explaining the information to decision-makers.

Aims and Objectives

The modern accounting system has to accomplish the following four objectives :

(i) To identify financial events and transactions that occur in an organisation,

(ii) To measure the value of these occurences in terms of money,

(iii) To organize the accumulated financial data into meaningful information, and

(iv) To analyze, interpret and communicate that information to a broad range of persons and groups, both within and outside the organisation.

Informative Sources

Financial information is needed by both investors and management. Financial information is required to predict, compare and evaluate the firm's earning ability. It is also required to aid in economic decision-making investments and financing decision-making. Every enterprise should know the activities carried by it together with their financial implications. The financial score of an enterprise is kept by the accounting system. It points out the problems faced or likely to be faced by the enterprise. It also brings to the notice of the firm opportunities that are likely to arise. It indicates possible action, when needed. In fact, accounting is the guide-post and language of management.

The Motives : To understand the objectives of accounting well, let us define it. Accounting may be defined as :

The process of identifying, measuring and communicating economic information to permit information, judgement and decisions by users of the information. The objectives of accounting are to provide information for the following purposes :

(i) Making decisions concerning the use of limited resources, including the identification of crucial decision areas, and determination of objectives and goals,

(ii) Effectively directing the controlling of an organisation's human and materials resources,

(iii) Maintaining and reporting on the custodianship of resources, and

(iv) Facilitating social functions and controls.

The main objective of accounting is to provide information to the users to make relevant decisions and form judgements. Besides decision-making, the control and custodianship aspects of accounting should also be emphasised. Accounting is also required to serve some broad social obligations since the accounting information is used by a large body of people such as customers, employees, investors, creditors and government.

The decision-making aspect of accounting has also been emphasised yet in another definition, given by the Accounting Principles Board (APB) of the American Institute of Certified Public Accountants :

"Accounting is a service activity, its function is to provide quantitative information, primarily financial in nature, about economic entities that are intended to be useful in making economic decision-in making reasoned choices among alternative courses of action."

The Working : In providing information to users, accounting performs three functions :

Accumulation : The accounting system identifies and gathers relevant data. The process of data accumulation involves recording and analysis of economic events. These records are essentially historical in nature, as the events recorded are the ones which have already occurred.

Measurement : Accounting also performs the measurement function. It assigns monetary value to economic events. While performing this function, it acts in accordance with the generally accepted principles. Some economic events cannot be measured accurately, they are estimated.

Communication : Accounting is the source of business information. Therefore, the information accumulated and measured should be periodically communicated to users. The information is communicated through statements and reports. The financial statements and reports should be reliable and accurate. For the internal use of management, a variety of reports, depending on the information need, may have to be prepared. In communicating information to outsiders, standard criteria of full disclosure, materially, consistency and fairness should be adhered to.

The Users : As stated above, the major job of the accounting system is to collect and provide information. It gathers, classifies, analyses, processes, interprets and communicates data about the economic activities of the firm. The accounting information is needed by a variety of people. Some users of the accounting information have a direct interest in the firm, while others have indirect interest. Those who are directly interested in the financial information are owners, managers, creditors, investors, employees, customers and tax authorities. The indirect users include financial analysts, trade associations or trade unions.

Important Uses : The following are the important users of the accounting informations :

Owners : Owners have the primary interest in the financial information. They have entrusted their financial resources to the firm and, therefore, would like to know periodically its performance. Managers are the custodians of their investments and, therefore, they must submit periodical financial reports to owners.

Managers : Managers are responsible for the overall performance of the firm. They make several decisions and, therefore, need information. Accounting provides relevant information in which managers have a direct interest.

Creditors : Creditors supply financial resource to the firm. They are interested in the continuing profitable performance of the firm so that they may regularly receive interest and repayment of the principal sum. They need accounting information to evaluate the firm's performance and to determine the degree of risk to which they are exposed.

Potential Investors : Potential investors, get an idea about the firm's financial position and performance from its financial reports. They are generally interested in the earnings, dividend and growth trends of the firm. Usually they take the services of financial analyst in evaluating the performance of the firm.

Employees and Trade Unions : They also make use of the financial information revealed in the financial statements. They can bargain on masters relating to salary determination, bonus, fringe benefits or working conditions on the basis of the accounting information. Thus, financial information is useful to employees and unions, as they get insight into matters affecting their economic and social interests.

Customers : Customers might be interested in the financial information because a careful study of the financial statements may provide information about the prices being charged by the firm.

Government : Government also has an interest in the financial statemenl for regulatory purposes. The tax department of government has an interest in determining the taxable income of the firm.

Financial accounting is useful to management as well as to external users such as potential owners, creditors, government agencies and other interested persons. It provides information regarding the status of the business and results of its operations. The following functions of financial accounting are discussed here:

Recording of Information : Accounting is an art of recording financial facts of a concern. It is not possible to remember each and every transaction of the business. Accounting is necessary to supplement human memory. The information is recorded in journal and other subsidiary books. The subsidiary books to be used may be Purchase Book, Sales Book, Return Outward Book, Journal Proper, Cash Book etc. These books are used to record various transactions in such a way that the information is properly classified and analysed so that management may lake use of that information.

Classification of Data : The classification of information means that the data of nature is placed at one place. This is done in the book called 'Ledger'. The entries relating to different items are brought at one place, so that full information of these items may be collected under different heads. For example, we may have accounts called, Salaries, Rent, Interest, Advertisement etc. These accounts will be opened in the Ledger under their heads and all entries relating to these accounts will be posted into these accounts. We will then be able to get full information about these accounts from the Ledger.

Making Summaries : Another function of financial accounting is to make summaries of recorded and classified data. The classified data is used to prepare final accounts, *i.e.,* Profit and Loss Account and Balance Sheet. Profit and Loss Account is prepared from various revenue items for a given period. The Balance Sheet is a summary of various assets and liabilities. The final accounts are prepared to find out operational efficiency and financial strength of the business.

Dealing with Financial Transactions : Only those transactions arc recorded which are measurable in terms of money. Money is taken as a common medium and all economic transactions are expressed in monetary terms. Anything which cannot be expressed in monetary terms does not form a part of financial accounting even though it has a significant bearing on the working of the business. The good behaviour of production manager might have encouraged workers to work more but this vital factor will riot be a part of financial accounting because quality of an individual is not measurable in money.

Interpreting Financial Information : Accounting information is modified in such a way that it is interpreted by the management for drawing conclusions. The interpretation part is very important for decision-making. The outsiders such as creditors, investors, bankers, shareholders are able to form an opinion about the profitability and over all financial position of the business.

Communicating Results : Financial Accounting is not only concerned with the recording of facts and figures but it is also connected with the communication of results. The profitability and financial position of the business are communicated through Profit and Loss Account and Balance Sheet. The persons interested in knowing the results of the business can make their own conclusions from financial statements. The information is supplied at regular intervals.

Making Information more Reliable : Another important function of financial accounting is to make the information more useful and reliable. This is done by the use of internationally accepted accounting standards for preparing accounts. The same accounting principles should be consistently used otherwise the reliability of accounts will not be possible. If we change method of charging depreciation and valuation of stock every year then reliability of accounts will be adversely affected. An effort is made to make the information useful and reliable.

The Shortcomings : The Financial Accounting is mainly concerned with the preparalion of final accounts, *i.e.*, Profit and Loss Account and Balance Sheet. The business has become so complex that mere final accounts information is not sufficient in meeting informational needs. The management needs information for planning, controlling and co-ordinating business activities. It is because of the limitations of financial accounting that Cost Accounting and Management Accounting have developed. Some of the limitations of financial accounting are discussed below :

Historical Nature : Financial accounting is of historical nature. It records only those transactions which have taken place in the business during a particular period of time. The impact of future uncertainties has no place in financial accounting. It does not provide the necessary information to the management for planning control and decision-making. It does not tell how to increase the profit and maximise the return on the capital employed.

Recording of Actual Costs : In financial accounting assets and properties are recorded at their cost. No effect of changes in their value is recorded in the books after their acquisition. The prices of goods and assets go on varying time to time. The present prices of assets may be absolutely different from the recorded costs. Financial accounts do not record price level changes. Thus, it has nothing to do with their realisable or replaceable value.

Financial Accounting Provides Information about the Concern as a Whole : Under it, information is recorded for the whole concern. With the help of financial accounting one can find information about total expenses and total receipts only. The information is not recorded product-wise, department-wise or any other line of activity. It is essential to record information activity-wise, so as to be helpful for cost determination and cost control purposes.

No Provision for Cost Control : Costs cannot be controlled through financial accounting. The cost figures are known only at the end of financial period. When the cost has already been incurred then nothing can be done to control it. There is no technique in financial accounting which can help to ascertain whether the cost is more or less while the expenses are being incurred. There is no procedure to assign responsibility for higher costs, if any. The costing process requires a constant review of actual costs from time to time and this thing is not possible in financial accounting.

No Evaluation of Business Policies and Plans : It is not possible to evaluate business policies and plans in financial accounting. There is no technique for comparing actual performance with budgeted targets. Whether the work is going on as per schedule or not, cannot be determined. The profitability is the only yard-stick for evaluating managerial performance. Profits of an enterprise are influenced by a number of outside factors also, so it is not a reliable test for ascertaining efficiency of the management.

No Help in Decision-making : As the data available is of historical nature, the financial accounting is not of much help to the management in selecting a profitable alternative. There are many situations where management is required to take decision but information provided by financial accounting is not adequate.

Not helpful in Price Fixation : Financial accounting is not helpful in fixing the prices of products. The cost of product can be obtained only when all expenses have been incurred. It is not possible to determine the price in advance. The concern may be required to quote a price for the supply of goods in the near future for submitting tenders etc., but financial accounting can not supply these information. Price fixation requires information about variable and fixed costs, direct and indirect costs, but these can not be obtained through financial accounting. Thus, it is not helpful in price determination.

Chances of Manipulation : There are chances of using financial accounts to suit the whims of management. The over-valuation and under-valuation of inventory may change the figures of profits. More profits may be shown to get more remuneration. The possibility of manipulating financial accounts reduces their reliability.

Lack of Unanimity about Accounting Principles : Accountants differ on the use of accounting principles. In spite of the efforts of International Accounting Standards Committee, there is a lack of unanimity on the use of accounting principles and procedures. The methods of valuing inventory and methods of charging depreciation are the most controversial issues on which unanimity has not been possible. The use of different accounting methods reduces the usefulness and reliability of accounts.

Not Helpful in Taking Strategic Decisions : Management has to take strategic decisions like replacement of labour by machinery, introduction of a new product, discontinuation of an existing line of production, expansion of capacity, etc. Financial accounts cannot provide necessary information for taking important decisions because information is recorded for the whole concern and it is available only when the event has taken place.

Technical Subject : Financial accounting is highly technical in nature. Financial accounting can be prepared only by those persons who possess adequate knowledge of accounting concepts and conventions and are well conversant to the practice of accounting.

Cost Accounting

Evolution : Evolution of Cost Accounting took place because of industrial development and limitations of financial accounting. A business needs classified cost figures for departments, products, processes etc. in order to ascertain cost. It requires adequate cost data for fixing the selling price. It wants to know the reasons for the variation in the costs of any two or more periods. It wants expenses classified into direct and indirect, controllable and uncontrollable. It also needs to analyse losses owing to wastage of materials, idle time, etc. and to control costs of materials, labour and overheads. Additionally, it requires standards for the measurement of operations efficiency and cost data for taking various managerial decisions. Financial accounting does not serve the above business needs. To fill this gap, cost accounting was evolved.

Meaning : Cost accounting is a branch of accounting which deals with the accumulation, classification, analysis, recording, allocation, summarisation, interpretation, reporting and control of current and prospective costs. It also includes determination of forecasted future costs, standard costs and historical costs of products, services, activities, functions, responsibilities etc..

The costing terminology of *I.C.MA. London* defines cost accounting as, "the process of accounting for cost from the point at which expenditure is incurred or ommitted to the establishment of its ultimate relationship with cost centres and cost units. In its widest usage it embraces the preparation of statistical data, the application of cost control methods and the ascertainment of the profitability of activities carried out or planned."

Aims, Motives and Working System : The objectives and functions of cost accounting are :

To ascertain and analyse Costs : The primary objective of cost accounting is to ascertain and analyse cost incurred on the production of various products, jobs, and services, etc.

To Control Costs : Cost accounting has developed various techniques such as standard costing and budgetary control for controlling costs.

To fix the Selling Price : Cost accounting provides reliable data on basis of which selling price can be fixed.

To Reduce Costs : The objectives of cost accounting have been extended to reducing costs. Under the cost reduction plan products, processes, procedures, organisation and methods are continuously scrutinised to improve efficiency and reduce costs. Value analysis, time and motion study, standardisation, simplification, etc. are important techniques of cost reduction.

To Prepare Periodic Statements : Under cost accounting system monthly or quarterly cost statements for periodic review of operating results are prepared.

Provide Information : Cost accounting provides useful information for planning and control and for taking various decisions regarding increase in production, installation or replacement of machines, making or buying of components, continuing or closing down of a business etc.

The Significances : The importance of cost accounting lies in the fact that for the success of any organisation, it is essential that scarce resources such as materials, labour, overheads are used in the best possible way. An efficient system of costing is an essential factor for industrial control under modern conditions of business and, therefore, may be regarded as an important part of the-efforts of any management to secure stability this is possible through effective planning and control, and proper decision-making. In fact, cost accounting has become essential tool of the management. Cost accounting provides necessary information for (i) Planning and control and (ii) Decision-making.

Planning and Control : Planning and control are the basic functions of management. Planning involves the deciding of goals of an organisation and the manner in which they are to be achieved.

On the other hand, control is the process of analysing whether action is being taken as planned, whether results conform to plans and in case of deviations, taking corrective actions to move along the desired course. Thus in control, the activities of an organisation are conformed to the desired plan of action and feedback about actual results is provided through performance evaluation reports.,

Decision Making : Decision-making is the process of selecting a course of action from various possible or available alternatives. Cost accounting plays an important role in the decision-making process. It provides necessary information for a viable decision in given circumstances. Cost accounting techniques serve the management in taking various decisions such as :

(i) What should be the price of a product in normal and special circumstances ?

(ii) Should a component be produced in the factory itself or bought from the market ?

(iii) Should the production of a product be given up ?

(iv) What priority should be accorded to a product?

(v) Should investment be made in a new product ?

(vi) Given a selling price and a cost structure, how much should be produced to earn a desired profit ?

The Merits : The following are the advantages of cost accounting :

(i) Cost accounting is very helpful in controlling expenditure and economizing in the manufacture of product,

(ii) Cost accounting relates various expenses to their functions and provides an effective tool for control over such expenses,

(iii) Cost accounting provides useful data not only about product costs but also about production efficiency and performances,

(iv) It helps the management to initiate action to rectify delays, inefficiencies and wastage. Additionally, it determines normal levels of wastage of materials during storage or in process,

(v) Centralisation of purchasing is facilitated by the use of cost accounting. This results in economical purchasing,

(vi) Maintenance of time and job records for workers reveals losses incurred due to idle time. Such records assist in taking steps to minimise these losses,

(vii) A cost accounting system provides information about availability of materials, labour and machine capacity. In the absence of such information, proper production plans can not be drawn up.

(viii) Cost accounting entails identifying normal and abnormal losses and gains.

This task becomes simpler when standards are got up. Although the getting up of physical standards is primarily the duty of the industrial engineering department, cost accounting also helps a great deal by providing relevant information in this regard,

(ix) Cost accounting lays the basis of the system of standard costing and budgetary control. These two are instrumental in the control of expenditure. Variance analysis and comparison of actual performance with budgets pinpoint areas where economies can be affected,

(x) Cost accounting data help the management in appraising the performance of various units and managers. On the basis of such appraisal the management can encourage the concerned people with suitable rewards and incentives,

(xi) Cost accounting data are very useful for the management for planning various activities. A wise manager takes a decision only after he has carefully studied the cost implications of various alternatives,

(xii) A system of cost accounting provides an independent and reliable check on the accuracy of financial accounts through reconciliation of profit as ascertained by cost accounts and by financial accounts,

(xiii) Management is assisted in its process of routine and special decision-making by various cost concepts, *i.e.*, opportunity cost, relevant cost, marginal cost, etc.

(xiv) The cost department functions as in service department and provides useful and relevant information to various line managers such as sales manager, production manager, etc., which immensely helps them in their day-to-day affairs. For example, the following statements may be provided by the cost department, particularly for the use of managers :

(a) Periodical statements showing the total actual and budgeted costs of each activity.

(b) Statement showing the cost volume profit relationship of various products, *i.e.*, marginal cost and contribution of each product towards fixed overheads and profit.

(c) Sales budget showing the sale quantities of various products and also a summary of the total sales.

(d) Details of budgeted selling and distribution costs analysed territory- wise and product-wise.

(e) Periodical statements comparing actual figures with budgeted figures, classified territory-wise and product-wise.

(f) Statement showing the analysis of cost variances and sales variances.

(g) Ad-hoc statements for pricing purposes or for submitting tenders, etc.

(h) Any other cost statement required by managers for day-to-day decision- making.

The Shorcomings : In spite of so many advantages, some people feel that cost accounting is an unnecessary luxury for business establishments. But this is not true. Perhaps they feel so because of a few limitations of cost accounting such as :

(i) Cost accounting is not an exact and fool proof science, (ii) Classification of cost into its elements, pricing of material issue on the basis of average or standard costs, etc., apportionment and allocation of joint costs and overheads to joint and by-products and cost centres, division of overheads into fixed and variable, division of costs into normal and abnormal, controllable and uncontrollable, etc. are based on conventions, estimation and arbitrariness. The information provided by a cost accountant may not necessarily be absolutely true.

It may be noted that such limitations are also found in any other system of accounting. Principles and practice of cost accounting are based on sound reasoning and keen common sense. The advantages of cost accounting clearly establish that it is useful and necessary for the success of a modern industrial firm.

Management Accounting

Evolution : The financial accounting is mainly concerned with the preparation of final accounts, *i.e.,* Profit and Loss Account and

Balance Sheet. It only ensures that all transactions done with funds entrusted to management have properly been recorded and capital has been kept intact. It measures the income of the concern as a whole by distinguishing between revenues and costs and gives assurance to owners and creditors that their investments are safe. Though, Financial accounting conveys meaningful information to the outsiders, it fails to communicate valuable and varied information to management. Such varied information can be had by interpreting and analysing the results. Thus, recording of transactions is now considered to be the secondary function of the accountant. His primary function is now to analyse and interpret? the results and to report them to various levels of management. It is also alleged that financial accounting does not consider those factors which cannot be quantified. It is also said that financial accounting provides post-mortem records of business events.

A small undertaking with a local character is generally managed by the owner himself. The owner is in touch with day-to-day working of the enterprise and he plans and co-ordinates the activities himself. The use of simple accounting enables the preparation of Profit and Loss Account and Balance Sheet for determining profitability and assessing financial position of the enterprise. All informational needs for managerial purposes are met by simple financial statements. Since the owner is both the decision maker and implementor of such decisions, he does not feel the necessity of any communication system and no additional information is required for managerial purposes. The evolution of joint stock company form of organisation has resulted in large-scale production and separation of ownership and management.

The introduction of professionalism in management has brought in the division of organisation into functional area and delegation of authority and decentralisation of decision-making. The decision-making no more remains a matter of intuition. It requires the evolution of information system for helping management in planning and assessing the results. The accounting information is required as a guide for future. The management is to be fed with precise and relevant information so as to enable it in performing managerial functions efficiently and effectively.

Management accounting was not known to the business world until 1950. The term was first formally described in a report entitled *'Management Accounting'* in 1950. The report was published by the *Anglo American Council of Productivity* Management Accounting Team after its visit to united states during April, May and June 1950. The terminology of cost accountancy had no reference to the word management accountancy before the report of this study group. The complexities of business environment have necessitated the use of management accounting for planning, co-ordinating and controlling functions of management.

Additionally, at present, when the tempo of our thinking and way of life in general having become faster, technological changes taking place day-after-day, economic and social values being obsolete over the night, the business or management can no longer wait upto the end of the year to know the relationship and problems arising from the day-to-day business transactions. He must know the effects of his policies sooner than it is too late and he is totally overpowered by the economic forces. In other words, correct information regarding the effect of each business transactions must be gathered often from week to week or from month to month.

Further, cost accounting, no doubt, serves the internal management by directing their attention on inefficient operations and assisting in a day-to-day control of activities of the enterprise. But even costing information fails to meet informational needs for managerial functions. The costing data needs to be arranged, re-analysed and processed further for playing more effective role in the managerial process. In addition to costing and accounting data, managerial functions need the use of socio-economic and statistical data. These informations are beyond the scope of cost accounting and financial accounting which pave the way of emergence of management accounting. Management accounting provides all possible information required for managerial purposes. Probably, these are the main reasons which provided impetus to the development of the techniques which is now commonly known as management accounting.

The Concept : Management Accounting is comprised of two words 'Management and Accounting'. It is the study of managerial aspect of accounting. It is the presentation of accounting information in such a way as to assist management in the creation of policy and the day-to-day operation of an undertaking. Thus, it relates to the use of accounting data collected with the help of financial accounting and cost accounting for the purpose of policy formulation, planning, control and decision-making by the management.

Some leading definitions of management accounting are as follows :

1. "Management accounting is concerned with accounting information that is useful to management."

   - R.N. Anthony

2. "Management accounting is the term used to describe the accounting methods, systems and techniques which, coupled with special knowledge and ability, assist management in its task of maximising profits or minimising losses."

   J Batty

3. "Management accounting is the adaptation and analysis of accounting information and its diagnosis and explanations in such a way as to assist management."

   -T.G. Rose

4. "The essential aim of management accounting should be to assist management in decision making and control."

   —Brown and Howard

5. "Management accounting is the presentation of accounting information in such-a way as to assist management in the creation of policy and the day-to-day operation of an undertaking."

   —Anglo-American Council on Productivity

6. "Such of its techniques and procedures by which accounting mainly seeks to aid the management collectively have come to known as management accounting."

   — The Institute of Chartered Accountants of India

7. "Management accounting is a system of collection and presentation of relevant economic information relating to an enterprise for planning, controlling and decision making."

— The Institute of Cost and Works Accountants of India

8. "Any form of accounting which enables a business to be conducted more efficiently can be regarded as management accounting."

—Institute of Chartered Accountants of England and Wales

From the various definitions discussed above it becomes clear that financial data is recorded, analysed and presented to the management in such a way that it becomes useful and helpful in planning and running business operations more effectively and systematically.

Salient Features : The following points may be considered as the characteristics or the nature of management accounting :

Technique of Selective Nature : Management accounting is a technique of selective nature. It takes into consideration only that data from the income statement and position statement (Balance Sheet) which is relevant and useful to the management. Only that information is communicated to the management which is helpful for taking decisions on various aspects of the business.

Concerned with Future : Management accounting unlike the financial accounting deals with the forecast with the future. It helps in planning the future because decisions are always taken for the future course of action.

Providing Accounting Information : Management accounting is based on accounting information. The collection and classification of data is the primary function of accounting department. The information so collected is used by the management for taking policy decisions. Management accounting involves the presentation of information in a way it suits managerial needs. Management accounting is a service function and it provides necessary information to different levels ofmanagement.

Taking Important Decisions : Management accounting helps in taking various important decisions. It supplies necessary information to the management on the basis of which decisions are taken. The historical data is studied to see its possible impacts on future decisions. The implications of various alternative decisions are also taken into account while taking important decisions.

Increase in Efficiency : The purpose of using accounting information is to increase efficiency of the concern. The efficiency can be achieved by sotting up goals for each department. The performance appraisal will enable the management to pin point efficient and inefficient spots. An effort is made to take corrective measures so that efficiency is improved.

No Specific Rules Followed : In financial accounting certain rules are followed for preparing defferent accounting books. On the other hand, no specific rules arc followed in management accounting. Though the tools of management accounting are the same but their use differ from concern to concern. The analysis of data depends upon the person using it. The deriving of conclusions also depends upon the intelligence of the management accountant. Every concern has its own rules and by-rules for analysing the data.

No get Formats for Information : Management accounting does not provide information in a prescribed proforma like that of financial accounting. It provides the information to the management in the form which may be more useful to the management in taking various decisions on the various aspects of the business.

Analysis of Different Variables : Management accounting helps in analysing the reasons as to why the profit or loss is more or less as compared to the past period. Moreover, it tries to analyse the effect of different variables on the Profits and Profitability of the concern.

Provides Data and not the Decisions : The management accountant is not taking any decision but provides data which is helpful to the management in decision- making. It can inform but cannot prescribe. It is just like a map which guides the traveller when he will be if he travels in one direction or another. Decisions depend on the efficiency and wisdom of the management.

Use of Special Techniques and Concepts : Management accounting uses special techniques and concepts to make accounting data more useful. The techniques usually used include financial planning and analysis, standard costing, budgetary control, marginal costing, project appraisal, control accounting etc. The type of technique to be used will be determined according to the situation and necessity.

Achieving Objectives : In management accounting, the accounting information is used in such a way that it helps in achieving organisational objectives. Historical data is used for formulating plans and setting up objectives. The recording of actual performance and comparing it with targeted figures will give an idea to the management about the performance of various departments. In case there are deviations between the standards got and actual performance of various departments corrective measures can be taken at once. All this is possible with the help of budgetary control and standard costing.

Sphere and Scope : The scope of Management Accounting is very wide and broad based. It includes all information, which is provided to the management for financial analysis and interpretation of the business operations. The following field of activities are included in the scope of this subject :

Financial Accounting : Financial accounting though provides historical information but is very useful for future planning and financial forecasting. It is an essential perquisite of any discussion of management accounting. Financial statements contain enough information that is used by management for decision-making. Management accounting contains only tools and techniques and it gets the data for interpretation and analysis mainly from financial accounting. Thus, without efficient financial accounting system, management accounting cannot be operative.

Cost Accounting : Cost accounting provides various techniques for determining cost of manufacturing products or cost of providing service. It uses financial data for finding out cost of various jobs, products or processes. Business executives depend heavily on accounting information in general and on cost information in particular because any activity of an organisation can be described by its cost. They make use of various cost data in managing organisations effectively. Cost accounting is considered as the backbone of management accounting as it provides the analytical tools such as Budgetary Control, Standard Costing, Marginal Costing, Inventory Control, Operating Costing, etc., which are used by management to discharge its responsibilities effectively.

Financial Management : Financial management is concerned with the planning and controlling of the financial resources of the firm. It deals with the raising funds and their effective utilisation. Its main aim is to use the fund in such a way that the earning of the firm is maximised. Today finance has become the life blood of any business concern. Although, financial anagement has emerged as a separate subject, management accounting includes and extends to the operation of financial management also.

Financial Statement Analysis : The various parties (users) concerned with the financial statements may need information, which can be obtained by financial statement analysis and developing certain trends and ratios. A person can gain meaningful insights and conclusions about the firm with the help of analysis and interpretation of the information contained in financial statements. Different techniques have been developed which can be used for the proper interpretation and analysis of financial statements.

Interpretation of Data : The work of interpretation of financial data is done by the management accountant. He interprets various financial statements to the management. This interpretation of data gives an idea about the financial and earning position of the concern. These statements may be studied in comparison to statements of earlier periods or in comparison with the statements of similar other concerns. The significance of these reports is explained to the management in a simple language. If the statements are not properly interpreted then wrong conclusions may be drawn. So, interpretation is as important as compiling of financial statements.

Management Reporting : Clear informative, timely reports are essential management tools in reaching decisions that make the best use of firm's resources. Thus, one of the basic responsibility of management accounting is to keep the management well informed about the operations of the business. The reports are presented in the form of graphs, diagrams, index numbers or other statistical techniques so as to make them easily understandable: The management accountant sends interim reports to the management and these reports may be monthly, quarterly, half yearly. These reports may cover Profit and Loss statement, fund flow statement, cash flow statement, stock reports and reports on orders in hand, etc. These reports are helpful in giving a constant review of the working of the business.

Quantitative Techniques : Modern managers believe that the financial and economic data available for managerial decisions can be more useful when analyzed with more sophisticated analysis and evaluation techniques. The techniques such as time series, regression analysis and sampling techniques are commonly used for this purpose. Further, managers also use techniques such as linear programming, game theory, queuing theory etc., in their decision-making process.

Budgeting and Forecasting : Budgeting means expressing the plans, policies and goals of the enterprise for a definite period in future. Budgetary control, controls the activities of the business through the operation of budget by comparing the actuals with the budgeted figures, finding out the deviations, analysing the deviations in order to pinpoint the responsibility and take remedial action so that adverse things may not happen in future. Forecasting, on the other hand, is a prediction of what will happen as a result of a given set of circumstances. Forecasting is a judgement whereas budgeting is an organisational object. Both budgeting and forecasting arc useful for management accountant in planning various activities.

Inflation Accounting : Inflation accounting attempts to identify certain characteristics of accounting that tend to distort the reporting of financial results during the period of rapidly changing prices. It devises and implements appropriate methods to analyse and interprete the impact of inflation on the financial information.

Inventory Control : Inventory control is used to devote stock of raw materials, work-in-progress and finished products. Inventory has a special significance in accounting for determining correct income for a given period. The management should determine different levels of stocks, *i.e.*, minimum stock level, maximum stock level, re-ordering level, danger level, etc. for inventory control. The control of inventory will help in controlling costs of products. Management will need effective inventory control for controlling stocks. Management accountant will guide management as to when and from where to purchase and how much to purchase. Thus, the study of inventory control will be helpful for taking managerial decisions.

Tax Accounting : In the present complex tax system, tax planning is an important part of Management Accounting. Taxation plays an important role in the profitability of a commercial concern. Therefore, it is essential for a management accountant to have a complete knowledge of business taxation. The Business Profit and tax thereon is to be ascertained as per the provision of taxation. The filing of tax returns and the payment of tax in due time is exclusively the responsibility of management accountant.

Cost Control Procedure : These procedures are integral part of the management accounting process and includes inventory control, cost control, labour control, budgetary control and variance analysis, etc.

Methods and Procedures : It includes in this study all those methods and procedures which help the concern to use its resources in the most efficient and economical manner. It undertakes special cost studies and estimations, reports on cost volume profit relationship under changing circumstances.

Internal Audit : The internal audit is a discipline of management accounting. It makes arrangements for performance appraisal of the firm's various departments. Thus, a management accountant must possess knowledge about the fixation of responsibilities and measurement of results.

Office Services : To discharge the responsibilities efficiently a management accountant has to deal with data processing, filing, copying and duplicating. His area of responsibilities also includes the evaluation and reporting about the utility of different office procedures and machines.

The Distinction : Financial accounting and management accounting both are the two branches of the accounting information system of business enterprise. Financial accounting is concerned with the recording of day-to-day transactions of the business. These transactions are classified according to their nature. These transactions enable the concern to find out Profit and Loss for a particular period and financial position of the concern is also judged on a particular date through Balance Sheet. On the other hand, management accounting uses financial account. The accounts are used in such a way that they are helpful to the management in planning and forecasting various policies. Thus, financial accounting has a significant influence on management accounting. Further the principles of financial accounting are equally useful in management accounting. Both financial and management accounting arc complemen-tary and are necessary in running the concern effectively.

Despite the close relationship, there are certain points of distinction between financial accounting and management accounting. The main points of distinction are discussed below :

Objects : The main object of financial accounting is to measure business income and communication of information to the various categories of persons, such as, management, creditors, supplier's of goods, bankers, investors, etc. whereas, the main objectives of management accounting is to help the internal management in formulating policies and plans.

Nature : Financial accounting is objective in nature. It lays emphasis on the past activities and represents historical records just to show the results of the business. On the other hand, management accounting is subjective in nature. It stresses the future and uses historical costs and data for estimating the future. Thus, management accounting has prospective character.

Compulsion : The Indian Companies Act, 1956 has made financial accounting obligatory for joint stock companies to maintain a system of financial accounting. At the same time, the benefits as offered by a financial accounting system have made it more or less compulsory for the non-company organisation. On the other hand, the setting up of management accounting system is at the discretion of the management.

Subject Matter : Financial accounting considers the business as one entity and accordingly financial accounting reports have been confined to the business operations as a whole. Such statements present the position and the performance of the entire business. On the other hand, under management accounting system each unit/department is treated as a separate entity in order to ensure effective planning and control. Therefore, profitability and performance reports are prepared for each unit or division of the business separately.

Accounting Principles : Financial accounting system is based on sonic accounting principles and conventions which a financial accountant has to strictly follow, while preparing financial accounts and statements. On the other hand, management accounting is not bound by generally accepted accounting principles and conventions. The preparation of reports and statements under management accounting are governed by the requirements of the management. Management can frame its own ground rules and principles regarding form and content of information required for internal use.

Precision : Financial accounting pays more emphasis on precision and considers only actual figures in the preparation of its statements. There is no scope for approximate figures in financial accounting. On the other hand, the reports and statements prepared under management accounting system contain more approximate figures than the actual figures. Thus, management accounting is less precise as compared to financial accounting.

Frequency of Reports : The financial statements are prepared at the end of financial period which is usually a period of twelve months. But the management accounting reports and statements are prepared at a regular intervals so that management may not face any difficulty in decision-making. Management is constantly informed about the business performance through these, reports and statements. Thus, the reporting frequency of management accounting is much higher as compared to the reporting of financial accounting.

Nature of Data Used : The financial statements as prepared under financial accounting contain only such transactions that are expressed in monetary terms. The non-monetary events such as nature of competition, business reputation, change in fashion, are not at all considered by financial accounting. But management accounting uses both monetary and non-monetary data.

Recipients : Financial statements such a Profit and Loss account and balance sheet, are extensively used by outsiders, *i.e.*, shareholders creditors, tax authorities etc. on the other hand, management accounting reports and statements are exclusively meant for management. Such reports are not easily available for outsiders.

Methodology : Financial accounting records the transactions relating to income, revenue, personal accounts and property accounts, etc. whereas management accounting reports, cost and revenue by profit centre or responsibility centre.

Reporting : Financial accounts are prepared to find out profitability and financial position of the concern. These reports are useful for outsiders like bankers investors, shareholders, Government agencies, etc. These reports arc prepared nol only for the benefit of the concern but also for outsiders. On the other hand, management reports are meant for internal use only. These are prepared for the benefit of different levels of management. Financial report such as profit and loss account is prepared for a specific period and not on a particular date. On the other hand, there is no such binding for preparing management accounting reports. The main idea for preparing these reports is to enable the management to have a view about the position of the concern and no consideration is given to the period. Management accounting reports are rather future projections of figures.

Period : Financial accounts are prepared for a particular period. Profit and Loss account is generally prepared for one year. All the items relating to that year are taken to Profit and Loss Account. Balance Sheet is prepared on a particular date. It reveals the financial position of the concern on that date. Management accountant supplies information from time to time during the whole year. There are no specific period for which management accounts are prepared.

Audit : Financial accounts can be got audited. Under Companies Act, 1956 auditing of financial accounts is compulsory.

On the other hand, management accounts can not be audited. They are not based on actual figures and projected data are also used in management accounting. So it is not possible to get management accounts audited.

Publication : The financial accounting statements are almost published by every business concern for the information of the general public. The Indian Companies Act, 1956 has made it compulsory for every company to publish its final account, *i.e.*, Profit and Loss Accounts and Balance Sheet. On the other hand, management accounting reports and statements are not published.

From the above discussion we can conclude that financial and management accounting are necessary for a concern. While financial accounting lays more emphasis on the past but is very essential for future forecasting of the events. Management accounting though deals with the future events but has to take into consideration the past events also. For becoming a successful management accountant, knowledge of financial accounting is very essential.

The Difference : Cost accounting and management accounting both have the same objectives of helping the management in planning, control and decision-making. Both are internal to the organisation and use common tools and techniques like standard costing variable costing, budgetary control etc. Inspite of these similarities there are certain differences between these two.

The main distinction between these two are discussed as follows:

Object : The object of cost accounting is to record the cost of producing a product or providing a service. The cost is recorded product-wise or unit-wise. Besides recording, it deals with cost control, matching of costs with revenue and decision- making. On the other hand, the object of management accounting is to provide information to the management for planning and co-ordinating the activities of the business.

Scope : The scope of cost accounting is narrow as compared to management accounting. It deals primarily with cost ascertainment. On the other hand, the scope of management accounting is very wide. It includes Financial accounting, cost accounting, budgeting, tax planning, reporting to management and interpretation of financial data.

Nature : Management accounting is generally concerned with the projection of figures for future. The policies and plans are prepared for providing future guidelines. On the other hand, cost accounting uses, both past and present figures.

Nature of Data Used : In cost accounting only those transactions are recorded which can be expressed in figures. In other words, only quantitative aspect is recorded in cost accounting. On the other hand, Management accounting uses quantitative and qualitative data both.

Deals With : Cost accounting deals with ascertainment, allocation, apportion- ment and accounting aspect of cost. On the other hand, Management accounting deals with the effect and impact of cost on the business.

Base : Cost accounting provides a base for the management accounting. On the other hand, Management accounting is derived from both cost accounting and financial accounting.

Status : The status of cost accountant comes after the management accountant. On the other hand, management accountant is senior in position to cost accountant.

Tools and Techniques : Cost accounting has standard costing, variable costing break-even analysis etc. as the basic tools and techniques. On the other hand, alongwith these, the management accounting has funds and cash-flow statements, ratio analysis etc. as accounting tools and techniques.

Period of Planning : Cost accounting is concerned with short-term planning. On the other hand, management accounting is concerned with both short-term and long-term planning and uses techniques like sensitivity analysis, probability structure etc. Its special field is evaluation of capital investment projects.

Assistance: Cost accounting merely assists the management with functioning. On the other hand, management accounting assists and evaluates the management performance.

Principle Followed : Certain principles and procedures are followed for recording costs of different products. The same rules are applicable at different time too. On the other hand, no specific rules and procedures are followed in reporting management accounting. The information is prepared and presented as is required by the management.

Installation : Cost accounting can be installed without management accounting. On the other hand, in management accounting, financial and cost accounting are taken as the base for its installation.

Development : The development of cost accounting is related to industrial revolution. Financial accounting could not satisfy information needs of management. Cost accounting was thus evolved as a supplementary accounting method. On the other hand, management accounting has developed in the last fifty years. Thus, management accounting and cost accounting are both complementary subjects. ′

Significant Role : The main objectives of the management is to manage the business in a systematic way following a plan, allocating responsibilities to implement the plan, organising methods to execute the plan and also obtain efficiency. To achieve this, the management accountant is required to present the information to the management in such a form so that it may be helpful in formulating policies, making-decisions, planning activities and controlling business operations. The main objectives of management accounting are discussed below:

Helpful in Planning and Formulation of Policies : Management accounting assists management in planning the activities of the business. Planning is deciding in advance what is to be done, when is to be done, how is to be done and by whom it is to be done. It involves forecasting on the basis of available information, setting goals, framing policies, determining the alternative courses of action and deciding on the programme of activities to be undertaken.

Thus, planning is making intelligent forecasting. This forecasting is based on facts. Facts are provided by past accounts on which forecast of future transactions is made. Management accounting helps management in its function of planning through the process of budgetary control.

Helpful in Organising : Organisation is related to the establishment of relationship among different individuals in the concern. It also includes the delegation of authority and fixing the responsibility. Management accounting is concerned with establishment of cost centres, preparation of budgets, preparation of cost control accounts and fixing the responsibility for different functions. This all needs the intensive study of the organisational structure. In turn, it helps to rationalise the organisational structure or efficient organisational frame work.

Helpful in Interpreting Financial Information : Accounting is a technical subject and may not be easily understandable by everyone till the user has a good knowledge of the subject. Management may not be able to use the accounting information in, its raw form due to lack of knowledge of accounting techniques. Management accountant presents the information in an intelligible and non-technical manner. This will help the management in interpreting the financial data, evaluating alternative courses of action available and guiding the management in taking decisions. If necessary, management accountant uses statistical devices like charts, diagrams, index numbers, etc. So that the information is easily followed.

Motivating Employees : Management accounting helps the management in selecting the best alternatives of doing the things. Targets are determined by the employees. They feel motivated in achieving their targets and further, incentives may be given for improving their performance.

Helpful in Co-ordination : Management accounting helps the management in co-ordinating the activities of the concern. It provides tools which are helpful in co-ordinating the activities Of different departments. The work of co-ordination is done through functional budgeting. Management accountant acts as a coordinator and reconciles the activities of different departments. Thus, management accounting is a useful tool in co-ordinating the various operations of the business.

Helpful in Controlling Performance : Management accounting devices like standard costing and budgetary control are helpful in controlling performance. For this work is divided into different units and separate goals are set up for each unit and the responsibility of a particular person is determined. The actual results are compared with pre-determined objectives. The management finds out the deviations and takes necessary corrective measures. Different departmental heads are associated with preparing budgets and setting up goals. The management accountant acts as a co-ordinating link between different departments and he also monitors their performance to the top management. Thus, the management is also to control performance of each and every individual with the help of management accounting devices.

Helps in Decision-making : The management of any concern has to take certain important decisions. Whenever there is a question of starting a new business, expanding or diversifying the existing business, strategic business problems has to be faced and solved. Similarly when in a particular situation, there are different alternatives as whether labour should be replaced by machinery or not, whether selling price should be reduced or not, whether to export the item or not etc., the management accountant helps in solving such problems and decision-making. For such decisions, the management accountant may take the help of marginal costing, cost volume profit analysis, standard costing, capital budgeting etc. Management accounting provides feed back to the management such as, what business to engage in or diversify, how to run that business efficiently. This is the most important contribution which the management accountant has made.

Communicating-up-to-date Information : One of the primary objectives of management accounting is to keep the management fully informed about the latest position of the concern. Management needs information for taking decisions and for evaluating performance of the business. The required information can be made available to the management by means of reports which are an integral part of the management accounting. Reports are means of communication of facts which should be brought to the notice of various levels of management so that they may be guided for taking suitable action for the purpose of control.

Helpful in Evaluating the Efficiency and Effectiveness of Policies: Management accounting also lays emphasis on management audit which means evaluating the efficiency and effectiveness of management policies. Management policies are reviewed from time to time to make an improvement in them so that maximum efficiency may be achieved.

Helpful in tax Administration : The complexities of tax system are increasing day-after-day. Management accounting helps in assessing various tax liabilities and depositing correct amount of taxes with the concerned authorities. Various tax returns are to be filed under different tax laws. Tax administration is carried on with the advice and guidance of the management accountant.

Various Methods : Management accounting is an information system designed to communicate meaningful economic and financial information to the managers so that they may discharge their functions efficiently. The management accounting system consists of a number of tools and techniques which are frequently used by the management accountant to meet the increasing needs of the business. The main techniques and methods of management accounting are discussed below :

Financial Planning : Planning is necessary not only for efficient utilization of resources but also for better and progressive business results. Financial planning is the process of deciding in advance financial objectives, policies and procedures. An organisation can achieve long-term as well as short-term financial objectives by employing financial planning. In the short-term, it can help a concern in meeting its obligations by balancing the flow of funds. At the same time, its proper application can ensure efficient utilization of available financial resources in the long period.

Analysis of Financial Statement: The analysis of financial statement is meant to classify and present the data in such a way that it becomes useful for the management. The meaning and significance of the data is explained in non-technical language. The techniques of financial analysis include comparative financial statements, trend analysis, ratio analysis, fund flow statements, etc.

Historical Cost Accounting : The historical cost accounting provides past data to the management relating to cost of each job, process and department so that comparison may be helpful to the management for cost control and future planning.

Marginal Costing : This is a method of costing which is concerned with changes in costs due to changes in the volume of production. Under this system, cost of product is divided into variable and fixed costs. Marginal costing is helpful for measurement of profitability of different lines of production, different departments and divisions of an enterprise. The decision about short-term utilisation of capacity is also assessed with the help of marginal costing.

Budgetary Control : It is a system of costing which uses budgets as a tool for planning and control. The budgets of all functional departments are prepared in advance. The budgets are based on historical data and future possibilities. Under this system, the actual performance is recorded and compared with the pre-determined targets. With the help of budgetary control, the management is able to assess the performance of each and every in the organisation. Thus, budgetary control is an important technique of directing business operations to achieve a satisfactory return on investment.

Standard Costing: Standard costing is an important technique for cost control purposes. Under this technique, costs are determined in advance. The actual costs are recorded and compared with the standard costs. The variance, if any are analysed and their reasons are ascertained. It helps to increase the efficiency of the concern and also 'management by exception'.

Decision Accounting : Taking-decision is the important work of management. Decision-taking involves a device from various alternatives. There may decisions about capital expenditure, whether to make or buy, what price to be charged, expansion or diversification etc. The management accounting helps the management through the techniques of marginal costing, capital budgeting, differential costing to select the best alternative which will maximise the profits of the business.

Funds Flow Statement : The management accountant uses the technique of funds flow statement in order to analyse the changes in the financial condition of the concern between two period. It explains, wherefrom the funds are coming in the business and how these are used in the business. It helps a lot in financial analysis and control, future guidance and comparative studies.

Revaluation Accounting: Revaluation accounting is also known as Replacement Accounting. The management accountant assures the maintenance and preservation of the capital through this technique. It brings into account the impact of changes in the prices on the preparation of the financial statements. According to J. Batty "Revaluation accounting is used to denote the methods employed for overcomingthe problems connected with fixed asset replacement in a period of rising prices."

Communicating : The success or failure of the management is dependent on the fact, whether requisite information is provided to the management in right form at the right time so as to enable them to carry out the functions of planning, controlling and decision-making effectively. The management accountant will prepare the necessary reports for providing information to the different levels of management by proper selection of data to be presented, organisation of data or selecting the appropriate method of reporting.

Control Accounting : Control accounting is not a separate accounting system. Different systems have their control devices and these are used in control accounting. Standard costing and Budgetary control can be exercised through variance analysis reports. In control accounting we can use internal check, internal audit, statutory audit for control purposes.

Statistical and Graphical Techniques : The management accountant uses various statistical and graphical techniques in order to make the information more meaningful and presentation of the same in such form so that it may help the management in decision-making. The techniques used are master chart, chart of sales and earnings, investment chart, linear programming, statistical quality control, etc.

Management Information System : With the development of electronic devices for recording and classifying data, reporting to management has considerably improved. The data planning coordination and control is supplied to the management. Feed back of information and responsive actions can be used as control techniques.

Working System : Management accounting is a special part of accounting. It has developed out of the need for making more and more use of accounting for taking managerial decisions. Management accounting is assigned the functions of classifying, presenting and interpreting data in such a way that it helps management in controlling and running the business in an efficient and economical manner. The major functions of management accounting are summarized below :

Planning and Forecasting : Planning is an activity of the management that requires an efficient system of decision-making. In any type of enterprise, plan should be made to guide future operations of the business. Thus, one of the major functions of* the management accountant is to help management in the selection of company's goals and in the formation of policies and strategies to allocate resources to achieve these goals. Different accounting techniques are used by the management to discharge the function of planning efficiently. The important among them are financial statements analysis, budgeting, direct costing, capital budgeting, standard costing, marginal costing, trend ratios, funds flow statement, probabilities, etc. These techniques are useful in planning various activities.

Modification of Data : Management accounting helps in modifying accounting data. The information available is modified in such a way that it becomes useful for the management. If sales data is required, it can be classified according to product, area, season-wise, type of customers and time taken for getting payments, etc. Similarly, if production figures are required, these can be classified according to product, quality, time taken by the manufacturing processes, rate of production, etc. The modification of data makes the data more understandable and useful. Management accountant classifies the data according to the need of the management.

Financial Analysis and Interpretation : Management accountant performs the work of presenting financial data in a simplified way. Financial data is generally collected in a technical way. But, top managerial personnel may lack technical knowledge. So management accountant analyses and interprets financial data in a simple way and presents it in a non-technical form. Further, he gives his opinion about various alternative courses of action so that it becomes easy for the management to take a correct decision.

Co-ordination : The co-ordination among different departments or units is essential for smooth functioning of the concern. The management accountant acts as the oo-ordinator in this regard. The techniques such as budgeting, financial reporting and analysis and interpretation are commonly used by management accountants to co-ordinate efficiently the various activities of the; business. The efficient co-ordination increases the efficiency of organisation which in turn increases the profitability of a concern.

Communication : The management accountant prepares various reports to communicate the results to the different levels of management, to motivate the employees, to exercise effective control on their activities and to enable the management to take sound decisions. He also communicates with the outside world account the progress of the business through published accounts.

Helpful in Taking Strategic Decisions : Management accounting helps in taking strategic decisions. It supplies analytical information regarding various alternatives and the choice of management is made easy. These decisions may be regarding seasonal or temporary stoppage of production, replacement decisions, expansion and diversification of works, etc. with the help of management accounting, correct decisions are taken in this regard.

Special Studies : Modern business is operating under such dynamic conditions where even a minor change in business can have a significant impact on the business results. Therefore, management is always interested to know the area of business which can contribute to the stability and profitability of the concern. To meet this objective, management accountant undertakes various special studies such as sales analysis, economic forecasts, price spread analysis, etc.

Information to Various Levels of Management : Every management level needs accounting information for decision-making and policy execution. Top management takes broader decisions and leave day-to-day decisions for the lower levels of management. Management accountant feeds information to different levels of management so that further decisions are taken. The supply of adequate information at the proper time will increase efficiency of the management.

Helps in Managerial Control : Management accounting is very useful in controlling performance. For this, the standards of various departments and individuals are set-up. The actual performance is recorded and deviations are ascertained. It enables the management to assess the performance of everyone in the organisationand corrective measures are taken, if necessary. Performance evaluation is possible through standard costing and budgetary control which are an integral part of management accounting.

Qualitative Information : Management accounting is not restricted to the use of monetary data only rather it is concerned also with the use of qualitative information. While preparing a production budget, management accountant may not only use the past production figures, but he may rely on the assessment of persons dealing with production, productivity reports, consumer surveys and may other business documents. The use of qualitative information is as useful as monetary information.

The Significance : In the present complex industrial world, management accounting has become an integral part of management. Management accountant guides and advices management at every step. Management accounting not only increases efficiency of the management but it also increases the efficiency of the employees. The main advantages of management accounting are discussed below :

Determination of Aim: Management accounting on the basis of the information available determines its goal and tries to find out the route through which it can reach the goal.

Helpful in the Preparation of Plan : Present age is the age of planning. That producer is considered as most successful producer who produces articles according to the plan and needs of the consumers. Before taking any plan the manager must study and analyse the present and future of the business.

Easy to Take Judgement : Before taking any plan or to determine policy, there are several plans or policies before the management and on the basis of their study he decides which plan or policy to be adopted so that it may be more useful and helpful.

It Increases Efficiency of the Business : Management accounting increases efficiency of the business concern. The targets of different departments of the enterprise are determined in advance and the achievement of these goals is taken as a tool for measuring their efficiency.

It Provides Effective Management Control : The tools and techniques of management accounting are helpful to the management in planning, controlling and co-ordinating activities of the business. The getting of standard and assessing actual performance regularly enables the management to have 'management by exception'. Everybody assesses his own work and immediate actions are taken in case of deviation in performance.

Better Service to Customers : The cost control devices used in management accounting enables the reduction in prices. All employees in the concern are made cost concious. The quality of products becomes good because quality standards are pre-determined. The customers are supplied goods of good quality at reasonable prices.

Measurements of Performance : The technique of budgetary control and standard costing enables the measurement of performance. In standard costing, standards are determined first and then actual cost is compared with standard cost. It enables the management to find out deviations between standard cost and actual cost. The performance will be good if actual cost does not exceed the standard cost. Budgetary control system too helps in measuring efficiency of all employees.

Maximum Profits can be Obtained : In this process every possible efforts are made to control unnecessary expenses. The incapability or inefficiency is removed. New systems or techniques are found out to achieve the goal, so that there may be maximum profit out of the capital invested in the business.

Safety and Security from Trade Cycle : The information received from the management accounting gives more or throws enough light over the past trade cycles. The management tries to ascertain the causes of trade cycle and its affect. Thus, management accounting tries to safeguard the organisation from the affect of trade cycle.

The Shortcomings : Despite of the fact that the management accounting is very useful for the business concern, still it has got certain limitations which are discussed below :

It is based on Financial Accounting : Whatever information the management accounting gets, they are of the financial accounting. The accuracy of the management decisions is based on the correctness of these informations. If financial data is not reliable then management accounting will not provide correct analysis. Its effectiveness is limited to the reliability of those sources.

Lack of Knowledge : For taking a sound decision it is necessary that the management must have knowledge of various fields like accounting, statistics, economics, taxation, production, engineering and so on. But it has been observed that the person who is taking the decisions may not have comprehensive knowledge of all such subjects.

Lack of Continuity and Co-ordination : In order to make the conclusions drawn bymanagement accountant meaningful, they must be implemented in the organisation at various levels. But in actual practice they loose their significance because it is not feasible to implement such conclusions.

Lack of Objectivity: There is every possibility of personal bias and manipulation from the collection of data to the interpretation stage in financial accounting. Thus, it losses objectivity and validity.

Costly : The installation of management accounting system in a concern requires large organisation and a wide net work of rules and regulations and thus requires a heavy investment. Therefore, it can not be utilized by the small organisations.

Evolutionary Stage : The management accounting is in a recent origin and still in an evolutionary stage. New theories and new techniques are being introduced every now and then. Thus, it is essential to keep a continuous track for the latest theories and their application.

Effect of Time Element: The information received in management accounting are all past and by the time the information and statistics are introduced, the situations are all changed and this condition puts the organisations in difficulties.

It cannot be Treated as an Alternative to Management : It must be remembered that by seeing its activities it can be said that management accounting can not be treated as an alternative to management. By providing a system for relevant data reporting, management accounting assists the management in taking proper decisions rather than making available to it readymade decisions.

Difficulty of Psychological Resistance : There is the difficulty of psychological resistance by the staff. Introduction of a new system needs a corresponding change in the style and attitudes of personnel. It calls for a rearrangement of personnel as well as their activities. But this is a time consuming process and during initial stage, staff difference certainly possesses a problem.

Wider Scope : The scope of management accounting has become so wide that the task to be performed becomes too difficult and complex. Sometimes the objectives laid down are so ambitious that they seems unattainable.

Unquantifiable Variable : There are various problems in business which cannot be expressed in monetary terms. Such problems cannot be interpreted for the future.

The Conventions : As discussed earlier, management accounting is a science but not an exact science. Most of the conclusions derived on the basis of management accounting depend upon the intelligent interpretation of data. It is well known that even in the case of Financial Accounting some conventions have been developed with the passing of time. No such rules have been propounded for management accounting as in the case of Financial Accounting. The common practices, which have been adopted by management accountants to deal with a special problem from time to time, have taken the form of management accounting conventions. Some important concepts or conventions are discussed below:

Management by Exception : The concept 'management by exception' should be followed in communicating the accounting information on the basis of management accounting. According to this concept the management should pay attention only to those business problems which are 'unusual' or 'exceptional' of the planned programme. The practical application of this concept is possible through various reports, such as,

(a) Management reports related to :

  (i) Comparison between actual performance and standard determined,

  (ii) Comparison between previous year and current year, and

  (iii) Actual and budgeted results.

(b) Special Extra ordinary Reports in connection with unusual events.

(c) Reports in respect of Variance Account, Discount and Doubtful Account, Wastage Account, etc.

Principle of Key Areas : There are some key areas of operation almost in all business concern. The success or failure of the whole business depends upon the success or failure of these areas. For example, stocks may comprise of many items, but only few items may account for neerly 70 to 80% of total stocks. The management may control the total stocks by concentrating over these few items only. Therefore, Management Accounting should especially lay more emphasis on these few areas of the life of a business concern.

Responsibility Accounting : The organisational structure of an enterprise should present a clear picture about the authority and responsibility of each employee, executive, manager and departments also.

If an accounting report and internal control is designed in respect of each level of centre, then the person responsible for any particular task can easily be pointed out. This method of preparing accounting reports on the basis of level of centre is known as

Responsibility Accounting, which depicts not only as what is happening in the business but also as who is responsible for such happening. Thus, it is accepted convention of Management Accounting that for every event someone of the personnel is held responsible.

In addition to the above, J. *Batty* in his book *'Management Accounting'* has stated the conventions of Management Accounting as under :

(i) There should be integration of all management information.

(ii) Management Accounting should be forward looking.

(iii) Accounting is concerned with the recording of business transactions only.

(iv) Cost and revenues should be matched as far as possible.

(v) Capital employed should be kept intact at current price.

(vi) All future losses should be considered in the calculation of profit, but expected profit or unrealised profit should not be considered.

(vii) The form of accounting information (past, present or future) should be designed to meet the special need of the business.

(viii) There should be consistency and stability in methods, procedures and principles followed.

(ix) Managerial reports and statements should not be used as substitute for personal dealing.

(x) Direct costs should be apportioned to cost centres or recovered by products.

Controller-status

The Definition : Management Accountant or Controller is the Chief Accountant under Management Accounting. In America, he is called controller. In the industrial country the work done by the accountant is considered as very important and wide-spread. Therefore, the chief accountant finds himself unable to cover the work in the absence of administrative and technical capacity. In other words, any person responsible for the supply of accounting information to the management is known as management accountant. He feeds informational needs of different managerial levels. The position of Management Accountant is different in different business.

The Status : The organisational status of Management Accountant varies from concern to concern depending upon the character of management accountant as well as upon the pattern of management system in that particular concern. He may be considered as Executive in some concerns, while he may be a member of Board of Directors in case of some other concerns. Generally, he occupies a key status in the organisation heading the Accounting Department by a number of specialists such as, Financial Accountant, Cost Accountant etc. At the same time, he functions in perfect co-ordination with executive heads of all functional and service departments. He collects information regarding the various departments through financial and cost accountants and after making suitable analysis of it sends it back to the concerned department along with his suggestions. Sri P. L. Tandon in his paper 'The Role of Accountants in General Management' presented in the Fourth All India Seminar on Management Accounting, Lucknow, has described the status of Management Accountant as under :

"The Management Accountant is exactly, like the spokes in a wheel, connecting the rim of the wheel and the hub receiving the information. He processes that information and then returns the processed information back to where it came from."

However, the controllers institute has suggested the following organisational status of the management accountant :

(i) He should be an executive officer at the policy-making level responsible directly to chief executive officer of the business. His appointment or removal should require the approval of the Board of Directors.

(ii) He should be required by the Board of Directors to present directly Periodic reports covering the operating results and financial conditions of the business.

(iii) He should preferably be a member of Board of Directors and all other top policy-making-groups. At least, he should be invited to attend all meetings of such groups.

A closely related to status of Management Accountant is the question of responsibility of Management Accountant. As discussed earlier, Mangement Accountant assists the various levels of management by furnishing alternative plans and their profitability. He is not concerned with the task of decision-making, which remains the job of top management. As such, if a wrong decision is being taken, who should be held responsible for that? If the decision taken happens to be wrong one on account of inaccuracy biased and fabricated data furnished by the Management Accountant, he shall be held responsible for the wrong decision taken by the management.

Significant Factors : A Management Accountant must possess the following qualities :

Knowledge of Accountancy : Management accountant must have a thorough knowledge of financial accounts and cost accounts. If he will not have the knowledge of these accounts, he can not gather the proper information concerning these accounts.

Knowledge of Statistics : He must have the knowledge of statistical methods, so that he may classify and analyse the data collected over charts, diagrams, tables etc. and can be placed before the management.

Knowledge of Economics : Many facts of the business are based on economic laws. On the basis of demand and supply the price is determined. Determination of the production, full use of capital, are taken into consideration at the time of deciding future policy. Therefore, the management accountant must have the knowledge of economics.

Knowledge of Law : Present business is surrounded with the complexities of law. So many decisions of the business are based on legal decisions. Issue of new capital, distribution of dividend, depreciation and reserve, publication of final accounts, audit, etc. are also many problems which have its own legal importance. No body can ignore them. Therefore, the management accountant must have the knowledge of law.

Knowledge of Psychology : Management accountant controls not only the costs but he has to control the workers as well. If he has knowledge of psychology then he can take better work from the workers and can supply current and up-to-date information to the management.

Personal Qualities : The management accountant can make best use of his status and opportunities, if he possesses the following personal qualities :

(i) Acceptable Personality

(ii) Ability to receive the views of management and to apprehend the desired information.

(iii) An understanding to fill the role of a specialist and adviser.

(iv) A comprehensive knowledge of management theory and practice.

(v) A balanced outlook.

(vi) Ability to think and confer with top management.

Working System : The functions of Management Accountant depend upon his status in the organisation, needs of the enterprise and personal capabilities of the persons. But whatever may be the status of management accountant in a business concern, his main function is to help management in performing the various functions. In addition to his routine duties an accountant has a responsibility to analyse, inlerprete and report the operating results to top management with an objective to assist in framing policy and in directing and controlling day-to-day operation. It is his duly to keep management at all levels duly informed of their actual positions.

The Financial Executives Institute, America has specified the functions of the controller (Management Accountant) as follows :

Planning for Control: Management accountant establishes, co-ordinates and maintains an integrated plan for the control of operations. Such a plan would provide cost standards, expenses budgets, sales forecasts, capital investment programmes, profit planning and the system to effectuate the plans.

Reporting : Management accountant measures performance against given plans and standards. The results of operations are interpreted to all levels to management. This function will include installation of accounting and costing system and recording of actual performance so as to find out deviations, if any.

Evaluating : He should evaluate various policies and programmes. The effectiveness of planning and procedures to attain the objectives of the organisation will depend upon the calibre of the management accountant

Administration of Tax : Management accountant is expected to report to government agencies as required under different laws and to supervise all matters relating to taxes.

Appraisal of External Effects : He is to assess the effect of various economic and fiscal policies of the government and also to evaluate the impact of other external factors on the attainment of organisational objects.

Protection of Assets : The protection of business assets is another function assigned to the management accountant. This function is performed through the maintenance of internal controls, auditing and assuring proper insurance coverage of assets.

The Responsibility : The primary duty of management accountant is to help management in taking correct policy decisions and improving efficiency of entrepreneurial operations. This duty may require him not only to help management with the necessary information from the business sources but he may have to collect information from outside sources too. The information is made useful by arranging and re-adjusting in such a way that the management is able to understand its significance and utility for managerial purposes. Institute of America has defined the following duties of management accountant or controller :

(i) The installation and supervision of all accounting records of the corporation;

(ii) Collection of information from business sources as well as from outside sources too;

(iii) The preparation and interpretation of financial reports and statements of the corporation;

(iv) The Audit of accounts and records;

(v) The compilation of production costs and distribution costs;

(vi) The taking and costing of all physical inventories;

(vii) The preparation and filing of tax returns and the supervision of all matters relating to taxes;

(viii) The maintenance of adequate records of all contracts and leases;

(ix) The approval for payment of all cheques promissory notes and other negotiable instruments;

(x) The preparation and interpretation of all statistical records and reports of the corporation.

(xi) The ascertainment that all properties are properly and adequately insured,

(xii) The ascertainment that financial transactions covered by minutes of the Board of Directors and are properly executed and recorded;

(xiii) The examination of all warrants for withdrawal of securities and determination that such withdrawals are made in conformity with the bye-laws and regulations established;

(xiv) The preparation or approval of the regulations or standard practices required to assure compliance with orders or regulations issued by government and its agencies.

(xv) As budget director, the preparation of annual budget covering all activities for submission to the Board of Directors.

The Organisation : For the effective operation of the business concern it is necessary that the organisation of controller's division should be designed in an effective manner. He must organise the whole accounting division in such a way that there is prompt and immediate recording of the entire information flowing into his department from other functional and service departments. The organisation depends upon the size of business and nature and pattern of business. If the size of business is small, then one or more accounts clerks may be appointed in management accounting department and the work of recording the original records may be assigned to them and accounting activities can be performed by appointing general accountant. But, in the case of large scale concerns the organisation of accounting department may be functional or divisional.

Organisation of management accounting can be divided under three heads, which are as follows:

I. On the basis of Accounting (Functional) system.

II. On the basis of Divisional or Departmental system.

III. On the basis of Tax Accounting Division system.

The organisation of this department includes cost departments Budget department, General Accounting department and Internal Audit department. These departments are given under the charge of Chief Cost Accountant, Supervisor of Budgets, Chief Accountant and Chief Auditor.

The Distinction : The important difference between the workings of the financial accountant and management accountant are as follows :

Writing of Accounts : The working of the financial accountant is restricted only to the writing of the accounts of business according to the law. This work is done according to the fixed customary rules laid down and does not require more intelligence and efficiency. On the other hand, the work of management accountant is to execute the information in a planned and well organised manner. The execution of the information requires more intelligence, better imagination and efficiency.

Its use and Benefit : The information supplied by the financial accountant is prepared for the use and benefit of the outsiders. Whereas, the information given by the Management accountant is mostly for the use of insiders and are prepared for their benefit.

Information in General not in Parts : The information prepared by the financial accountant is always related to the complete business. Whereas the information prepared by the management accountant indicates to the specific department of the business and are divided in separate parts and division.

Work : The work of financial accountant is related with the transactions of the business already done. Whereas, the work of the management accountant relates to the work of future plan and accounts preparation of the future.

Principles Followed : Financial accountant does the accounting work under certain fixed principles. He is surrounded with the law of accounts and he cannot deviate even an inch with the principles laid down. Whereas, the work of management accountant is not surrounded with laws and rules. He prepares accounts as per convenience and to suit the business. He is not to follow the rules laid down and is not binding on him to follow the principles.

Correctness and Accuracy : Financial accountant maintains complete correctness and accuracy and his account gives a correct statement of even one paisa. Whereas, management accountant while preparing information put emphasis on the nearest of the accuracy.

Monetary Transactions : Financial accountant in his accounts gives the information of monetary transactions. Whereas, management accountant keeps in mind non-monetary transactions, for example, changes in the value of money competition, etc.

3

Concept and Perception

Life Cycle Costing is the accumulation of costs for activities, that occur over entire life cycle of a product from the inception to the abandonment by the manufacturer and consumer. It focusses on total cost (capital cost + revenue cost) over the products life including design, development, acquisition, operation, maintenance and servicing. Service costs include marketing, distribution, administration and after-sales service costs. The terms "cradle to grave" and "womb to tomb" are the different terms which are used in the context of life cycle costing to convey the attempt to capture fully all costs associated with the product during life span. CIMA defines life cycle costing as the practice of obtaining over their life time, the best use of physical asset at the lowest cost of entity. Terotechnology is another term which is used as synonym for life cycle costing. This life cycle costing is a technique, which takes account of total cost of owning physical asset, or making a product during its economic life.

The term 'Life Cycle Cost' has been defined as follows, *"it includes the costs associated with acquiring, using, caring for and disposing of physical asset including the feasibility studies, research, design, development, production, maintenance, replacement and disposal as well as support, training and operating costs generated by the acquisition use, maintenance and replacement of permanent physical assets."*

Life cycle costing is specially important in industries that face rapid technological or style changes. Periodic external financial statements may make a product appear to be worthwhile, because its development costs were initially expensed. But, in total, the company may have not even have recovered its original investment. Over the product or service life cycle, companies need to be aware of and attempt to control the total cost of making a product or providing a service.

Life Cycle

Each product has a life cycle. The product life cycle spans from the time of initial R & D to the time at which support to customers is withdrawn. The life cycle of a product vary from a few months to several years. For motor vehicles, this time may span from 5 to 10 years. For some pharmaceutical products, product life cycle may be 3 to 5 years. Intensive global competition and technological innovation combined with increasingly discriminating and sophisticated customers demands have resulted in dramatic decline in product life cycles. It is now being realised increasingly that in order to be successful, companies must now speed up the rate at which they introduce new products to the market. Being later to the market than the competitors may have a dramatic effect on product profitability.

Phases of Product Cycle : A typical product life cycle has four stages, *i.e.*, introduction, growth, maturity and saturation and decline as follows:

Introduction : When the product is introduced to the market, already heavy expenditure will have been incurred on product development and perhaps also on the purchase of new fixed assets and building up stocks for sale. On introduction to market, the product begins to earn some revenue, but initially demand is likely to be small. Potential customers will be unaware of the product or service and the organisations may have to spend further on advertising to bring the product or service to the attention of the market.

Growth : The product gains a bigger market as demand builds up. Sales revenues increase and the product begins to make a profit. The initial costs of the investment in the new product are gradually recovered.

Maturity : A point comes eventually when the growth in demand for the product will show down it will enter a period of relative maturity. It will still continue to be profitable. The product may be modified or improved as a means of sustaining its demand.

Saturation and Decline : At last a point comes, when it starts appearing that market has bought enough of the product. It will, therefore, reach a saturation point. Demand will start to fall. For some time, the product will be still profitable in spite of declining sales, but eventually it will become a loss maker. This is the time when organisation should decide to stop selling the product or service and so the product's life cycle should reach its end.

Salient Features

This major characteristics of product life cycle are as follows:

(i) After all products have limited life and they pass through the phases of introduction, development, growth, maturity and decline as discussed earlier,

(ii) Product's revenue, cost and profit patterns tend to follow predictable courses.

(iii) Profit per unit varies as products evolve through life cycle.

(iv) Each phase throws a new challenge and calls for a specific strategic decision.

(v) By finding new uses and new users, it is possible to extend life of a product.

Different Levels

Life cycle of a manufactured product follows following stages:

Ascertaining Relevant Market Segment : First step is to attempt a market survey. Effort is made to find out what the customer wants, what customer is ready to pay, status of competition, potential demand.

Specification : After search in the market, it is possible to establish, what is to be made. A detailed specification of what is required is given to engineering and designing department. It is necessary to tell engineering department about maximum permissible manufacturing cost, the number required, delivery date and required functional nature of the product.

Decision : Based on the specifications given, the design engineers produce drawings and process schedules, which define the geometry ofproject and some of its manufacturing processes.

Prototype Manufacture : From the drawings, first of all attempt is made to produce a prototype. This prototype will help to ascertain whether the product will meet the laid down parameters.

Development : When a product is made for the first time, it rarely meets the requirements. A lot of work is done in development stage to make the product to conform to the laid down specifications.

Manufacture : When it has been established that the product will meet the laid down specifications and it will be profitable as well, attempt is made to manufacture the product. It means arranging for input material, labour and facilities for manufacture.

Marketing : This involves arranging for market expansion and ensuring that the product reaches the desired market. This stage may involve a lot of expenditure on advertisement.

After-sale Service : After the product has been sold, it is necessary to maintain reputation to provide after-sale service to the customer. Sometimes it requires maintaining the whole after-sale service group.

Decommissioning and Withdrawal : After the life of the product, the plant used to produce the product is sold/scrapped/or disposed of in a manner, that is suitable. Even this stage may involve expenditure, as at times decommissioning is very expensive.

Life Cycle Costs : Life cycle costs are incurred for both: (i) Product and services from design stage through development to market launch, production and sale and their eventual withdrawal from market, and (ii) Fixed cost, *i.e.*, capital equipment, etc.

The component elements of a product's cost over its life cycle should include:

(a) Acquisition cost, *i.e.*, costs of research design, testing, production, construction or purchase in case of capital equipment.

(b) Product distribution, i.e., transport and handling.

(c) Maintenance cost, i.e., such costs as customer service, field maintenance and "in factory" maintenance.

(d) Operation costs *i.e.*, the costs incurred in operations such as energy costs and various facility and other utility costs.

(e) Training, *i.e.*, operator and maintenance training.

(f) Inventory costs, *i.e.*, cost of handling and warehousing costs.

(g) Technical data costs, i.e., costs of purchasing any technical input.

(h) Retirement and disposal, *i.e.*, cost at the end of product's life or life of capital equipment.

The advocates of life cycle costing argue that all these costs should be evaluated together as an integrated package of cost over the product life cycle, when the initial decision to design the product or purchase the capital equipment in first taken. It is being realised that habit of budgeting for these costs separately after the product launch decision or purchase decision has been taken, is a bad management accounting practice.

Life Cycle Costs of a Capital Asset

The life cycle costs of a capital asset are summarized below:

(a) If the asset is constructed 'in-house':

(i) Research and development,

(ii) Design specifications,

(iii) Manufacturing,

(iv) Quality control and testing,

(v) Design modifications,

(vi) Recruitment and training of operating staff and maintenance engineers.

(b) If the asset is purchased from the supplier:

(i) Acquisition cost,

(ii) Installation,

(iii) Commissioning,

(iv) Obtaining spares,

(v) Recruitment and training of operating staff and maintenance engineers,

(vi) Purchase of auxiliary maintenance equipment. The operating costs for an item of capital equipment include not just operator costs and maintenance costs but also indirect materials, tools, and cost of support services such as materials handling, quality control, energy costs, continued training requirement for new stan, etc.

Factors to be taken into account with operating cost include:

(a) the cost of lost production during down time due to preventive maintenance work on breakdown repairs;

(b) the cost of poor performance if the equipment produces poor quality of output;

(c) the cost of low utilisation, because the equipment does not match the original specifications.

Disposal costs for a fixed asset can be significant because the asset must be demolished or dismantled and removed and the site is made good for alternative use. These costs may be off-set by the disposal value of the assets.

Different Perspective : 1. From a manufacturing standpoint, profitability is viewed on a long-range basis rather than period by period basis. Basically, producers of goods and providers of services are concerned about maximising profits over a product's or service's life cycle, because revenue must be generated in excess to product cost (not just current cost) for a product to be truly profitable. This approach is different from finding out periodic profit for the related accounting period. 2. For financial purposes, cost incurred for R & D is expensed during those periods, development cost is amortised. Here, capitalisation of R & D cost would provide a better long-range profitability information. This may be against the treatment laid down in accounting standards, but it will be good for management decision-making. The purpose of life cycle costing is different than finding out periodic results.

Thus, companies desirous to focus on life cycle costs and profitability will need to change their internal accounting treatment of costs.

Life Cycle Costing as an Aid to Operational Decision-making: Life cycle costing as a concept can be used to help decision-making by evaluating alternative courses of action:

(a) alternative methods of maintenance and logistic support.

(b) alternative equipment design specifications.

(c) alternative inventory policies.

(d) alternative quality control policies.

(e) alternative product transportation, distribution and handling methods.

(f) alternative product guarantee or warrantee options.

(g) alternative disposal methods.

Other benefits of Product Life Cycle Costing:

(a) Results in adoption a course of action which is viable technically and financially.

(b) Better decisions ensue due to realistic and accurate assessment of revenue and costs.

(c) It results in adoption of long-term rewarding project.

(d) It provides framework for considering total incremental costs over the entire span of a product. Analysis on these lines facilitates to ascertain the areas where cost effectiveness might be improved.

Life-Cycle Budgeting : Life-cycle budgeted costs can provide important information for pricing decisions. For some products, the development period is relatively long, and many costs are incurred prior to manufacturing.

To be profitable, TCS must generate revenues to cover costs in all six business functions. A product life cycle budget highlights the importance of setting price and budgeting revenues to recover costs in all the value-chain business functions rather than costs in only some ofthe functions (such as production). The life-cycle budget also indicates the costs to be incurred over the life of the product.

Three combinations of the selling price per package and predicted demand are shown. The high non-production costs at TCS are readily apparent in the above statement. For example, R & D and product-design costs constitute over 30% of total costs for each of the three combinations of selling price and predicted sales quantity. TCS should put a premium on having as accurate a set of revenue and cost predictions for General Ledger as possible, given the high percentage of total life-cycle costs incurred before any production begins and before any revenue is received.

Above statement assumes that the selling price per package is the same over the entire life cycle. For strategic reasons, however, TCS may choose to "skim the market" by charging higher prices to customers eager to tryGeneral Ledger when it first comes out, and lower prices to customers who are willing to wait. The life-cycle budget will then express this strategy.

Life Cycle Reports : Most accounting systems emphasize reporting on a calendar basis— monthly, quarterly, and annually. In contrast, product life cycle reporting does not have this calendar-based focus.

Developing life cycle reports for each product requires tracking costs and revenues on a product-by-product basis over several calendar periods. For example, the R & D costs included in a product life cycle cost report are often incurred in different calendar years. When R & D costs are tracked over the entire life cycle, the total magnitude of these costs for each individual product can be computed and analysed.

A product life cycle reporting format offers at least three important benefits:

1. The full set of revenues and costs associated with each product becomes visible. Manufacturing costs are highly visible in most accounting systems. However, the costs associated with upstream areas (for example, R & D) and downstream areas (for example, customer service) are frequently less visible on a product-by-product basis.
2. Differences among products in the percentage of their total costs incurred at early stages in the life cycle are highlighted. The higher this percentage, the more important it is for managers to develop, as early as possible, accurate predictions of the revenues for that product.
3. Inter-relationships among business function cost categories are highlighted. For example, companies that cut back their R & D and product-design costs may experience major increases in customer-service costs in subsequent years. Those costs arise because products fail to meet promised quality-performance levels. A life cycle revenue and cost report prevents such causally related changes among business function costs from being hidden (buried) as they are in calendar income statements.

Life cycle costs further reinforce the importance of locked-in costs, target costing, and value engineering in pricing and cost management. For products with long life cycles, a very small fraction of the total life cycle costs are actually incurred at the time when costs are locked-in. But locked-in costs will determine how costs will be incurred over several years. Automobile companies combine target costing with life cycle budgeting. For example, Ford, General Motors, Mercedes, and Toyota determine target prices and target costs for their car models on the basis of estimated costs and revenues over a multi-year horizon.

Management of environmental costs provides another example of life cycle budgeting. The enactment of strict environmental laws has introduced tougher environmental standards and increased the penalties and fines for polluting the air and contaminating subsurface soil and groundwater. Environmental costs are often locked-in at the product and process design stage itself. To avoid these environmental liabilities, companies design products, processes, and procedure to prevent and reduce pollution over the product's life cycle.

A different notion of life cycle costs is customer life cycle costs. Customer life cycle costs focus on the total costs to a customer of acquiring and using a product or service until it is replaced. Customer life cycle costs for a car, for example, include the cost of the car itself plus the costs of operating and maintaining the car minus the disposal price of the car. Customer life-cycle costs can be an important consideration in the pricing decision.

Life Cycle Costing and Management Control : When life cycle costing is used for capital investment appraisal, the aim of life cycle management then switches to control, i.e., monitoring actual life cycle costs and comparing them with the expected costs. Cost targets are allocated to specific stages in product life cycle. As the product evolves through its life cycle and through each stage of its development or use, cost figures should be gathered for what the various costs of products are and these should be compared with original targets. Where there is excess spending over the target, the variance should be reported and corrective action should be taken where appropriate. Control action might consist of action to reduce costs of the existing asset, but it will also include (a) action to improve the design or specifications for future capital purchases, and (b) action to improve the life cycle costing technique that are being used so that future capital asset purchase decision will be better.

Life Cycle Costing and Capital Investment Appraisal : It is a healthy practice to take into account life cycle costing for capital investment appraisal. Following considerations are relevant to optimise life cycle costs:

(i) Ascertaining capacity and quantity of capital asset.

(ii) Quantification of life cycle costs besides purchase costs for each option.

(iii) Optimise a trade-off between acquisition costs, commissioning costs, operating costs, maintenance costs and disposal costs, etc. over the economic life of each asset.

At times, a company has to decide between two alternative items of capital investments to buy, i.e., item *x or* y. This decision should not be taken based on which alternative is cheaper. This would mean buy now and pay later attitude.

The cheaper alternative may cost more to operate and maintain and it may be worth much less on eventual disposal. A higher capital cost may have the advantage of lower maintenance cost for the whole of the asset's operational life of asset. The inter-active nature of elements calls for a total assessment of physical asset life cycle costs. The trade-off between capital costs, maintenance costs and disposal costs or value can be important for the design of a product as well as the purchase of capital equipment.

The Advantages : 1. It can provide important information for pricing decisions. This is essential in present-day context because for some products, development period is relatively long and many costs are incurred prior and after manufacturing. 2. It helps the manager to develop insight and plan so that it is possible to generate revenue from the product; which covers costs relating to all six categories, (i.e., research and development, product design, manufacturing, marketing, distribution, customer service) and not only one sub-set of the categories *i.e.,* manufacturing. In a software packaging company, research development and product design cost contributes to approximately 30% of total cost. In these situations, life cycle costing is of immense value. 3. It broadens the perspective of manager because complete life cycle relating to product is kept in view and for this reason the term "cradle to grave" and "womb to tomb" are often used in the context of life-costing. It does not have calendar based focus, but considers whole life span of the product. 4. Pull costs associated with each product becomes relatively more visible. Manufacturing costs are highly visible in most accounting system. However the costs associated with upstream areas (for example, research and development) and down-stream areas (for example, customer service) are often less visible at a product-by-product level in the lorganisation following traditional costing. Life cycle costing finds solution to this problem. 5. Life cycle costing highlights inter-relationships across cost categories. Many companies, who cut R & D costs, later experience major increases in customer-service-related costs in subsequent years. The products of these companies also failed to meet promised quality performance level. A life-cycle revenue and costs statement highlight hidden area, which get obscured in cost statements having calendar-based focus. 6. The life cycle costing is immensely useful in capital budgeting decisions (*i.e.,* long-term decision-making). It considers both capital costs and revenue costs relating to the product/project over its life span. It makes explicit the trade-off between higher capital costs and lower maintenance running costs.

Target Costing **:** Target costing is one of the few "proactive" costing activities, that an accounting department performs. Most of the costing work involves an after -the-fact review of costs, that have already been incurred. Only in the case of target costing, a cost accountant takes an active part of the new product design team apprising the design team of the current cost of a design as well as the impact of contemplated design change on cost.

The basic idea beneath target costing is that all product costs are pre-determined before a product even reaches the production floor. For example, types of material to be used, production method to be used, etc. can be determined before actual production.

In this types of situation cost reduction focus of any company should be to review the costs of products, while they are still in the design stage. Every effort at the design stage is done to keep these costs to a minimum.

Definitions **:** Target costing has been described as a process, that occurs in a competitive environment, in which cost minimisation is an important component of profitability. It is based on the promise that cost planning, cost management and cost reduction must necessarily occur in the design development process of the product to minimise the total life cycle cost of the product. All acceptable definition of target costing does not exist, following important definitions have been given:

Sakurai says, "Target costing can be defined as a cost management tool for reducing the overall cost of a product over its entire life cycle with the help of production, engineering, research and design, marketing and accounting departments."

Cooper writes, "The purpose of target costing is to identify the production cost for a proposed product such that the product, when sold, generates the desired profit margin."

Horwath on behalf of Consortium of Advanced Manufacturing International (CAM-I) defines it as, "Target costing is a set of management methods and tools to drive the cost and activity goals in design and planning for new products to supply a basis for control in the subsequent operations phase and to ensure that those products reach given life cycle profitability targets."

Kato defines it as, "In reality, target costing is not a quantification technique, but rather a complete cost reduction programme starting even before the first drawings of the product have been prepared. It is an approach aimed at reducing the cost of new products throughout their life cycle, while meeting customer requirements in terms of quality and reliability among others, examining all conceivable ideas relating to cost reduction at the planning, development and prototyping stages. Target costing is not a simple cost reduction technique but a complete profit management system."

Based on the above, common themes relating to target costing can be summarised as follows:

(i) They emphasise the importance of target price and profit determination before calculating the target cost.

(ii) They emphasise the importance of early cost planning to reduce costs incurred over the products entire life cycle.

(iii) They indicate that a cross-functional team is needed to successfully implement target costing.

Major Themes : Following major thoughts permeate target costing: (i) *Price-based cost targets.* In target costing a company starts by predicting the market place. It attempts to draw a map of customer segments. It, then, focusses on these attractive market segments to determine what level of quality and function will succeed in that customer segment and what price customers will be willing to pay for the product (i.e., target price). Target selling price is first established based on perceived value of the product to customer. Then target profit or margin is determined. The estimated cost to produce the product is typically higher than the target cost because market forces require a company to lower its cost and reduce profit product engineering is than used to reduce the estimated cost to target cost (which is also the allowable cost). Suppose target price of the hypothetical product MRs. 750. The hypothetical target profit is Rs. 200. In this situation target cost can be calculated as Rs. 550. Suppose estimated (drifting) cost by the product in Rs. 675. Now in this situation, cost reduction efforts of target costing team will focus on reducing the estimated cost of the product by Rs. 125, so that product can be sold in market at a profit, that company seems acceptable. (ii) *Early cost planning*. A major advantage of target costing is that it forces the company to plan its forces, profits and costs much earlier than is typical for most companies. Target costing requires that considerable cost calculations be made before a product is introduced. Once target cost is established, cost must be allocated to products' parts and sub-assemblies. (iii) *Cross-functional involvement*. Target costing is basically a cross-functional company exercise. It is essentially a multi-functional activity. A basic requirement is inter-disciplinary teams. It requires simultaneous involvement of marketing, technical and economic skills. Normally a target costing team includes people from such diverse functions as production technology, design, purchasing, development, marketing, manufacturing, product planning, finance or accounting.

Four Steps Approach of Process of Target Costing : Target costing process involves following four steps:

(i) *Conduct Market Research*. A thorough review of the market place is done to see what products are in market place. This also involves finding out what new products the competitors are trying to bring in the market. Effort is also made to ascertain customer requirements. All these efforts on these lines give the company a general outline of revenue plan in terms of number of units, that can be sold and the price, at which they will sell. (ii) *Determining Margin and Cost Feasibility*. Based on the market survey, as referred to in step 1, effort is made to determine a price, at which the product is likely to sell. On the selling price, a standard margin is determined to finally come to a cost figure, that a product cannot exceed. Now efforts are made to see whether the product based on approved design can be produced within the range of 'cost figure' arrived at above. If this is not possible, design product is cancelled as unfeasible. (iii) *Meet margin targets by design improvement.* Sometimes it so happens that product designed cannot be produced in the 'cost range' decided. In this type of situation, value-engineering is used to drive down the product cost to a level, at which target price and margin can be attained. After it is ensured that product of specified design can be produced in desired cost range, the design is finalised and resulting bill of materials is sent to purchasing staff for procurement and the engineering staff proceeds to install all required changes to the production facility needed to implement low-cost production process. (iv) *Implement Continuous Improvement.* The production is launched first through a pilot production run and afterwards it is produced at full production volumes. Cost accountant plays an important role by collecting actual cost and reporting variances. He tries to ensure that targeted cost levels are maintained subsequent to design phases. This is known as ongoing continuous improvement programme known as 'Kaizen Costing', that focusses on the reduction of waste in the production process, thereby lowering cost below the initial targets specified during the design phase.

Implementing Target Pricing and Target Costing : Developing target prices and target costs require the following four steps:

Step 1: Develop a product that satisfies the need of potential customers.

Step 2: Choose a target price based on customers' perceived value for the product and the prices competitors charge, and a target operating income per unit.

Step 3: Derive a target cost per unit by subtracting the target operating income per unit from the target price.

Step 4: Perform value engineering to achieve target costs. Value engineering is a systematic evaluation of all aspects of the value-chain business functions, with the objective of reducing costs while satisfying customer needs. Value engineering can result in improvements in product designs, changes in materials specifications, or modifications in process methods.

Managers often find the distinction between value-added and non-value-added activities and costs useful in value engineering. A *value-added* cost is a cost that customers perceive as adding value, or utility (usefulness), to a product or service. Determining value-added costs requires identifying attributes that customers perceive to be important. Activities and the costs of these activities do not always fall neatly into value-added or non-value-added categories. Some costs fall in the gray area in between, and include both value-added and non-value-added components. The following examples are drawn from classifications made by operating personnel at a General Electric medical equipment assembly plant:

Category	***Examples***
Value-added costs	Costs of assembly, design, tools, and machinery
Non-value-added costs delivery, and obsolete	Costs of rework, expediting, special inventory.
Gray area	Costs of testing, materials movement, and ordering.

Problems with target costing. Certain limitations levelled against target costing are:

(i) Product development can be lengthened to a considerable extent because design team may require a number of design iteration before it can devise a sufficiently low-cost product; that meets the target cost and margin criteria.

(ii) Large amount of mandatory cost cutting can result in finger pointing in various parts of the company. For example, the industrial engineering staff will not be happy if it is required to completely alter the production layout to generate cost savings, while purchasing staff is not required to make any cost reductions through supplier negotiations.

(iii) Different representatives of design team from different departments may not see an eye to eye with each other and there may be a difficulty in reaching a consensus on the proper design, because there are too many opinions regarding design issues.

For every problem outlined above, dominant solution is retaining strong control over the design team, which calls for a good team leader. The team leader should have exceptional knowledge of the design process, a good impersonal skills and a commitment to stay within time and cost budget for a design project.

Impact of Target Costing on Profitability : (i) Target costing improves profitability in two ways. *First,* it places a detailed continuing emphasis on product cost throughout the life cycle of every product. *Secondly,* it improves profitability through precise targeting of correct prices at which the company feels it can field a profitable product. (ii) Target costing is really part of a larger concept called concurrent engineering which requires participants from many departments to work together on project team. Clustering representatives from many departments on a single design team can be quite a struggle. This problem can be solved by senior management. (iii) The cost accountant should continue taking lead role in continuing review of suppliers' cost. (iv) A company, which issues a stream of new products should make target costing a central part of its strategy.

Target Costing Data Flow : (i) Data can be obtained from central accounting data base carefully stocked form such a variety of sources as, accounts payable, billing, bills of materials and inventory records. (ii) In initial stages of product design, the cost accountant must make the best possible guesses regarding the costs of proposed designs. (iii) The cost accountant may include best estimate as well as the highest possible cost, that may be encountered. This additional information lets the management grow whether there is significant degree of risk, that the project may not achieve the desired cost target. (iv) Data can also be obtained from competitors information collected by the marketing staff or an outside research agency. This database contains information about the prices at which competitors are selling their product as well as the discounts allowed at various price points. This information is used to determine the range of price points at which company should sell its existing or anticipated products. (v) Sometimes information is compiled by a combined effort of the marketing and engineering staff through a process called reverse engineering. This source can, also serve as a data base for the project team. (vi) Engineering staff also compiles their own cost data relating to different designs/components. This data is collected over the years and can be useful for target costing. (vii) The data base available with cost accounting department regarding previous quality, cost and on-time delivery performance of all key suppliers as well as the production capacity of each one.

Based on the wide variety of sources mentioned in this section, a cost accountant, who is an integral part of the design team can have access to a considerable amount of information that is of great use in determining product prices and costs. The important point is that cost accountant, who collects the data should be well trained in its uses as well as its shortcomings. He should be able to realistically portray expected cost and margin levels despite its imprecise nature.

Target Costing Control Points : Following control points should be taken care of in all target costing projects: (i) *Identification of principal control point.* Experience shows that there always comes a point, where the cost of maintaining the design team exceeds the savings garnered from additional iterations. It is also necessary that most products should be launched within a reasonably short time or they will miss the appropriate market, where they will beat the delivery of competing products to the market. This emphasises that the principal control points over the course of target costing programme should be properly taken care of. (ii) *Point of "Go/No Go" decision.* If target cost is not reached, management retains power to abandon the design project. There comes a point, when actual performance is very close to expected performance in matter of cost incurrence. For example, if a situation has reached, where target cost has not been attained, but results are very close to target cost. In this situation, a "Go/No Go" decision is to be taken by management overriding the cost target. Final decision involves either terminating the design project or sending the design to production for implementation. (iii) *Milestone can be in terms of time or points.* A milestone can be in terms of time, say one month. It can also be on the points in design process, at which specific activities are completed. For example, a milestone review can occur as soon as successive design iteration is completed.

Implementing a Target Costing System : A target costing initiative requires the participation of several departments. Therefore, there is a possibility of project getting delayed and resulting in serious cost overruns. These problems can be mitigated, if following points are taken care of: (i) *Creating a project charter.* It is always good if target costing effort starts with a document approved by senior management, which describes its goal and what it is authorised to do. (ii) *Active participation and interest of top* management There should be someone in corporate hierarchy, who strongly believes in the project outcome. He supports fund sanctioning and solicits support of other members of top management. (iii) *Funds approval.* It is necessary that funds should be got approved by higher management so that well-staffed design team can complete target costing tasks. As far as possible funding should be based on a formal allocation of money through the corporate budget. (iv) *Assign a strong team manager.* Implementation of target costing programme involves so many people with different background. It may become difficult to weld the group together into smooth functioning team focused on key objectives. A proper manager with leadership qualities should be asked to manage the team. (v) *Full time participation.* It will always be in the interest of organisation, if members of target costing team are fully focused on target costing. For this, it is necessary that they should be relieved of all other responsibilities. (vi) *Usage of management tools.* Target costing may come out to be a complex effort. This specially holds true in case of high cost projects with many features and components. To ensure that the project stays on track, the team should use all project management tools.

Value Engineering Review in Target Costing : Value engineering plays a dominant role in target costing. Following are some of the issues, that are dealt with during value engineering review conducted for the purpose of target costing: (i) *Elimination of Junctions from the production process.* A very detailed review is undertaken to see if there are steps in production process, that add no value. By eliminating these no-value added steps, it is possible to take their associated cost and overheads out of product cost. These steps must have been put in for some reason. The value engineering reviews ascertain the possibility of successfully getting rid of these no-value added steps without defeating the primary objective (function of the product/process). (ii) *Ascertaining possibility of eliminating.* It is possible that product had been designed for excessive degree of sturdiness into a product. For example, Euroclean Vacuum Cleaner can also be designed to withstand a one-ton impact; although there is only remote possibility that such an impact will even occur. However, in such instances savings can be effected through change in design, whichjloes not stress sturdiness so much. (iii) *Determining whether substitution is possible.* This approach encourages search for less expensive components, which can replace expensive part currently used in a product design. It is becoming increasingly valid approach since new materials are being developed every year. This step is known as component parts analysis. (iv) *Combining steps.* A detailed review of all processes associated with a product sometimes reveals that some steps can be consolidated. It may mean that one step can be eliminated or several can be accomplished by one person. This is called as process centering. This approach can result in saving some of the transfer or queue time from the production process. This approach also means avoiding risk of damage of material in transfers. (v) *Searching a better way of accomplishing the target.* This step strikes at the core of cost reduction issue. The improvements resulting from this step tend to have the largest favourable impact on cost reductions, but it is also most difficult for the organisations to adopt this approach. (vi) A mix of all value engineering steps noted above must be applied to each product design to ensure that maximum permissible cost is safely reached.

Target Costing for Target Pricing : An important form of market-based price is the *target price.* A *target price* is the estimated price of a product (or service) that potential customers will be willing to pay. This estimate is based on an understanding of customers' perceived value for a product and competitors' response. A *target operating income per unit* is the operating income that a company wants to earn on each unit of a product (or service) sold. The target price leads to a *target cost. A target cost per* unitis the estimated long-run cost per unit of a product (or-service) that, when sold at the target price, enables the company to achieve the target operating income per unit. Target cost per unit is derived by subtracting the target operating income per unit from the target price. What relevant costs should we include in the target cost calculations? All costs, both variable and fixed. Why? Because in the long run, a company's prices and revenues must recover all its costs. If not, the company's best alternative is to shut down. Relative to the shutting-down alternative, all costs, whether fixed or variable, are relevant. Target cost per unit is often lower than the existing full product cost per unit. To achieve the target cost per unit and the target operating income per unit, the organisation must improve its products and processes.

Cost Incurrence and Locked-in Costs : Two key concepts in value engineering and in managing value-added and non-value-added costs are *cost incurrence* and *locked-in costs. Cost incurrence* occurs when a resource is sacrificed or used up. Costing systems emphasize cost incurrence. They recognise and record costs only when costs are incurred. Locked-in costs (Designed-in costs) are those costs that have not yet been incurred but that will be incurred in the future on the basis of decisions that have already been made.

Why is it important to distinguish between when costs are locked-in and when costs are incurred? Because it is difficult to alter or reduce costs that have already been locked-in. For example, if a company experiences quality problems during manufacturing, its ability to improve quality and reduce scrap may be limited by product design. Scrap costs are incurred during manufacturing, but they may be locked-in by a faulty design. Similarly, in the software industry, costs of producing software are often locked-in at the design and analysis stage. Costly and difficult-to-fix errors that appear during coding and testing are frequently locked-in by bad designs.

In some industries, such as mining, costs are locked-in and incurred at about the same time. When costs are not locked-in early, cost-reduction activities can be successful right up to the time that costs are incurred. In these industries, the key to lowering costs is improved operational efficiency and productivity rather than better design.

Fixed Costs or Variable Costs : Surveys indicate that most managers use full product costs, that is, they include both fixed costs per unit and variable costs per unit in the cost base when making their pricing decisions. The advantage cited for including fixed costs per unit for pricing decisions include the following: (a) *Full product cost recovery.* For long-run pricing decisions, full product costs inform managers of the bare minimum costs they need to recover to continue in business rather than shut down. Using variable costs as a base does not give managers this information. There is then a temptation to engage in excessive long-run price cutting as long as prices give a positive contribution margin. Long-run price cutting, however, may result in long-run revenues being less than long-run (full product) costs, resulting in the company going out of business. (b) *Price stability.* Managers believe that full-cost formula pricing promotes price stability, because it limits the ability of managers to cut prices. Managers prefer price stability because it facilitates planning. (c) *Simplicity.* A full-cost formula for pricing does not require a detailed analysis of cost-behaviour patterns to separate costs into fixed and variable components for each product. Calculating variable costs for each product is expensive and prone to errors. For these reasons, many managers believe that full-cost formula pricing meets the cost-benefit test.

Including unit fixed costs when pricing is not without its problems. Allocating fixed costs to products can be somewhat arbitrary. Calculating fixed cost per unit requires an estimate of expected future sales quantities. If actual sales fall short of this estimate, the actual full product cost per unit could exceed price.

Target Pricing : The selling prices computed under cost-plus pricing are prospective prices. The target pricing approach eliminates the need to go back and forth among cost-plus prospective prices, customer reactions, and design and cost modifications. Instead, the target pricing approach first determines product characteristics and price on the basis of customer preference and competitor responses. The target price then serves to focus and motivate managers to achieve the target cost to earn the target operating income. Sometimes the target cost is not achieved. Managers must then redesign the product, adjust the price, or work with a smaller margin.

Suppliers who provide relatively unique products and services— accountants and management consultants, for example, frequently use cost-plus pricing. Professional service firms set prices based on hourly cost-plus billing rates of partners, managers, and associates. These prices are, however, reduced in competitive situations. Professional service firms also consider a multiyear client perspective when choosing prices. Certified public accountants, for example, sometimes charge a client a low price initially and higher prices later.

Refined cost driver and cost information play an important role in both cost-plus pricing and target costing and pricing. The identification of cost drivers is critical as managers do value engineering to "cost down" their products. *Cost down* refers to reducing the cost of a product while still satisfying customer expectations.

Target Costing vs. Traditional Costing

Following table contrasts target costing with traditional costing:

Target costing	***Traditional costing***
Production specification	Production specification
↓	↓
Target price and volume	Product design
↓	↓
Target profit	Estimated cost
↓	↓
Target cost	Target cost
↓	↓
Product design	Target price

Fisher contrasted the target costing sequence with traditional costing sequence. In target costing, a 'company first develops a preliminary product concept. Then company determines a target price and product volume based on perceived value to the customers. A product's target profitability is derived from a long-range profit plan, which in many Japanese companies is based on a return-on-sale metric.

Cost Accountant's Role in a Target Costing Environment (i) The cost accountant should be able to provide for the other members of the design team a running series of cost estimates based on initial design sketches and activity-based costing reviews. (ii) The cost accountant helps the project team in capital budgeting decisions. (iii) The cost accountant works with the design team to help it understand cost-benefit-trade offs of using different design or cost options in the new product. (iv) The cost accountant continues to compare a product's actual cost to the target cost even after the design is completed.

The Advantages : Following advantages ensue, when a company follows target costing:

(i) *Forced planning.* Target costing ensures proper planning well ahead of actual production and marketing.

(ii) *Competitive atmosphere.* Target costing starts with customer study or market study. It cannot work properly, till a company has got a charged competitive atmosphere. Ways and means are found out to succeed in competition.

(iii) *Cohesive team spirit.* For success of target costing, a inter-function team is essential. Therefore, it promotes cohesive team spirit in the organisation. This spirit impels the team members to attempt higher-level performance.

Value Chain Analysis : Competitive advantage of an organisation cannot be understood by looking at a firm as a whole. It comes from many discrete activities, that a firm performs in designing, producing, marketing, delivering and supporting its product. Each of these activities can contribute to a firm's relative cost position and create a basis for differentiation. Value chain is a basic tool for systematically examining all the activities and determining how these activities interact to contribute to competitive advantages. The value chain disaggregates a firm into strategically relevant activities to understand behaviour ofcost and potential sources of differentiation. An organisation gains competitive advantage by performing these strategically important activities more cheaply or better than its competitors. The concepts, tools and techniques of value chain analysis apply to all organisations, which produce and sell a product or provide a service. There are three sources of competitive advantage, known collectively as generic strategies. They are low cost, differentiation and focus.

Value Chain : The idea of a value chain was first suggested by Michael E. Porter in his acclaimed book, "Competitive Advantage". In 1985 Michael E. Porter wrote, "Every firm is a collection of activities that are performed to design, produce, market, delivery and support its product. A firm's value chain and the way it performs individual activities are a reflection of its history, its strategy and the underlying economics of the activities themselves." Value chain analysis is a method of decomposing the firm into strategically important activities and understanding their impact on the cost behaviour and differentiation.

Porter classified business activities under two heads, i.e., primary line activities and support activities.

Primary Activities : (i) Inbound Logistics. (ii) Operations. (iii) Outbound Logistics. (iv) Marketing and Sales. (v) Service.

Support Activities : (i) Firm Infrastructure. (ii) Human Resource. Management. (iii) Technology Development. (iv) Procurement.

In other words, a value chain is "linked set of value creating activities all the way from basic raw materials sources to ultimate end products." Value chain is the entire set of processes that transform raw materials into finished products. The companies, that operate in many segments of value chain, are called vertically integrated.

The major oil companies are good examples, as they explore and drill pump oil from fields, transport to refine it and sell it to customers. Companies try to gain advantage in the value-chain by establishing co-operative relationships with suppliers and customers. Compaq Computers, the world's largest manufacturer of personal computers had awash in inventory of parts, until it began to work with its suppliers to improve relations. Several suppliers agreed to build plant near Compaq's main plant in exchange for Compaq's giving them information on its production in advance. The suppliers were thus able to plan better, produce in smoother cycle and avoid costly rush orders for needed parts.

These days firms are concentrating on the delivery of value to customers. Accountants and managers refer to value chain as the set of activities required to design, develop, produce, market and deliver products and services to customers. When an activity is performed, central concern is to ascertain whether it is important to customer. In order to be effective, cost management system must track information relating to wide variety of activities important to customers *(i.e.,* product quality, environmental performance and delivery performance). For example, with regard to delivery performance, customers these days count the delivery of the product or service as part of the product. These days companies compete not only in technological terms and manufacturing terms, but also in terms of the speed of delivery and response. Today, many customers believe that delivery delayed is delivery denied. It is important to note that companies have internal customers as well. The staff functions of a company exist to serve the line functions. For example, accounting department creates cost reports for production managers. Accounting departments, that are "customer driven" assess the value of reports to be sure that they communicate significant information in a timely and readable fashion. The reports, that do not measure up to the expectation, are dropped. Value to the customer is at the heart of cost management system. Thus concept of value chain is integrated throughout an organisation in its activities both to internal and external customers.

Competitive Advantage : To diagnose competitive advantage, it is necessary to define a firm's value chain for competing in a particular industry. Individual value activities are identified in the particular firm. Defining relevant value activities requires that activities with discrete technologies and economies be isolated. Broad functions such as manufacturing or marketing must be sub-divided into activities. The study of product flow, order flow or paper flow can be useful in doing so. Every machine in a factory could be treated as a separate activity. The appropriate degree of disintegration depends on the economics of the activities and the purpose for which the value chain is being analysed. Basic point is that those activities should be isolated and separated, which (i) have different economics, (ii) have a high potential impact of differentiation, or (iii) represent a significant or growing proportion of cost. In using value chain, necessarily finer disaggregations of some activities are made, as the analysis exposes differences important to competitive advantage. Selecting the appropriate category in which to put an activity may require judgement, which can be illuminating in its own right. Value activities should be assigned to categories, that best represent their contribution to a firms competitive advantage. If order processing is an important way in which a firm interacts with its buyers, it should be classified under marketing. Many firms have gained competitive advantage by redefining the roles of traditional activities.

Competitive Scope and Value Chain : Competitive scope can have a powerful effect on competitive advantage; because it shapes the configuration and economics of value chain. (i) *Segment scope, i.e.,* the product varieties produced and buyers served. (ii) *Degree of integration,* i.e., the extent to which activities are performed in-house instead of independent firms. (iii) *Geographic scope, i.e.,* range of regions, countries, or groups of countries in which a firm competes with a coordinated strategy. (iv) *Industry scope, i.e.,* range of related industries in which the firm competes with a coordinated strategy.

Broad scope can allow a firm to exploit the benefit of performing more activities internally. It may allow the firm to exploit inter-relationships between the value chains, that serve different segments, geographic areas or related units. Narrow scope can allow tailoring of a chain to serve a particular target segment, geographic area or industry to achieve lower cost or to serve the target in a unique way. Broad and narrow scope can be combined. A firm may create competitive advantage by tuning its value chain to one product segment and exploiting geographic inter-relationships by serving that segment worldwide. It may also exploit inter-relationships with business units in related industries.

Segment Scope : Differences in the needs or value chains required to serve different products or buyer segments can lead to a competitive advantage of focussing. For example, value chain required to serve sophisticated mini- computer buyers with in-house servicing facilities is different from that required to serve small business users, who need extensive sales assistance, less demanding hardware performance, user-friendly software and service capability.

Degree of Integration : Vertical integration defines the division of activities between a firm and its suppliers, channels and buyers.

A firm may purchase components rather than fabricate them itself, for example, or contract for service rather than maintain a service organisation. Similarly channels may perform many distribution, service and marketing functions instead of a firm. The value chain allows a firm to identify more clearly the potential benefits of integration by highlighting the role of vertical integration. The exploitation of vertical linkages does not require vertical integration, but integration may sometimes allow the benefits of vertical linkages to be achieved more easily.

Geographic Scope : Geographic inter-relationships can enhance competitive advantage if sharing and coordinating value activities, lower cost or enhances differentiation. There may be cost of coordination as well as differences among regions or countries that reduce the advantage of sharing.

Industry Scope : Inter-relationships among business units can have a powerful influence on competitive advantage, either by lowering cost or enhancing differentiation. A shared logistical system may allow a firm to reap economies of scale. Shared sales force offering related products can improve the sales persons effectiveness with the buyer and thereby enhance differentiations. All inter-relationships do not lead to competitive advantage. Not all activities benefit from sharing. There are always costs of sharing, that must be offset against the benefits.

The Value Chain and Industry Structure : Industry structure both shapes the value chain of a firm and is a reflection of the collective value chains of competitors. Structure determines the bargaining relationships with buyers and suppliers that is reflected in both the configuration of a firm's value chain and how margins divided with buyers suppliers and coalition partners. The threat of substituting of an industry influences the value activities desired by buyers. The array of competitor's value chain is the basis for many elements of industry structure. Many elements of industry structure can be diagnosed by analysing the value chain of competitors in an industry.

The Value Chain and Organisational Structure : The value chain is a basic tool for diagnosing competitive advantage and finding ways to create and sustain it. The value chain can play a valuable role in designing organisational structure. Organisational structure groups certain activities together under organisational units such as marketing or production. The logic is that these activities have similarities, that should be exploited by putting them together in a department. At the same time departments are separated from other groups of activities because of their differences. This separation of like activities is what organisational theorists call differentiation. With separation of organisational units come the need to coordinate them. This is termed as integration. This integrating mechanism must be established in a firm to ensure that the required coordination takes place. Organisational structure balances the benefits of separation and integration. The value chain provides a systematic way to divide a firm into its discrete activities. This can be used to examine now the activities in a firm are and could be grouped. The need for integration among organisational units is a manifestation of linkages. There are often many linkages within the value chain and organisational structure often fails to provide mechanisms to coordinate or optimise them. An organisation structure that corresponds to the valve chain will improve a firm ability to create and sustain competitive advantage.

The Value Chain and Cost Analysis : The behaviour of a firm's cost and its relative cost position stems from the value activities that a firm performs in competing in an industry. A meaningful cost analysis examines the cost of these activities and not the cost of the firm as a whole. Each value activity has its own cost structure and behaviour of its cost may be affected by linkages and inter-relationships with other activities both within and outside the organisation. Cost advantage results if the firm achieves a lower cumulative cost of performing value activities than its competitors.

Defining Value Chain for Cost Analysis : The starting point for cost analysis is to define a firm's value chain and to assign operating costs and assets to value activities. Each activity in the value chain involves both operating costs and assets in the form of fixed and working capital. Purchased inputs make up part of the cost of every value activity and can contribute to both operating costs and assets. The need to assign assets to value activities reflect the fact that the amount of assets in an activity and the efficiency of assets utilization are frequently important to the activity's cost. For purposes of cost analysis, the disaggregation of value chain into individual activities should reflect three principles, which are mutually exclusive:

(i) the size and growth of the cost represented by the activity,

(ii) the cost behaviour of the activity, and

(iii) differences with competitor in performing the activity.

Activities should be separated for cost analysis, if they represent a significant or rapidly growing percentage of operating costs or assets. While most firms can easily identify the large components of their cost, they frequently overlook smaller but growing value activities, that can eventually change their cost structure. Activities must be separated, if they have different cost drivers. Activities with similar cost drivers can be safely grouped together. For example, advertising and promotion usually belong in a separate value activities because advertising cost is sensitive to scale while promotional costs are largely variable. The initial breakdown of the value chain into activities will inevitably represent a best guess of important differences in cost behaviour. Value activities can be further aggregated or disaggregated as further analysis exposes differences or similarities in cost behaviour. A final test for separating value activities is the behaviour of competitors. Significant activities should be treated separately when a competitor performs them in a different way. Differences among competitors raise the possibility that an activity is the source of a relative cost advantage or disadvantage.

***Assigning Costs and Assets to Value Activities* :** After identifying its value chain, a firm must assign operating costs and assets to value activities. Operating costs should be assigned to activities in which they are incurred. Assets should be assigned to the activities that employ, control or must influence their use. The assignment of operating costs is straightforward in principle, although it is time consuming. Accounting records must often be recast to match costs with value activities rather than accounting classifications. Assets are expensive and their selection and use often involve trade-offs with operating costs. Assets must be assigned to value activities in the same way, that will permit an analysis of cost behaviour. Assignment of cost to activities is more complex than assignment of operating cost. Assets accounts must usually be regrouped to correspond activities and assets must be valued in some consistent way. Initially the costs and assets of shared value activities should be allocated to the value chain of the business unit using whatever methodology the firm currently employs typically based on some allocation formula. As the analysis proceeds, the costs of shared activities can be refined using more meaningful allocation methods based on the cost behaviour of the activities. It should also be remembered that assigning costs and assets to value activities do not require the precision of financial reporting purpose. Estimation are more than sufficient to highlight strategic cost issues and can be employed in assigning costs and assets to value activities, where generating accurate figures would require substantial expenditure. As the analysis proceeds and particular value activities prove to be important to cost advantage, greater efforts at precision can be made. Finally, a firm may find that competitors assign their costs differently. The way in which competitors measure their cost is important, because it will influence the cost behaviour. It helps to diagnose competitors' costing practices.

The allocation of costs and assets will produce a value chain, that illustrates graphically the distribution of a firm's costs. It can prove revealing to distribution the cost of each value activity into three parts, i. e,, purchased operating inputs, human resource costs and assets by major category. The proportions of value chain can be drawn to reflect the distribution of costs and assets among activities. Even initial allocation of operating costs and assets to the value chain may suggest areas for cost improvement. Purchased operating input will often represent larger proportion of costs than commonly perceived. Other insights can result from grouping valued activities into direct, indirect and quality assurance activities and cumulative activities. Managers often fail to recognise burgeoning indirect cost and have a tendency to focus almost exclusively on direct cost. In many firms not only represent a large proportion of total costs but also have grown more rapidly than other cost elements. The introduction of sophisticatea information systems and automated processes is reducing direct costs but boosting indirect costs.

Accounting Data for Value Chain Analysis : In this section, some of the key concepts in value chain planning will be described and problems in obtaining the relevant accounting data discussed.

First *structural issues* (i.e., the cost objectives for the accumulation of cost assets and revenues) will be discussed. Next focus will be on the topic of *linkage and inter-relationships.* The we turn to *traditional budgeting mechanism* and compare them with the value chain concept of the cost of performing different activities. Finally, we point out some of the difficulties of performing value chain analysis.

Problems of Structures : First step in this direction is to define the Strategic Business Unit (SBU). This requires dividing the firm into SBUs in a manner appropriate for strategic decision-making. Once the SBUs have been defined, the planner can begin to divide the business into individual activities for further study.

The guiding principal in applying SBU planning is to determine what sub-units of the total firm can be considered autonomous for strategic decision-making. Autonomy in this context means that decisions about one SBU can be made in relative isolation from decisions about other SBUs. The planner is therefore seeking a vantage point for decision-making which will allow him to manage the most critical shared resources. In establishing SBUs, the planner will look inside the firm for shared costs and technologies and outside for shared markets, distribution, and customers. These two perspectives may not led to the same definition of SBUs.

A great deal of judgement is required in interpreting the information from these two perspectives and, when they conflict, in choosing which should dominate. Value chain planning recognises this dilemma by placing considerable emphasis on understanding the inter-relationships that, exist between business units because of shared resources.

The first obstacle to using accounting data for value chain analysis therefore occurs when the firm is not organised around

SBUs and consequently the accounting system does not recognise SBUs as a dimension for data accumulation.

Identifying Critical Activities **:** Having defined the boundaries of the SBU, the next step is to identify its component critical activities. A critical activity is one which has a large impact on competitive advantage. This means that an activity becomes key if it creates a large potential for cost reduction or differentiation. The critical factors, as determined in the market place, should translate into key activities for creating value.

The second obstacle to using cost accounting data for value chain analysis is that there is no obvious correspondence between critical activities as defined in the value chain and responsibility centres as defined in accounting systems.

Defining Products **:** The last structural dimension for the accumulation of costs and revenues is the product. The costs of each primary activity must be split down by product (or product group). Following three difficulties are encountered:

The *first* is that it may not be the physical product that creates value for buyers. An obvious example would be IBM's initial dominance of the personal computer market. Its products were outclassed by many competitors in terms of performance, quality and price. Nevertheless IBM's products dominated their market segments because of software, service, advertising and because IBM was going to stay around. If the physical product is not responsible for creating buyer value, or does not account for a major part of it, then the accounting system's accumulation of costs by product will be of little help.

The *second is* that traditional accounting systems do not attempt to trace non-manufacturing costs to products. Thus manufacturing costs are classified as product costs and non-manufacturing as period costs. The reason for this distinction is that the former are used for valuing inventories and determining income and the latter are not.

The value chain analyst must therefore construct his own theoretical models of how resource inputs to non-manufacturing primary activities are related to products and find ways of expressing this theoretical model in terms of data which are

Impact of 'JIT' System on Waste :' A JIT system relently focuses on eliminating all waste from a system. This can be a waste of asset, in the case of unneeded inventory. It can also be a waste of time in case of assets, that are not used for a long time after production. It can also be a waste of materials such as unnecessary levels of obsolete inventory, defective products, rework and the like. When fully installed, a JIT system vastly reduces all these types of wastes. When it happens, there is a sharp drop in several aspects of a product's costs. For example, if incoming part from another work station is defective, the operator can notify the preceding work station of the problem before it makes any more parts. This reduces the quantity of rework, that might have been necessary. This type of warning system lowers the amount of the labour costs charged to a product. Similarly, any material, that would have been scrapped because of improper rework is no longer lost. All this eventually reduces a product's cost. Overhead costs charged to a product also go down, as other types of waste decline. For example, by clustering machines into cells the materials handling costs previously incurred in shifting materials between widely scattered machines can be eliminated. This reduces the amount of materials handling costs, that used to be charged to overhead. Machine cells tend to reduce the amount of floor space needed, since there is no longer a need for large aisles for materials handling people to drive their fork lifts through. By reducing floor space, one can also reduce facility costs, which no longer appear in cost pool. Another form of waste is the quality inspections, which are performed on many machines. Under JIT system machine operators conduct their own quality check, so there is no need for a separate group of inspectors. Accordingly cost of their pay can be eliminated from overhead costs. All costs which do not add value to products, are wasteful costs, that are subject to elimination. JIT system also focuses on reducing various kinds of wasted time so that entire time is spent only in actually producing products. For example, inspection time, movement time, queuing time and storage time are either eliminated or at least substantially reduced. This ultimately reduces cost. Under JIT system, cost drivers are charged to wasteful activities, that accumulate costs. For example, overhead cost can be charged out based on number of components in a product, number of material moves on the number of units scrapped. In this way, cost of these activities become apparent to management and as a result these will be considerable focus on reducing these cost drivers, since the accounting system places so much emphasis on their total burdened cost. In this way, the cost accounting system can be continually altered so that it has a direct and active role in reducing wasteful activities.

Impact of JIT System on Overhead Costs : It has already been discussed that costs of materials handling, facilities and quality inspection decline, when JIT system is installed. Reduction in all types of inventory results in a massive shrinkage in the amount of space required for warehouse facility. This results in reduction of cost of staff, equipment, fixed assets, facilities and rent associated with warehouses. When manufacturing cells are created under JIT system, there will be a lot of shift of cost from overhead cost pool to direct cost. This means that the depreciation, maintenance labour and utility costs of each cell can be charged straight to product. Thoughts there is no increase or decrease in cost, it does increase the reliability of allocation for many more costs than was previously the case. In short, overhead costs decline, as some costs are eliminated, while other costs shift between products, as more costs are charged directly to products and the remaining overhead costs are charged out using different allocation methods.

Impact of JIT System on other Costs : When JIT system is created, the amount of inventory retained in a company drops precipitously. Raw materials inventory is reduced because supplier delivers them near the machine, which uses raw materials first. WIP inventory drops by use of 'Kanban' system. Finally, finished goods inventory drops, because production is carried out when there are orders in hand. For this reason, cost of maintaining inventory declines, which in turn reduces the overhead costs associated with inventories. Some of these inventory-related costs, which get considerably reduced due to JIT system are:

(i) interest cost related to the debt that funds the inventory investment.

(ii) cost of rent for storage facility.

(iii) cost of all equipment used in the warehouse.

(iv) cost of warehouse utilities,

(v) cost of warehouse employees.

(vi) cost of insurance needed to cover the possible loss of inventory.

(vii) cost of taxes on the inventory.

Besides, a reduction in the level of working capital and inventory-related costs, a company can also reduce its investment in capital assets. This happens, when a company with large machines replaces them with a larger number of much smaller, more easily configured machines. Then equipment set-up time becomes shorter, which in turn makes it profitable to have shorter runs, thereby eliminating an excess investment in inventory. All these savings releases cash for other uses while reducing the depreciation to be charged to overhead. Thus JIT system exerts a significant influence in reducing other costs.

Impact of JIT System on Product Prices : It has been experienced that customers are willing to pay high prices, when a company achieves a higher level of product quality. This is particularly true in industries, where quality, delivery or reliability is low. Where every one else is offering same level of quality and service, a company new-found lower costs initiates price war; that results in a drop in prices. Hence, impact of JIT system on product pricing is primarily driven by customer perceived need for higher product quality and reliable delivery times, installation and operations base.

JIT Cost Allocation Differences : The main impact of JIT system is that many items of overhead (as perceived in traditional system) get converted to direct cost. For example, a machine cell is designed to produce either a single product or a single component. All costs generated can be charged directly to products, that manufacturing cells are producing. JIT system results in accurate cost and considerably reduce the debate over where costs should go. The costs, which can be charged directly to product, are:

(i) *Depreciation.* Depreciation can be charged directly to concerned product,

(ii) *Material handling.* Most materials handling costs in JIT systems are eliminated. Only the costs for materials handling between cells should be charged to an overhead pool for allocation.

(iii) *Operating supplies.* Supplies are mostly charged to machine cells, so majority of expenses can be separately tracked by individual cell and charged to products.

(iv) *Repairs and maintenance.* They are all grouped according to machine cells and these charges are made against the products directly.

(v) *Supervision.* If a supervisor takes care of more that one machine cell, the cost of the supervision can be split among the cells supervised. However the cost of general facility management as well as of any support staff must still be charged to an overhead cost pool.

Performance Measurement in a JIT System : Many measurements used in traditional accounting system are not used in JIT environment. New measurements can be implemented, that take advantage of unique characteristics of this system. For example, machine utilisation is a key measurement in a traditional system. This is used to ensure that every asset of the company is being thoroughly utilised. This is particularly important, where been a large investment in automation or large .high speed machinery.

In JIT, the approach is different. Under JIT system, producing only what is actually needed, is the underlying rule. Machine cells under JIT system are relatively smaller and less costly than the highly automated juggernauts used in more traditional systems. In other words, machine utilisation measurement can be thrown to backdoor, when JIT system comes in the front door.

In traditional systems, employees are paid by piece rates. Under a JIT system, emphasis is on producing only what is needed. Thus an employee who is producing more than requirements is going against the rule of the system. Therefore, piece rate system does not work under JIT system. Here measurement to be used is one, that focuses on quality of output or invites productive suggestions from employees.

Labour efficiency tracking is most talked about performance measurement. In JIT system, it is highly inappropriate to track labour efficiency. JIT system does not go on how fast an employee works. Major emphasis is on quality of product manufactured.

Labour variances in traditional system require considerable time tracking. All this labour tracking is non-value added activity, which a JIT system wants to avoid as unnecessary activity. JIT system also uses following performance measures:

(i) Inventory turnover. (ii) Set-up time reduction, (iii) Customer complaints. (iv) Scrap (v) Cost of quality (vi) Customer service (vii) Ideas generated

Backflushing in a JIT System : The time honoured picking system is inundated with paper work. This system does not work under JIT system, where companies use backflushing. Backflushing requires no data entry of any kind, until a finished product is completed. At that time total amount of information of finished product is entered into computer. Information is also fed based on bill of materials, which shows list of components, that should have been used in the production process. This is subtracted from the beginning inventory balance to arriving at the amount of inventory, that should have been left now in hand. Backflushing is good because data entry occurs once in the entire production process. However, there are some serious limitations of backflushing, that must be corrected before it will work properly:

(i) *Production reporting.* The total production figure entered must be correct or else wrong component types and quantities will be subtracted from stock.

(ii) *Scrap reporting.* All abnormal scrap must be diligently tracked and recorded. Otherwise these materials will fall outside the backflushing system and will not be charged to inventory.

(iii) *Lot tracing.* Lot tracing is almost very difficult in backflushing system. It is required when a manufacturer needs to keep records of which production lots were used to create a product in case all items in a lot must be recalled.

(iv) *Inventory accuracy.* It becomes difficult to know accurately the inventory balance, as in a backflushing system, data is fed into the system only once a day. This makes it difficult to maintain an accurate set of inventory records in the warehouse. Given below are main points of backflush costing, which is used under JIT system:

(i) There are no department in JIT. There are only cells and stations,

(ii) A 14-day lead time is reduced to hours, and it will be absurd to trace costs from station to station.

(iii) Production cycle is in minutes or hours.

(iv) Goods are shipped immediately upon completion.

(v) Then all of each day's cost flows to cost of goods sold. Backflush costing eliminates separate raw materials and work-in-progress account. There is single Raw Material in Process Account (RIP). The RIP account is used only for tracking of the cost of raw materials. Under JIT system, materials are immediately placed into process. For this reason, there is no need to record it under separate inventory account. Combining direct labour and overhead into one category is a second feature of backflush costing. As firms implement JIT and automate, traditional direct labour category disappears. Multi-skilled workers intermingle set-up activities, maintenance and material handling etc. As labour becomes multifunctional, the ability to track and report direct labour separately becomes impossible. Backflush costing combines labour costs with overhead costs in a temporary account called conversion cost control. This account accumulates the actual conversion cost on debit side and applied conversion cost on the credit side.

Example. (Journal entries—Traditional Costing vs. Backflush Costing). SV & Co had following transactions in April 2003:

1. Raw materials were purchased on account for Rs. 1,60,000.
2. All materials were placed into production.
3. Actual direct labour costs Rs. 25,000.
4. Actual overhead costs Rs. 2,25,000.
5. Conversion costs applied Rs. 2.35,000.
6. All work was completed for the month.
7. All completed work was sold.
8. Difference between actual and applied costs is computed.

SV & Co. follows JIT system. Pass both (a) Traditional journal entries, and (b) Backflush journal entries.

Transaction	Traditional Journal Entries		Rs	Backflush Journal Entries		Rs.
1. Purchase of raw	Materials A/c-Dr	1,60,000		Raw Materials-in		
materials	To Accounts Payable		1.60,000	process A/c Dr	1,60,000	
				To Accounts Payable		1,60,000
2. Materials issued to	Work-in-Progress Dr.	1,60.000		No entry		
production	To Materials A/c		1,60.000			
3. Direct labour cost	Work-in-Progress Dr.	25.000		Combined with overhead		
incurred	To Payroll		Rs. 25.000			
4. Overhead cost	Overhead Control Dr.	2.25,000		Conversion Cost		
incurred	To Account Payable		2.25,000	Control Dr.	2.50,000	
				To Payroll		25,000
				To Accounts Payable		2.25,000
5. Application of	W.I.P A/c Dr.	2,10,000		No Entry		
overhead	To Overhead Control A/c		2,10.000			
6. Completion of	Finished Stock Dr.	3,95.000		Finished Goods Dr.	3.95,000	
goods	To W.I.P. A/c		3.95.000	To R.I.P. A/c		1.60,000
				To Conversion		
				Control A/c		2,35,000
7. Goods are sold	Cost of Goods Sold Dr.	3,95.000		Cost of Goods		
	To Finished Goods		3,95 000	Sold Dr.	3.95.000	
8. Variance is	Cost of Goods Sold Dr.	15.000		To Finished Goods		3.95.000
recognised	To Overhead Control A/c		15.000	Cost, of Goods		
				Sold Dr.	15,000	
				To Conversion		
				Cost Control		15,000

JIT's Effect on Job Costing and Process Costing Systems : For implementing JIT in Job-order setting, the firm should separate its repetitive business from its unique orders. Manufacturing cells can then be established to deal with repetition business. For those products, where demand is insufficient to justify its own manufacturing cell, groups of dissimilar machine can be set-up in a cell to make families of products or parts, that require the same manufacturing sequence. With this reorganisation of manufacturing layout, for orders are no more needed to accumulate product costs. Instead, costs can be accumulated at the cellular level. In JIT environment, it is difficult to have job order for each job. Because of time and space compression feature of JIT, it becomes difficult to track each piece moving through the cell. In effect, job environment takes on the nature of process costing system. (ii) JIT simplifies process costing. A key feature of JIT is lower inventories. If JIT is assumed to reduce work-in-process, then need to compute equivalent units vanishes, Calculating product costs follows the simple pattern of collecting costs for a cell for a period of time and dividing the costs by the units produced during that period.

Materials Requirement Planning (Mrp-I & Mrp-II) : Traditionally, materials requirements were determined by continuously reviewing stock levels and pre-determined quality was ordered, whenever stocks fell below the reorder level. This approach suffered from a grave limitations. It assumed that replenishment of stocks could be planned independently. The basic fact ignored was that materials requirements is dependent on demand for assemblies of which they a part. Materials Requirements Planning (MRP) originated in 1960 as a computerised approach for coordinating the planning of materials acquisition and production. In a way MRP is a flow control system, i. e., it orders only what components are required to maintain the manufacturing flow. The orders can be for purchased parts or manufactured parts. MRP thus provides a base for production scheduling and raw materials purchasing. MRP can be defined as computerised planning system, which first determines the quantity and timing of finished goods demanded, i.e., it starts with preparation of master production schedule. Then this schedule is used to determine the requirement of raw materials, components and sub-assemblies at each of prior stage of production. The lead times for the purchase of each part are also incorporated into the computer system so that it could determine for the purchasing staff the exact date on which orders for parts must be placed. This new level of automation was called materials requirement planning, since, as the name implies, it revealed the exact quantities and type of materials needed to run a production operation. This is explained below:

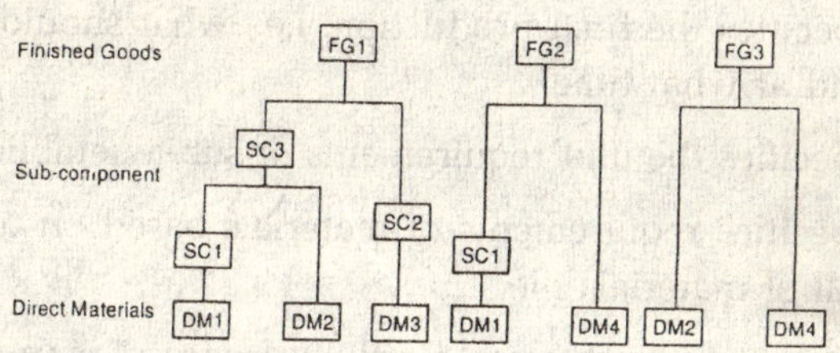

Fig. An overview of the structure of an MRP system.

Source: Colin Drury—*Management and Cost Accounting.)*

This diagram perfectly gives an overview of this approach. From this diagram, it is clear that top level items represent three finished goods items (FG1, FG2 and FG3). MRP breaks down the requirements of each finished goods into primary sub-components and sub-assemblies. These are in turn further broken down in terms of direct material items. For FG1, three sub-components are required. For FG2, these sub-components are required. For FG1, no sub-component is required.

Data Requirements to Operate Material Requirement Planning System : The prerequisites to operate an MRP system include the following:

(i) *A master production schedule.* It specifies both timing and quantity of each top-level finished goods items.

(ii) *A bill of materials file.* It specifies sub-assemblies components and materials required for each finished good.

(iii) *An inventory file.* This file specifies for each sub-assembly component and part, details of the number of items on hand, scheduled receipts and items allocated to released order but not yet drawn from stock.

(iv) *A master part file.* This file contains information regarding planned lead times of all items to be purchased and sub-assemblies and components produced internally.

MRP system takes into account items on hand and expected lead time. It is possible, then, to produce time-phased schedule of planned order releases of lower level items for purchasing and manufacturing. This time-phased schedule is called the *material requirement plan.*

Objectives of Materials Requirement Planning

(i) specifies the final production, i.e., what should be done and at what time.

(ii) specifies the unit requirements of sub-assemblies.

(iii) specifies requirements of materials based on up-to-date bill of materials file.

(iv) computer inventories, work-in-progress, manufacturing and packaging lead times.

(v) controls inventory levels by ordering bought-in-components and raw materials.

Material Resource Planning was afterwards extended to provide an integrated planning approach to the management of all manufacturing resources. This extended system is known as manufacturing resources planning or MRP-II. MRP-I is used to describe materials resources planning I.

Strategic and Tactical Importance of the MRP-II System : Basically MRP-II is an enormous scheduling tool. It is often used to bring structure to the chaos on the manufacturing floor. This system is designed to track and plan for existing manufacturing practice rather than to attempt to impose a new production methodology on a company.

MRP-II Reports : MRP-II system is capable of creating enormous number of reports. Some of these reports are:

(i) *Capacity Report :* This report lists the production utilization level of every piece of machinery in the facility. By going through this report, one can see, if there is an excess amount of capacity in some machines and shortfall in others, which would lead the cost accountant to recommend changes in the mix of machinery being used.

(ii) *Production Variances Report :* This report lists the production quantities, that were planned, but not actually manufactured. This report can be of interest to a cost accountant, who is investigating why the facility is not producing planned quantities.

(iii) *Rejection Report :* This reports reveals all the parts and suppliers who provided them. It also contains reasons for rejection.

(iv) *Scrap Variance Report :* This report itemises the excess quantities of scrap by identifying component number, that have been generated during the production process and which can be used to track down the causes of the scrap.

Impact of MRP-II on Waste Costs : An MRP-II system is good at itemising the waste in purchasing and production system. Here are some types of waste identified by the system:

(i) *Labour Variances :* This system contains Information regarding direct labour hours used at all stages of production process. The system then compresses it fo the standard labour quantities listed in the systems to generate variances at every work station in the production process, which management can use to investigate significant inefficiencies.

(ii) *Late Deliveries by Suppliers :* The system has all information about the supplies to be delivered by the suppliers. It compares it with date of actual receipts of supplies. The system is then able to bring out the list of suppliers, who delivered late.

(iii) *Production Variances by Machines :* The system keeps information relating to input to the work station and output from the work station. By comparison, it can generate reports of production variances due to work stations.

(iv) *Scrap Produced by Each Machine :* The system records any input to production floor. It is able to identify any missing part, etc. By reviewing the scrap report of work centre, managers can take remedial measures.

(v) *Work-in-process Quantities :* An excessive amount of work-in-process inventory is a source of waste since it requires an extra working capital investment to maintain it. The MRP-II system is able to create how much of inventory is located on the shop floor. The report generated in this regard pinpoints the area in the production flow, where inventory tends to build up and where low-quality parts are being produced.

(vi) *Enterprise Resource Planning (ERP):* Enterprise Resource Planning (ERP) covers the techniques and concepts employed for the integrated management of businesses as a whole from the viewpoint of the effective use of management resources to improve the efficiency of an enterprise. ERP packages are integrated (covering all business functions) that support the above ERP concepts. ERP software designed to model and automate many of the basic processes a company from finance to the shop floor with the goal of the integrating information across the company and eliminating complex and expensive links between computer systems that were never meant to talk to each other. When work station of Ghaziabad enters a customer order, data flows automatically to others in the company, who need to see it. *i.e.,* it is available at headquarters in Mumbai and it may also be available to factory in Kolkata. The line of information is primarily responsible for growth of ERP.

Advantages of ERP : Installing an ERP system has many advantages. The direct advantages include improved efficiency, information integration for better decision-making, fast response time to customer queries, etc. The indirect benefits include better corporate image, improved customer goodwill, customer satisfaction. Following are some of the direct benefits of ERP systems:

Business Integration : ERP promotes integration. ERP packages facilitate automatic data updation (automatic data exchange among applications). Under ERP packages, the data of related business function is also automatically updated at the time a transaction occurs. This helps management to grasp business details in time. This in turn facilitates timely decision-making.

Flexibility : Different languages, currencies, accounting standards can be packaged and implemented automatically. Flexibility is essential not simply for development but also in terms management.

Better Analysis and Planning Capabilities : Due to a powerful system, it is possible to have comprehensive and unified management of related business and its data. This system can utilize many types of decision support system and simulation functions. Thus, the system is able to give decision-makers, what they want.

Use of Latest Technology : ERP vendors often able to embrace latest developments in the field of information technology. They quickly adopt their systems to take advantage of the latest technologies like open systems, client/ server technology, internet/ intranet, CALS (Computer-Aided Acquisition and Logistics Support), electronic-commerce, etc. ERP includes many of the functions, that will be necessary for future systems.

Reduction of Lead-time : The elapsed time between placing an order and receiving it is known as the lead-time. It plays a significant role in purchasing and inventory control. Most purchasing departments urge the managers to anticipate materials demand well ahead of actual need. All inventory systems have safe mechanism like safety stock, reorder level, and so on built into them to avoid the situation, where material is out of stock. The consequences of non-availability of an item, that is required for production, can result in a lot of problems like missing the delivery schedule, losing the customer goodwill due to delayed delivery and even losing the customer competitors. The ERP systems help in automating the task and make inventory management more efficient and effective. ERP system is integrated. Material management module is integrated with other modules like sales, marketing, purchasing, manufacturing and production planning. Demand for a particular item can be known as early as an order is received. As soon as the order details are entered into the system, a lot of actions are triggered. The system will check whether the items are available in inventory. Then it will generate a BOM for the order and it will check whether all items required are available in inventory. Primary thing is that all records are available in data-base and updation is done immediately. Most suppliers are connected to the organisation's system. As soon as a purchase order is issued, supplier's system is updated with that information. This helps the supplier to know what items are required and when these items are required.

On-time Shipment : ERP systems provide freedom to change manufacturing and planning methods, as needs change without modifying or reconfiguring the work place or plan layouts. The use of ERP system helps to increase efficiency in design and development activities. By integrating the various business functions and automating the procedures and tasks, the ERP systems ensure on-time delivery of goods to the customers.

Reduction in Cycle Time : Cycle time is the time between receipt of the order and delivery of the product. ERP systems are helpful in both make-to -order and make-to-stock situations. In both cases, cycle time can be reduced by the ERP systems, but the reduction will be more in the case of make-to-order systems. ERP packages go a long way in reducing the cycle times due to automation achieved in material procurement, production planning and the efficiency achieved through the plant maintenance and production systems of the ERP packages.

Improved Resource Utilization : As manufacturing processes become more sophisticated and as the philosophies of elimination of waste and constraint management achieve broader acceptance, manufacturer place increased emphasis upon planning and controlling capacity. The capacity planning feature of ERP systems offer both rough-cut and detailed capacity planning. The system 'loads each resource with production requirements from Master Production Scheduling, Materials Requirements Planning and Shop-floor Control. The ERP systems have simulation capabilities that help the capacity and resource planners-to simulate the various capacity and resource utilization scenarios and choose the best option. The ERP systems help the organisation in drastically improving the capacity and resource utilization.

Better Customer Satisfaction : Customer satisfaction means meeting or exceeding customer's requirements for a product or service. The customer could get technical support by either accessing the company's technical support knowledge base (help desk) or by calling the technical support. Since all the details of the product and the customer are available to the person at the technical support department, the company will be able to better support the customer. All this is possible because of use of latest developments in information technology by the ERP systems.

Improved Supplier Performance : The quality of the raw materials or components and the capability of the vendor to deliver them ontime are of critical importance for the success of any organisation. For this reason, an organisation chooses its suppliers or vendors very carefully and monitor their activities very closely. To realise these benefits, corporations rely heavily on supplier management and control systems to help, plan, manage and control the complex processes associated with global supplier partnerships.

Total Quality Management (TQM) : Total Quality Management (TQM) is the integration of all functions and processes within an organisation in order to achieve continuous improvement of the quality of goods and services. The focus remains on customer satisfaction. It has been widely accepted that it is essential for global markets. TQM has broadened from its early concentration on the statistical monitoring of manufacturing process to a customer-oriented process of continuous improvement that focuses on delivering products or services of consistent high quality in a timely fashion. The efforts under TQM philosophy is to design and build quality in rather than trying to inspect it in, by focussing on the-causes rather than the symptoms of poor quality.

The concept of TQM is based on a number of ideas. It means thinking about quality in terms of all functions of the enterprise. TQM is a start-to-finish process that integrates inter-related functions at all levels. It is a systems approach, that considers every interaction between the various elements of the organisation. Thus, the overall effectiveness of the system is higher than the sum of the individual outputs from the sub-systems. The sub-systems include all the organisational functions in the life cycle of a product such as (i) design, (ii) planning, (iii) production, (iv) distribution, and (v) field service. The management sub-systems also require integration including (i) strategy with a customer focus; (ii) the total tools of quality, (iii) employee involvement (the linking process that integrates the whole). A corollary is that any product, process or service can be improved and a successful organisation is one, that consciously seeks and exploits opportunities for improvements at all levels. The load-bearing structure is customer satisfaction. The watch word of TQM is continuous improvement. The term TQM emphasises the following key issues :

(i) *The cost of quality* as the measure of non-quality (not meeting customer requirements) and a measure of how the quality process is progressing.

(ii) A *cultural change* that appreciates the primary need to meet customer requirements, implements a management philosophy that acknowledges this emphasis, encourages employee involvement and embraces the ethics of continuous improvement.

(iii) *Enabling mechanism of change,* including training and education, communication, recognition, management behaviour, teamwork and customer satisfaction programmes.

(iv) *Implementing TQM* by defining the mission, identifying the output, identifying the customer, negotiating customer requirements, developing a supplier specification, that details customer objective and determining the activities required to fill those objectives.

(v) Management behaviour that includes setting role model, use of quality process and tools, encouraging communication, sponsoring feedback activities and fostering and providing environment.

Elements of TQM. Key elements of TQM are: (i) Ensuring customer satisfaction. (ii) Managing process. (iii) Continuous improvement. (iv) Working together. (v) Encouraging personal initiative.

Customer Satisfaction : TQM starts with customer satisfaction in focus. Customers may be client, patients, students, guests and passengers. It is the customer, who defines the quality. It is good to avoid giving customer expectations, that a company cannot meet. The widespread tendency to ignore complains or track them and identify the causes can have very serious consequences. This is particularly true in services, where it is estimated that for every complaint a business receives, there may be many other customers, who feel the same way but do not air their feelings to the company. Failure to identify the root cause the complaints means that reduction of variation in the causative process is more difficult. If a customer is unable to get through to a sales representative, it is an evidence of malfunction in the sales and marketing function. Evidence indicates that part of the cause of failure to close customer-process loop is inadequate support from top management for the total quality management (TQM) infrastructure and a continued focus on the techniques of TQM particularly statistical process control (SPC).

Many researchers have found that quality performance measures such as defect rates and customer satisfaction levels play a key role in determining pay for senior managers in only focussed companies. Profitability is still the king. There is, of course, nothing wrong with a focus on cash flow and short-term profits, but long-term profits and market share require a base of satisfied customers that are retained by a focus on satisfaction. Another reason for lack of customer focus is the tendency of many firms to emphasize the techniques of TQM such as Statistical Process Control (SPC) and other outcome-oriented methods such as productivity and cost reduction. These are desirable and necessary but a singular emphasis on these areas is to put cart before the horse. The customer is not interested in the sophistication of a company's process control, its training programme or its culture. The bottom line for the customer is whether he or she obtains the desired product. This fact has been recognised by the pillars of quality like Deming, Juran and Crosby. By concentrating on customer satisfaction, a company can get customers for life, but this will require a complete change in approach and prospecting. The new thinking is that a company should strive not only for customer satisfaction but for customer delight.

Internal and External Customers : Mostly, when people think of customers, they think of ultimate purchaser or end-user of their product or service. But, there are other groups of customer exists—internal customer. Internal customers are those individuals or departments within an organisation to whom another department provides their products and services. In most large organisation, only a few departments actually have direct contact with external customers. The aim of every organisation is to satisfy external customers so that they will not only return to do business but will tell others about the company, with whom they are doing business. It should always be kept in mind ~lat external customer satisfaction results from a chain of satisfied internal 'Customers. The customer/supplier chain view of work requires teams or departments to continually talk to each other as customer and supplier so that they can provide each other with better products and services.

Internal customers are also important in a TQM programme. These are the people, the activities and the functions within the company, that are the customers of other people, activities or functions. Hence, manufacturing is the customer of design and several departments may be customers of data processing. Conflict frequently arises between the needs of internal and external customers. A balance needs to be struck between the needs of these two customer groups. The solution is to determining the real needs of each and design the process to meet both.

Quality Focus in Customer Service : These days companies go far constant bombardment of'quality' and 'satisfaction' messages in advertising on television and radio and in print media. But, the popular phrases 'satisfaction guaranteed' or 'low price guaranteed' do not state what the customer is supposed to get for his or her purchase. Many firms back up a satisfaction guarantee with promises of a reward if they fail to meet their own standards or those of the customer. Far at Pizza Hut in America, you get it free if not served in five minutes. An insurance company of Massachusetts sends a cheque of $ 50 if you get transferred from phone to phone while seeking an answer to an insurance question.

The Driver of Customer Satisfaction : The benefits of customers, who are satisfied are well known. The obvious way to determine what makes customers satisfied is to ask them. It is an appropriate practice to conduct an audit of company's TQM infrastructure. The key excellence indicators for customer satisfaction are:

(i) Service standards derived from customer requirements.

(ii) Understanding customer requirements

(a) thoroughness/objectivity

(b) customer types

(c) product/service features.

(iii) Front-line empowerment (resolution)

(iv) Strategic infrastructure support for front-line employees.

(v) High levels of satisfaction-customer awards,

(vi) Proactive customer service systems

(vii) (a) Product/service follow-ups

(b) Complaints

(c) Turnover of customers

(d) Employees

(e) Quality requirements of market segments.

Measurement of Customer Satisfaction : These days companies take accelerating interest in measurement of customer satisfaction. There are two basic steps in a measurement system:

(i) develop key indicators that drive customer satisfaction, and

(ii) collect data regarding the perceptions of quality received by customers.

Key indicators of customer satisfaction are what the company has chosen to represent quality in its products and services and the way in which these are delivered. The building blocks that the system is designed to track are:

(i) expectations of the customer, and

(ii) company perceptions of customer expectations.

The indicators for physical product are reliability, aesthetics, adaptability, etc. Some important areas to consider are outcome, friendliness/courteousness of employees, safety/risk of the service, billing/ invoicing procedures, responsiveness to request, competence, appearance of physical facilities, approachability of service provider, location and access, respect for customer feelings/ rights, willingness to listen to customer honesty and ability to communicate in clear language. These indicators, if appropriate and addressable, are converted to action items, that reflect specific delivery systems, where the product or service meets the customer. For example, in"^, bank, customer needs and systems would combine to deliver short teller lines, friendly and courteous staff, ATMs that work and low fees on accounts. Data collection is required in order to identify the needs of customers and the related problems of process delivery. The data gathering process surveys both customers and employees. By including employees, customer needs and barriers to service can be identified along with recommendation for process improvement. Different orientations are emphasised for customers and employees. The former are asked for their expectations and latter are asked what they think customer expect. Following points may be of great help in this regard:

(a) companies should ensure that the factors that customers assume will be handled, are indeed handled.

(b) Companies should address the issues, that customer has said are mandatory.

(c) Make it convenient for customers to get your products or use your service.

(d) Provisions should be made for additional products/ services, that customers would like to have.

(e) Efforts should be made to differentiate the organisation from competition.

(f) Efforts should be made to enhance your customers impression of the company.

(g) Pleasantly surprise the customer by visits/gifts and collect the feedback,

(h) Always efforts should be made to make customer experiences memorable.

(i) Efforts should be made to convey an "above and beyond the call of duty" attitude.

(j) Generate customers for life.

Steps in Understanding Customer Requirements : Understanding customer is pre-requisite to satisfy customer. Following steps should be taken in this regard:

(a) List team outputs to document the result of work performed.

(b) List customers to identify everyone who receives the outputs.

(c) Identify output requirements to pinpoint the output characteristics the customers want, require or expect.

(d) Meet the customers to verify output requirements, determining requirements importance and understand current level of satisfaction.

From the above, it is amply clear that customer satisfaction is a key for any organisation implementing TQM. For this purpose, achieving customer satisfaction, the pre-requisite is understanding customer requirements. A systematic, complete analysis of customer requirements lays the foundation for success of TQM.

Managing Process Quality : A statement such as "We are the Quality Company" convinces no one, *i.e.,* neither the employees and nor the customers. The company should be organised for managing process quality for TQM implementation. The management of process quality category examines the systematic processes, that the company uses to pursue the even-higher quality and company operational performance. The key elements of process management are research and development, design, management of process quality for all work units and suppliers, systematic quality improvement and quality assessment. The focus is on determining how well the processes are managed. Traditional management emphasises quality assurance, whereas under TQM emphasis is on controlling the continuous improvement of the process. Management of process quality under TQM goes beyond inspection, which has been used for a long time for quality assurance. Inspection is being replaced under TQM by efforts for zero defect situation. Moving from inspection to process control takes place in steps or phases as follows:

S.No.	*Step*	*Action*
1.	Process characterisation.	Definition of process requirements and identification of key variables.
2.	Develop standards and measures of output.	Involve work force.
3.	Monitor compliance to standards and review for better control.	Identify any additional variables that affect quality.
4.	Identify and remove causes of defects or variations.	This requires a step-by-step documentation of the process and process control charting.
5.	Follow-up	Ensuring achievement of process control with improved stability and reduced variation.

Continuous Improvement : What differentiates TQM from short-range improvement targets is continuous improvements. The idea is simple. TQM does not cease with implementing successfully a project. It is a continuous search for further improvement and thus this search permeates the whole gamut of activities in all various functions and parts of an organisation. This has been further discussed in detail under the heading "Seven Cs of TQM".

It emphasises the quest of an organisation to strive for further improvement as a way of life keeping in focus customer requirements.

Working Together : Working together for continuous improvement is the life-line of TQM. Working together, i.e., team work provides a real opportunity for people to work together to achieve quality improvement. People who work on their own or in a small group often have a picture of their organisation and work, that it does, which is very compartmentalised. They are often unfamiliar with the work, that is done even by people who work quite near to them. As a result, they are unaware of the consequences of poor quality in the work, they themselves do. Bringing people together in a team, with the common goal of quality improvement, aids communication between departmental or functional activities. Teamwork slowly breaks down communication barriers and acts as a platform for change. Communication is a cement, that holds together bricks of the total quality management process supporting the principle of people-based management. To communicate properly, it is necessary to focus on the receiver of the message. Teamwork enables a group of people to work as a task force, looking at cross-functional problems or as an action team solving local problems in order to identify and adopt new ways of doing things.

Encouraging Personal Initiative : This is, what bring forth the best result in the team mate. Getting quality results is not a short-term, instant-pudding way to improve competitiveness. Implementing total quality management requires hands-on continuous leadership. It is through encouragement that strategy, vision and action plans are implemented. Employees are encouraged to participate in setting and achieving measurable goals, senior management continuously tries to involve and energise employees towards formulation and implementation of quality goals and provide the participants opportunity to share with others.

Total Quality Management Principles : Under total quality management, all work is seen as process and special emphasis is on continuous process of improvement for individuals, groups of people and whole organisation. What makes total quality management different from other management processes is the concentrated focus on continuous improvement. Total quality management is not a quick management fix. It is about changing the ways things are done within the organisation's life time. To improve the process, therefore, people must know what to do, how to do it, have, the right methods to do it. It should also be possible to measure the improvement of the process and the current level of achievement. Total quality management encompasses a set of four principles and eight core concepts. The four guiding principles are:

Delight the Customer : This focuses on external customer and asks what would delight them. This implies a real need to understand the product or service requirements and a strong follow-up to ensure compliance. Delighting customer means being best at what matters most to customer. If there is change in it over a period of time, company has to take care of it. Being in touch with these changes and always satisfying the customer are an integral part of total quality management.

Management by Fact **:** Knowing the current quality standards of the product or service in customers' hand is the first stage of being able to improve. To bring about improvement, one has to know the base, that one is starting from. In TQM it is essential to have facts necessary to manage the business at all levels. Then this information (facts) are shared so that decisions are based on facts. This an integral part of continuous improvement.

People-based Management **:** TQM is based on a simple premise that employees should know what to do and how to do it. Based on the feedback received on their performance, they can be encouraged to take responsibility of their own work. The more the employees are involved, the greater will be their commitment to customer satisfaction. Systems, standards and technology will not themselves improve quality. The role of employees is extremely important in the continuous improvement of quality within an organisation.

Continuous Improvement **:** This is the pre-requisite of TQM. TQM is not a short-term programme or a project. TQM is based on the assumption that continuous improvement is possible because, in a state of competition, customers expect more. Continuous improvement is an incremental change and not a major break-through.

Core Concepts for Improvement under TQM **:** Following eight concepts are used to drive the process of continuous improvement under the environment of TQM:

Customer Satisfaction **:** A company with TQM philosophy never get bogged down with its internal problems to neglect its external customers. These companies use their customers to know what is important to the customers. Then effort is made by company to measure it outer performance against customer satisfaction. Asking from customers to set customer satisfaction goals is a clear sign of an outward looking company. Some companies have gone to the extent of weekly monitoring of customer satisfaction as measured by the customer.

Internal Customers are Real : Satisfying customers' requirements relate to internal customers as well as external one. For success of TQM, it is necessary to achieve successful internal working relations in order to satisfy the needs of the external customers. Whether product is being supplied or service is being rendered, the internal customers are as real as external customers. Thy also require speed, efficiency and accurate measurement. But achieving a quality service between internal customers can be, sometimes, very time-consuming. One way to deal with this is to assess poor quality in financial terms. Measuring the actual cost of poor quality and the way that amount is made up can provide and impetus for management to follow the quality improvement path. TQM philosophy emphasises in achieving the satisfaction of internal customers.

All work is Process : *TQM* emphasises improvement of business process. A process is a combination of methods, materials, manpower, and machines, which taken together produce a product or service. All processes contain inherent variability and one approach to quality improvement is to progressively reduce variation. This can be done, first by removing variation due to special causes and secondly by driving down the common cause of variation. Thus bringing the process under control and then improving its capability leads to total quality management.

Measurement : TQM philosophy pre-supposes, that products being produced or service being rendered should be capable of being measured. After measuring present performance relating to a product or service, it is possible to focus on internal customers' requirement and external customers' requirements. The measurement of internal quality may highlight such facts as:

(i) Breach of promise. (ii) Performance to standard. (iii) Reject level. (iv) Accidents. (v) Process in control. (vi) Yield/scrap. (vii) Time/cost due to non-available material. (viii) Number of changes to work orders, and (ix) Cost of quality.

Team-work : Team-work forges the different elements of a company into a force, that works bringing people together in teams with the common goal of quality improvement aids communication between departmental or functional activities. Team-work breaks down the communication barriers and acts as a platform for change. Communication is a cement, that holds together bricks of the total quality management process supporting the principle of people-based management. To communicate well, it is necessary to focus on the receiver. For successful communication, it is necessary to build credibility into the message and in the person, giving message. Any thing, that distracts from this causes damage to both. Team-work enables a group of people to work as task force; looking at cross-functional problems or an action team solving local problems, in order to identify and adopt new ways of doing things.

People Make Quality : Research have pointed out that most of the quality problems within an organisation are not normally within the control of the individual employee. As many as 80 per cent of these problems are caused by the way a company is organised and managed. The system often gets in the way of employees, who are trying to do a good job. In such a situation, it is difficult to solve the problem by simply telling the employees to do better. In these circumstances employees motivation alone cannot work. It requires real practical efforts on the part of managers to remove the barriers to quality management. The role of manages within an organisation is to ensure that everything necessary is in place to allow people to make quality. This in turn begins to create the environment when people are willing to take responsibility for the quality of their own work. Releasing the talent of every one within the organisation is the best way to create culture for quality improvement.

Continuous Improvement Cycle: The continuous cycle of establishing customers' requirements, meeting these requirements, measuring success and keeping on improving gives impetus to process of improvement in quality. By continually checking with customers requirements a company keep finding areas for improvement. This continuous supply of opportunities is used to keep the quality improvement plans up-to-date. It reinforces the idea that total quality journey is never-ending.

Prevention : This thought is central to total quality management and provides a positive approach to achieving continuous improvement. Prevention means seeking to ensure that failures will not occur. The continuous process of removing the problems and failures out of the system will create a culture of continuous improvement.

Seven Cs of TQM

Culture : Culture is the pattern of shared beliefs and values, that provides the members of an organisation rules of behaviour or accepted norms for conducting operations. It is the philosophies, ideologies, values, assumptions, beliefs, expectations, attitudes and norms that keep an organisation together and are shared by employees. For example, IBM's basic beliefs are (a) respect for the individual, (b) best customer service, and (c) pursuit of excellence. In turn, these beliefs are operationalised in terms of strategy and customer value. In simpler words, culture provides a framework to explain the way things are done. The acknowledged experts agree on the need for a culture or value system transformation for TQM.

(i) *Deming* called for a transformation of the American style.

(ii) *Feigenbaum* suggest a pervasive improvement throughout the organisation.

(iii) According to *Crosby*, "Quality is the result of carefully constructed culture, it has to be fabric of the organisation." Successful organisations have central core culture around which the rest of the company revolves. It is important for the organisation to have a sound basis of core values into which management and employees will be drawn. Without this central core, the energy of the members of the organisation will dissipate as they develop plans, and decisions communicate and carry on operations without a fundamental criteria of relevance to guide them. Research has shown that quality means different things to different people and levels in the organisation. Employees tend to think like peers and think differently from those at other levels. This suggests that organisations will have considerable difficulty in improving quality unless core values are imbedded in the organisation.

Embedding a Culture of Quality : It is one thing for top management to state a commitment to quality but quite another for this commitment to be accepted or embedded in the company. The basic vehicle for embedding an organisational culture is a teaching process in which desired behaviour and activities are learnt through experience, symbols and explicit behaviour. The components of total quality management provide the vehicle for change. Of course, demonstration of commitment by top management is essential. This commitment is demonstrated by behaviour and activities, that are exhibited throughout the company. Categories of behaviours include:

Signalling : It involves making statement or taking actions that support the vision of quality. Statements such as "it is a super market where shopping is a pleasure" or "customer is always right" indicate a vision of management.

Focus : Every employee must know the mission, his or her part in it and what has to be done to achieve it. What management pays attention to and how they react to crisis is indication of this focus. When all functions and systems are aligned and when practice supports the culture, every one is more likely to support the vision.

Employee Policies : These may be the clearest expression of culture at least from the viewpoint of the employees. A culture of quality can be easily demonstrated in such policies as the reward and promotion system, status symbol and other human resource actions.

A chart given below shown how focus change in a cultural change mechanism for TQM:

Focus	*From traditional*	To *quality*
Plan	Short-range budgets	Future, strategic issues
Organise	Hierarchy-chain of command	Participation/empowerment
Control	Variance reporting	Quality measures and information for key-control
Communication	Top down	Top-down and bottom-up
Decisions	*Ad hoc*/ crisis management	Planned change
Functional	Parochial, competitive	Cross-functioning, integrative
Management Quality management	Fixing/one-shot management	Preventive/continuous all functions and processes

Transition to a quality culture at Xerox is summarised below in a diagram:

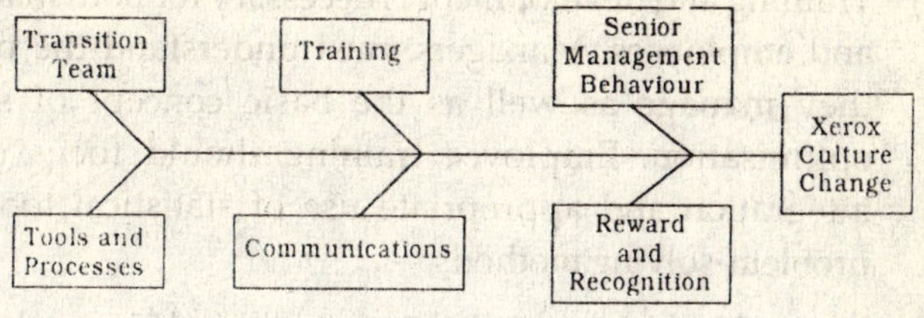

Communication : Communication is inextricably linked in the quality process, yet some executives find it difficult to tell others about the plan in a way that will be understood. An additional difficulty is filtering. As top management's vision of quality gets filtered down through the ranks, the vision and plan can lose both clarity and momentum. Thus, top management as well as manages and supervisors at all levels serve as translators and executors of top management's directive. The ability to communicate is a valuable skill at all levels from front line Supervisor to Chief Executive Officer. Quality conscious companies are interested in-cost of poor communication in terms of both employees productivity and customers perception of product and service quality. Limited or inaccurate facts parcelled out to employees may demoralise workers and lead to rumours. Effort should be made to adopt an easily understood and simple approach to help communicate the strategy, vision and actions plans related to TQM. Communication is defined as the exchange of information and understanding between two or more persons or groups. A special emphasis is laid on exchange and understanding without understanding between sender and receiver concerning the message, there is no communication. The simple model is as follows:

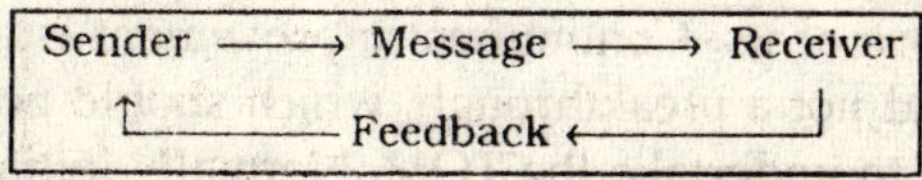

Unless sender gets back the message that receiver understands the message, no communication takes place. Communication is an extremely complex process. Communication mode specifically tailored for an organisation may be used as a vehicle for TQM implementation. Following points are relevant:

(a) Training and development is necessary for both managers and employees. Managers must understand the process they manage as well as the basic concept of system optimisation. Employee training should focus on the integration and appropriate use of statistical tools and problem-solving methods.

(b) There should be participation at all levels in establishing benchmarks and measures of process quality. Involvement is both vertical in the hierarchy as well as horizontal by cross-functional teams.

(c) Employees should be empowered by delegating authority to make decisions regarding process improvement within individual areas of responsibility so that the individual owns the particular process step.

(d) Quality assurance should be introduced not only in manufacturing or operations but also in business and supporting processes as well.

(e) There should be proper-emphasis on human resource management systems that facilitate contributions at all levels (up and down and across) of organisation chart.

Communication system should receive due attention in implementation of TQM.

Continuous Improvement : Total quality management is not a short-term activity, that will finish, when a set target has been achieved. It is not a programme or a project. It is a management process, that recognises that, however much a company may improve, competition will continue to improve and customer will expect more of us. Continuous improvement is an incremental change and not a breakthrough, which should be the aim of all who wish to undertake the TQM. Normally initial desires *fizzle,* excitement wanes and momentum disappears, but in case of TQM it does not happen. In case of TQM, methodology of continuous improvement is adopted as a way of life. Tools and concepts of

TQM require a structure, *i.e.*, a sequenced set of activities to follow. It is summarised in diagram given below.

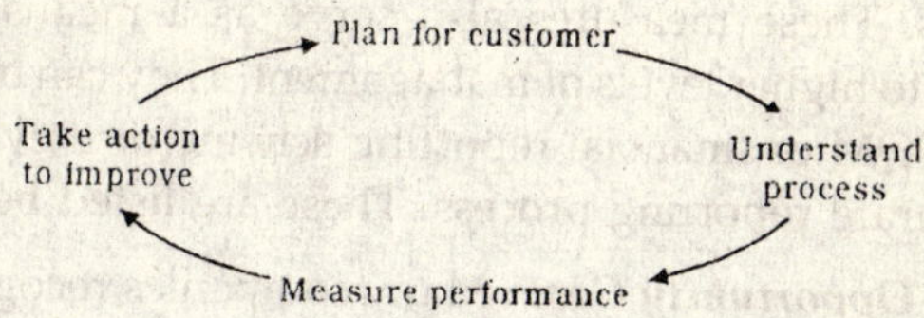

Fig. The continuous improvement cycle

Customer Focus and Satisfaction : In the words of Joel Ross, quality begins and ends with customer. For TQM, it is necessary to examine company's relationship with customers and its knowledge of customer requirements and of quality factors, that drive market place competition. Special emphasis is on company's methods to determine customer satisfaction, current trends and levels of customer satisfaction and retention. The widespread tendency to ignore complaints or track them and identify the cause(s) can have serious consequences. This is particularly true in services.

Commitment : For success of TQM, involvement or rather commitment of top management is essential. Top management must become convinced of the need for quality and must clearly communicate this to entire company by written policy, stating that each person is expected to perform according to the requirement or cause the requirement to be officially changed to what the company and the customers really need.

Cooperation : TQM does not mean conforming to a set routine. It requires involvement, participation" and imagination of employees. Efforts are made to make best use of on-therjob experience of employees. For continuous improvement imposition on employees some set guidelines will not do. For TQM employees have to be inspired to involve with the project/product/process mentally. This cooperation and participation of employees is essential for TQM.

Control : Imposition on employees is avoided. Rather they are invited to participate in development and execution, but still control mechanisms is essential for success of TQM. It will call for a system of documentation and feed- back. This may require collection analysis of data and use of statistical method, etc.

Others measures of Total Quality Management : Managers continue to seek creative means to demonstrate the value of TQM. These measures help direct activities and resources to solve the problems. These measures also serve as a means of reporting progress to higher levels of management. They can be a part of the regular TQM or financial reporting scheme or they may be used as a separate reporting process. These are listed below:

Lost Opportunity Cost : Many companies recognise the large hidden cost of losing customers because quality problems cause customer dissatisfaction. This is referred to as "cost of lost opportunity". Many companies have developed measurement systems to measure the expected business loss caused by customers, who do not order or who significantly reduce their business with the company. Some companies call it "defectives analysis" and place value on the stream of lost revenue. This loss is part of the cost of poor quality. Some companies employ outside consultants to conduct customer survey to rank the company's performance. To get the customer's perspective of quality i.e., meeting expectations), companies are relying increasingly on external surveys to provide reliable data for analysis.

Half-life Model : Analog Device employs a half-life model for evaluating TQM progress. *Art Schneiderman,* the originator of the programmes observes that any defect level subjected to a legitimate quality improvement process decreases at a constant rate. In this programme, a model (based on extensive data) that shows that for each type of defect, the defect level drops 50 per cent over a specific level of time. For example, if the initial defect level was 10 per cent and the defect half-life was six months, then after the first six months, the defect level would fall to 5 percent after the next six months the defect level would fall to 2.5 per cent, and so on. Analog Devices adopted the half-life systems as an integral part ofdivisional performance to balance the strictly financial point of view. Under this programme, focus remaining on following items:

(a) On-time delivery. (b) Outgoing defect level. (c) Lead time. (d) Manfacturing cycle time. (e) Process defect level (f) Yield. (g) Time to market.

The managers found this data very useful in measuring the

movement in continuous improvement or *Kaizen* (Japanese term). This measurement device serves the company well.

Common Characteristics : The new innovative measure of quality normally have three things in common:

(a) The use of time. (b) A willingness to use outside data sources. (c) Flexibility regarding the sources and mixture of data. Traditional accounting records do not capture the dynamics of most orgnaisations or the complexity of their processes. Operational data alone do not give managers the economic consequences of their decisions. To gain a complete view of the impact of TQM, a holistic approach involving all stake holders is necessary. Thus, companies are putting more reliance on the quality assessment of the customer. Operating managers want measures that made sense, provide valuable feedback and fit the value of the business being assessed. The mix is based on what is appropriate.

Balanced Scorecard Approach : Companies are rapidly learning that measuring performance using financial measures alone can distort performance and mislead mangers. Many companies are turning to the *balanced scorecard approach.* They incorporate measures from accounting, operating, human resources, customers and other stakeholders to arrive at a more integrative and holistic measure of performance. This trend also applies to measuring the impact of a TQM programme, which is natural because TQM is designed to influence the total orgnaisation. A table given below gives on balanced scorecard measures of TQM.

TQM Element	*Financial Measure*	*Non-financial Measure*
Customer satisfaction	External failure cost, field service expense.	Customer satisfaction survey results on-time delivery, Number of customer complaints.
Internal performance	Appraisal cost internal failure cost, preventior cost.	Defect rates yields lead times. Idle capacity unscheduled machine downtime.

Collect and Analyse Data using Statistical Methods : For success of TQM data collection, analysis and use of available techniques should be given due consideration. There are two types of data, *i.e.,* attributes and variables. Attributes data are counted, not measured. Variable data provide a more detailed history of the process. Rather than just reporting whether or not an event occurred, variables data also provide information about the frequency or severity of situation understanding how often certain events happen is a common starting point in collecting data. Most important point is to decide what data will be collected. It is necessary to be as specific as possible so that it is always possible into which category each event should fit. Experience should be used to identify what categories should be used. In analysis, emphasis should be to find out possible correlation between two factors. A correlation means a complementary relationship between two variables. There are different types of correlation, *i.e.*, a positive correlation, no correlation and a negative correlation. Run charts provide a lot of information about the performance of a process, but proper interpretation of time-sequenced data required statistical data analysis. Without proper analysis, every fluctuation in the data may seem significant.

Use of Creative Thinking Techniques : This is a fundamental truth that creativity is very helpful (if not necessary) in problem-solving. That is why it is said that creative thinking may have obvious link to problem-solving. It will involve such steps as:

Escape from Patterns : Mind is a pattern-making system. It creates and looks for pattern. Sometimes, a company has to do something different to break out of a set mould. The creative thinking techniques provide a means to escape from existing pattern.

Provide a Means for Restructuring: Minds absorb information. The pieces are placed and patterns are created. A pattern may develop in one way but had the information been available at the same time, the pattern may be quite different. Sometimes, the information needs to be restructured to create a better and more effective pattern. Every one has heard the phase: "We have done it, this way." This means that a pattern exists and immediately efforts should be directed to determine the best way to do the same activity. The techniques of creative thinking provide a means of restructuring existing patterns to create better patterns.

Challenge Assumptions : Assumptions are patterns that go unchallenged. For creative thinking it is necessary to challenge the basic assumptions, but one should be careful in challenging assumptions. Besides, challenging assumptions may not be popular. It creates special difficulties, when some senior members of management are resistant to challenges of existing assumptions.

Techniques of Creative Thinking : Some say that creativity cannot be taught. This may be true but technique that can be applied to generate creative ideas can be taught. Some techniques to promote creativity are as follows:

Application : There are two primary uses of creative thinking techniques, *I.e.,* identifying possible causes and identifying possible solutions. The focus is different for these two uses. After possible causes have been identified, focus shifts to identifying possible solutions for the causes.

Brainstorming : It is good to generate ideas. Sometimes brain storming session may become dry. Still brainstorming is an excellent way to get started with generating ideas.

Reversal : It is possible to become so familiar with a problem that identifying creative solution may become difficult. Changing the way to look at a problem frequently provides new perspectives resulting in new ideas. Reversing is one way to change the way to look at the problem.

Characteristic Changing: The characteristic changing techniques starts with an identification of the parts, that make up a key element of the problem statement. The parts are then further divided into characteristics, that describe the parts. For example, the characteristics of a computer monitor include its size, colour options, resolution and range of ergonomic adjustments. Once the characteristics are identified efforts are made to find ways to change them to help the problem.

Cost of Quality : Any discussion, regarding TQM will be incomplete without talking about cost of quality. The most obvious and relevant question, that often remains unanswered, is "How much quality is enough?" In theory, it is analogous to a principle of economics. Basic marginal cost equals marginal revenue (MC = MR), *i.e.,* spend on quality improvement until the added profit equals the cost of achieving it. This also brings to perspective such questions as: "What are the costs of added quality?" or "What are the hidden costs of non-quality?" The cost of poor quality in individual firm and the potential for improvement can be staggering. Experts agree that poor quality can cost about 25 per cent of the personnel and assets in a manufacturing firm and about 40 per cent in service firm. There appears to be a general agreement that the costs range between 20 and 30 per cent of sales. Three views about costs are: (a) Higher quality means higher cost. (b) The cost of improving quality is less than the resulting savings. (c) Quality costs are those incurred in excess of those that would have been incurred, if the product were built or the service performed exactly right the first time.

Quality Costs : The cost of quality are generally classified into four categories: (i) prevention; (ii) appraisal , (iii) internal failure, and *(iv)* external failure. *Prevention costs* include those activities, which remove and prevent defects from occurring in the production process. Included are such activities as quality planning, production reviews, training and engineering analysis. *Appraisal costs* are those costs incurred to identify poor quality products after they occur but before shipment to customers. Inspection activity is an example. *Failure costs* are those incurred either during the production process (internal) or after the product is shipped (external). *Internal failure costs* include such items as machine downtime, poor quality materials, scrap and rework. *External failure costs* include returns and allowances, warranty costs and the hidden costs of customer dissatisfaction and lost market share. Quality costs information can be used in a number of ways:

(a) to identify profit opportunities (every rupee saved goes to the bottom line).

(b) to make capital budgeting and other investment decisions.

(c) to improve purchasing and supplier related costs.

(d) to identify waste in overhead caused by activities not required, by the customer.

(e) to identify reductant systems.

(f) to determine whether quality costs are properly distributed.

(g) to establish goals for budgets and profit planning,

(h) to identify quality problems.

(i) as a management tools for comparative measures of input-output relationships (i.e., the cost of reliability efforts versus warranty costs).

(j) as a tool of 'Pareto Analysis' to distinguish between the 'vital few' and the 'trivial many'.

(k) as an objective performance appraisal measure.

Types of Quality Costs : It is useful to split quality costs into four categories as follows:

Prevention Costs

Administration of Quality Related Activities : Some staff time is required to plan for and administer quality prevention activities.

Education : A significant cost is spent in preparation of training materials, the cost of trainers and training facilities and the labour cost of all employees attending the training.

New Product Trial Costs : For organisations releasing new products, having customers test product designs is a central method for ensuring a high quality of design. Accordingly, the costs of products given to customers and survey administration can be clustered into this sub-category.

Preventive Maintenance : Ensuring that machinery is capable of running, when needed is a key prevention activity. This includes the cost of maintenance personnel engaged in preventive maintenance, as well as any related material and administrative costs.

Preventive Maintenance Scheduling Software : The preventive maintenance activities just mentioned can be more easily accomplished, if maintenance software is available to track the lost time such maintenance was conducted.

Procedure and Instruction Development : A major prevention activity is the creation of machine operation instructions, that give employees complete information about how to perform their jobs. The costs of initial investigation of activities, procedure deployment and distribution of the remitting materials are in the category.

Supplier Qualification Assessment : Products cannot have a high quality level, unless the supplier of their components has high quality standards. The cost of all employees time spent in reviewing and assessing the output of supplier falls into this category.

Tool Design Reviews : If a company uses a number of custom tools to create products, these tools must be carefully reviewed in terms of their ability to produce parts at minimum specification levels as well as their ability to do so consistently and with minimal failure rates. The cost of these reviews and any resulting tool revision costs are in this category.

Appraisal Costs

These are the costs incurred to measure products, the malerial components used in products and the processes used to manufacture products. These activities are designed to reduce the number of defective products shipped to customers. Examples are:

Incoming Component Testing : If there are particularly troublesome problems with materials received from suppliers, a company may have to initiate an extensive effort to review a large proportion of these materials, which results in costs not only for testing personnel but also for any materials destroyed during the testing process.

Material Appraisal : When removed materials are destroyed during testing, the cost of these materials is recorded as appraisal cost.

Outsourced Laboratory Testing : Some of the tests conducted on materials are of such a specialised nature that a company finds it more cost-effective to send them to an outside laboratory for review. The fee of such laboratories are charged to this cost sub-category.

Process Appraisal : The process appraisal is not confined to material reviews. It is also necessary to periodically analyse how well the production and supporting processes are functioning. The staff time denoted to this activity is charged to this cost sub-category.

Prototype Appraisal : The quality staff can spot problems with new products before they are produced by examining a variety of quality related issues for prototype products. The costs of testing and of destruction of prototypes are grouped under this cost sub-category.

Testing Equipment Calibration : The testing equipment used by the quality staff must be periodically recalibrated to ensure its accuracy. This task is services, which makes it itify their fees and charge them to this cost sub-category.

Testing Equipment : Depending on the kinds of quality tests performed the types of testing equipment can be expensive. When the cost of this equipment falls below a company's capitalisation limit, the entire cost is charged straight to this sub-category. When it is higher, the associated depreciation is charged here.

Internal Failure Cost

These are costs incurred when product defects are discovered prior to shipment. Examples are:

Correction of Related Paper Work : When a product failure occurs internally, resulting in rework or scrap, various paperwork activities are required. The staff time required to complete all these activities is recorded here.

Lost Profit on Products Sold as Seconds : When a company finds that it has products of a sufficiently low quality that they cannot be sold through normal sales channels, it can elect to sell them at a discount rather than expend extra rework effort to bring them up to higher quality standard. Then, loss in profit, that occurs. When these products are sold at lower price should be recorded in this sub-category as a cost or sales discount.

Machinery Downtime : This discovery of internal product failure can lead to machinery downtime for two reasons. The machines are needed to rework defective products, which keeps them from being used to create new products. The cause of the internal failures may be the machinery, which require some downtime, while it is being investigated and repaired. In either case, the cost of the machinery downtime should be charged to this cost sub-category.

Redesign : If a product continues to have high quality error rates over time, the problem may not be in the manufacturing process, but rather in the underlying product design. The engineering time charged to this work should be summarised in this cost sub-category.

Reinspection and Testing : Once a product has been reworked, it must be inspected and tested to ensure that it now meets quality specifications, which requires extra staff time.

Repurchasing : When products are scrapped, the purchasing staff may need to repurchase the components needed to create replacements. The cost of the time needed to do this can be recorded separately in this cost sub-category.

Rework : Depending on the extent of product rework required, separate staff may be needed for the activity. There may also be a charge for machinery required to perform rework tasks.

Safety Stock : If there is a significant volume of internal product failure, the management team may find it necessary to keep on hand large quantities of extra components to make up the shortfall of components, that occur because of the scrapping of low-quality products. An interest cost is associated with the investment in this extra inventory, as well as shortage, insurance and obsolescence costs that can be accumulated in this sub-category.

External Failure Costs

These are costs incurred when low-quality products are shipped to customers. This tends to be most difficult quality cost area to measure because it is hard to quantify some customer-related costs. Examples of external failure costs are:

Customer Surveys : A company may conduct customer surveys for the sole reason that it needs feedback about the quality of products sold to them. If this is the only reason for creating and operating a survey, then the cost of the survey can be charged to this account.

Customer Imposed Penalties : These penalties should certainly be segregated into a separate account so that management can easily determine their extent.

Loss of Customers : The opportunity cost of sales lost should still be itemised in this account because of its potential size.

*Loss of Reputation :*This is a difficult cost to calculate or even estimate, so most companies do not use this cost account preferring instead to simply itemize the potential for this cost in the narrative reactions of their quality cost reports.

Product Recall Insurance : This can be an expensive policy to obtain. The cost is certainly high enough to be placed in its own separate account.

Suppliers Warranty Ckdmprocessing : When customers returns products, there is a good chance that their complaints involve products components sold to the company by its supplier. In this case company also fills out warranty claim forms to send to its suppliers to obtain reimbursement for shoddy components. These administrative costs should be charged to this account.

Warranty Claim Administration : When there aremany productreturnsfrom customers, a company may find it necessary to create a full-time warranty claims department. The cost of the staff for this department, as well as all associated overhead costs should be charged to this account.

Major Considerations in implementing TQM

(i) Efforts should be made to use reliable estimates. Price measures may be too costly to obtain.

(ii) TQM measures should be used for process indication.

(iii) Team approach should be used to determine the parameters of the measures.

(iv) The frequency of reports can vary from daily to yearly. It takes time for TQM to make a measurable difference. Experience reveals that most companies opt for the longer reporting time of quarterly or annually.

(v) Training should be accepted as key to understanding the meaning of the measures.

(vi) Care should be taken to make measures based on natural business unit such as a subsidiary, a specific plant or an independent division,

(vii) Emphasis should be on setting realistic expectation.

(viii) Measures selected should be flexible and measures selected should be changed with the staff in TQM focus.

Cost Accountant and Total Quality Management : A cost accountant can make significant contribution in evaluating the cost implication of a TQM programme as follows:

(i) Use COQ (Cost of Quality) as part of regular reporting and control process. The traditional or emerging COQ model can be used with quality costs collected by cost categories. Most companies commit the cardinal mistake of not determining the optimal cost point. Rather they assess total quality costs and match the costs with changes in quality as a result of various TQM efforts.

(ii) *Focus the accounting and control efforts on non-conformance (internal and external failure) costs reduction.* Many international companies of repute concentrate on non-conformance costs. The conformance costs are a natural part of the TQM programme and can be considered like fixed cost of quality. Economic gains come from changing processes to reduce failure costs.

(iii) *Support the operations by focusing on specific non-financial hard SPC (Statistical Process Control) to monitor the progress of TQM.* Some companies choose to ignore COQ and rely on operation data as the real measure of success. Statistical process control, yield rates, waste amounts and defect percentage provide managers with data to measure the progress of TQM programme. It is assumed that these data correlate well with improved economic performance.

(iv) *Do not use COQ.* Certain financial heads aid the company with a focus on general and overall non-financial measures of conformance to monitor progress of TQM. IBM and Motorola are strong proponents of this approach. These non-financial measures drive the company to achieve specific level of quality performance and make the necessary investment to achieve the target.

These are a few of different strategies, of which first two are very popular.

Accelerating use of TQM : The increased acceptance and use of TQM is the result of three major trends:

(i) reaction to increasing domestic and global competition;

(ii) the pervasive need to integrate the several organisational functions for improvement of total output of the organisation as well as the quality of output within each function; and

(iii) the acceptance of TQM in a variety of service industries.

The paradigm of TQM applies to all enterprises both manufacturing and service and many companies in manufacturing, service and information industries have reaped the benefits. Industries as diverse as telecommunications, public utilities and health care have applied the principles of TQM.

4

Standard Costing

From Management's point of view, "What a product should have costed" is more important than "what it did cost". Managers are constantly comparing their product cost with "what it should have costed". Reasons for deviations are rigorously analysed and responsibilities are promptly fixed. Thus, "what a product should have costed" is a question of great concern to management for improvement of cost performance. A scientific answer to this problem, *i.e.* an answer based on reasons and consequences, is developed by use of standard costing. Standard costing is a managerial device to determine efficiency and effectiveness of cost performance. First of all, different terms to be used in this chapter have been taken up in detail.

Standard : It is a pre-determined measurable quantity set in defined conditions.

Standard Cost : Standard cost is a scientifically pre-determined cost, which is arrived at assuming a particular level of efficiency in utilization of material, labour and indirect services. CIMA defines standard cost as "a standard expressed in money. It is built up from an assessment of the value of cost elements. Its main uses are providing bases for performance measurement, control by exception reporting, valuing stock and establishing selling prices."

Standard cost is like a model which provides basis of comparison for actual cost. This comparison of actual cost with standard cost reveals a very useful information for cost control.

Standard cost has also been referred to as cost plan for a single unit. This cost plan will give element-wise outline of what the product cost should be according to management's thinking. This thinking is not merely an estimate or guess work. It is based on certain assumed conditions of efficiency, economic and other factors. Standard cost is primarily used for following purposes:

— Establishing budgets.

— Controlling costs and motivating and measuring efficiencies.

— Promoting possible cost reduction.

— Simplifying cost procedures and expediting cost reports.

— Assigning cost to materials, work-in-process and finished goods inventories.

— Forms basis for establishing bids and contracts and for setting selling prices.

Standard Costing : According to CIMA (London), *"Standard costing is a control technique which compares standard costs and revenues with actual results to obtain variances which are used to stimulate improved performance."* Use of standard costing is not confined to industries having repetitive processes and homogeneous products only. This technique has established the advantages of its use in industries having non-repetitive processes like manufacture of automobile, turbines, boilers and heavy electrical equipment.

Variances and Variance Analysis : Variances represent deviations of actual performance from standard performance. There can be cost variances, profit variances and sales value variances. Variances can be favourable or unfavourable depending upon their impact on the profits of the organisation. Variance analysis is an exercise involving efforts to classify variances according to causes for highlighting the situation demanding managerial attention.

Standard Hour or Minute : Production is generally expressed in terms of physical units like tonnes, pounds, gallons, numbers, etc. When different type of products are being manufactured in the factory, it is difficult or rather impossible to express all the products in one common unit. For example, in the coke oven factory, both coke and gas are produced. Coke is measured in tonnes, while gas is measured in cubic feet. Thus, difficulty arises in expressing heterogeneous products in one common measure—either in tonnes or in cubic feet . Standard hour approach is useful in expressing the output of an organisation, when it is producing a variety of products having different units of measurement. CIMA defines Standard hour or minute as "the quantity of work achievable at standard performance in an hour or minute". It is the media of converting production into allowed hours or minutes. It states in detail the standard relationship between time and output. Standard relationship implies that considerable amount of thought and energy is applied before specifying "time allowed" for a unit of output. In a manufacturing organisation work done, i.e., production is expressed in physical terms only, but with the aid of standard hours it can be converted or expressed in allowed hours or minutes also. Suppose production in coke oven factory is : 1,000 kg. of coke and 600 cft. of gas and the standard time allowed per unit is 8 hours and 16 hours respectively. The production in standard hours will be:

Coke 1,000 kg. x 8 hrs.	=	8,000 hrs
Gas 600 cft. x 16 hrs.	=	9,600 hrs
Production in standard hours	=	17,600 hrs

Standard Cost and Estimated Cost : Following are the points of difference between standard cost and estimated cost.

Scientific Determination : Standard cost is scientifically determined. It means considerable amount of time and energy is spent to decide how a task should be accomplished and what resources it should consume. Estimated cost is not scientifically determined. It is based on past data relating to product, which is adjusted according to anticipated changes in future.

Representation of Management's View : Standard cost represents management's view of efficient operation and relevant expenditure . For this reason, standard cost ensures a particular efficiency in utilization of material, labour and indirect services. The idea of efficiency does not dominate determination of estimated cost.

Different Aims : "What a product cost should be" and "What a product cost will be" point towards the two different attitudes, that dictate determination of standard cost and estimated cost.

Usage of Control : Standard cost primarily helps management in controlling cost performance. For this reason, precision, efficiency and analysis become important ingredients of standard cost determination.

Limitations

1. Data does not provide yardstick of comparison for actual cost.
2. Data is made available too late to correct inefficiencies, that are causing costs to go out of limits.
3. Data does not provide motivation to employees to strive for accomplishment of their objectives.
4. Data provides insufficiently for budgeting, planning, decision-making and price quotation.

These limitations of historical costing are primarily responsible for advent and wide usage of standard costing.

Standard Costing and Budgetary Control : Budgetary control and standard costing are two different terms. These techniques are complementary to each other. These are interrelated techniques, but these techniques are not inter-dependent. Standard costing is introduced primarily to ascertain efficiency and effectiveness of cost performance. Budgetary control is introduced to state in figures an approved plan of action relating to a particular period. Both standard costing and budgetary control have following common features:

1. Both have common object of improving managerial control.
2. Both techniques are based on the presumption that cost is controllable.

3. In both the techniques results of comparison are analysed and reported to management.

Despite these common features, these are two different techniques. The points of difference are summarised as follows:

Denote Different Ideas : Standard costing denotes a unit idea. It outlines what a unit should cost. Standard cost provides a cost plan for a unit whereas budget denotes a "a total idea". The statement clearly explains the difference: "Budgeted cost of material is Rs. 1,000 if 10,000 units are produced at a standard cost of Rs. 1 each."

Different Aims : Budget seeks to lay down a monetary limit of expenses which should not be normally exceeded. If this limit is exceeded , the actual profit will fall short of budgeted profit. Standard costing seeks to procure efficient unitization of material, labour and indirect services.

Different Scope : Budgets are laid down for all functions of an organisation like production, purchase, selling and distribution, and research and development. Standard costing relates primarily to one function *i.e.,* production. It mainly deals with manufacturing cost only.

Treatment of Income and Expenditure : Budget preparation considers both income and expenditure, whereas use of standard costing is mainly confined to expenditure only.

Difference in Treatment of Variances : In practical life, budgets are taken to be the monetary ceiling. Often, efforts are directed to see that budgets are not exceeded because failure to be in budgetary limit will call for a detailed explanation to higher management. In standard costing, variances are subjected to microscopic view with reference to causes and incidence. All distinct deviations are reported to higher management.

Different Junctions : Budgetary control prescribes a monetary limit which, if adhered to , will keep the business out of financial crisis. Standard costing emphasises a particular efficiency in utilisation of input resources. It may highlight new areas for probe and improvement.

General Advantages

1. Use of standard costing leads to optimum utilization of men, materials and resources.
2. Its use provides a yardstick for comparison of actual cost performance.
3. Only distinct deviations are reported to management. Thus, it helps application of the principle of management by exception.
4. It is very useful to management in discharging functions, like planning, control, decision-making and price fixation.
5. It creates an atmosphere of cost consciousness.
6. It motivates workers to strive for accomplishment of defined targets. It precipitates an attitude that is conducive to efficiency.
7. It highlights areas, where probe promises improvement.
8. Its introduction leads to simplification of procedures and standardisation of products.
9. Its introduction enables the management to reduce time required for preparation of reports for pricing, control or quotation purposes.
10. Its use enables to find out the cost of finished goods immediately after completion.
11. If standard costing is used, stock ledgers can be kept in terms of quantities only. This eliminates much clerical effort in pricing, balancing and posting on stores ledger cards.
12. Its use may encourage action for cost reduction.

Specific Advantages : Specific uses of standard costing in connection with different activities of organisation are summarised below:

Accounting Department is benefited by: (i) Planning and budgeting, (ii) Valuatton of inventories, (iii) Cost control, (iv) Pricing, sales and cost estimates, (v) Developing monthly operating results.

Producation Department is Benefited by : (i) Production planning, (ii) Matching scheduled production with machine capacity, and (iii) Preparing reports of business logs in terms of time.

Sales Department is benefited by: (i) Determining and checking selling prices, (ii) Preparing quotations on special products, and (iii) Determining the profitability of specific product lines.

The Limitations : Standard costing is a very good system, but it should be used giving regard to following limitations:

1. Establishment of standards may demand a lot of skill, imagination and experience. If all these factors are not in harmony, desired results will not be forthcoming.
2. Variance analysis is useful, whereas deviations are linked with responsibilities. Sometimes, it is difficult to fix responsibility, because the result happens to be the outcome of a number of contributory factors.
3. Standards should correspond to current conditions for best results. Current conditions change very rapidly. Revision of standard is a costly exercise and leads to a lot of associated problems. For this reason revision of standards may get ignored. This delay may be disastrous for effectiveness of the system.
4. It is difficult to use standard costing, when working conditions do not permit standardisation of material contents, labour contents or the use of indirect services relating to different jobs, processes and services.
5. Lack of interest by appropriate level of management renders the use of standard costing ineffective.
6. Isolating the controllable and uncontrollable elements of variances is a very difficult exercise and this difficulty restricts the application of standard costing.
7. Sometimes, use of standard costing creates adverse psychological effects, if standards are set at a high level.

Preliminaries to Establishment of Standards : Before standard cost for different elements of cost is determined, management must take decisions about the following:

Length of Period of Use: First of all, a decision is to be arrived at relating to the period, for which standards will be used. According to this decision, management will decide to use current standard, basic standard or normal standard. This decision is the starting point for establishment or standards.

Types of Standards to be Used : It means that management should decide how tight or loose standards ought to be. Policy of management will help to take this decision. If cost reduction is the aim, a tight standard will be the choice of management. Similarly, if pricing decision and planning the expenditure is the aim of management, standards corresponding to the current conditions will be the choice of management.

Review of Existing Procedures : The existing procedure should be subjected to review, because some activities may have to be routinised and wastages, rejections and losses may have to be standardised. This review will call for a complete study of technical and operational aspects of organisation.

Classification of Accounts : The existing accounts manual in an organisation may not be sufficient to comply with the requirements of cost collection, cost analysis and variance reporting. For this reason existing accounts manual may have to be suitably adapted to meet the requirements. This may call for a change in existing classification of heads of accounts.

Review of Existing Coding System : The existing coding system is subjected to review to adapt it to introduction of standard costing. This change may demand orientation of existing coding system.

Constitution of Standard Committee : An apex standards committee should be constituted. This committee should have representation of different functional Managers, like Personnel Manager, Production Manager, Planning Manager and Marketing Manager. The cost accountant coordinates the functions of standard committee. It will be the job of this committee to prepare a detailed plan dealing with: (a) introduction of standards; (b) computation of variances; (c) linking the deviations with responsibilities; (d) reporting to management, i.e., deciding now various reports dealing with variances will be sent to various levels of management; and (e) developing a system of follow-up.

Decisions to be Taken at Various Levels : For introduction of standard costing. Certain important decisions will have to be taken at various managerial levels. These are summarised below: (a) *Top Management decisions:* (i) Plant operating hours. (ii) Kinds and volume of goods to be produced and sold. (b) *Engineering Management decisions:* (i) Product designs. (ii) Product specifications. (c) *Manufacturing Management decisions:* (i) Personnel requirements. (ii) Indirect services requirements. (d) Sales *Management decisions:* (i) Prices at which goods can be sold. (ii) Personnel requirements. (iii) Other distribution requirements. (e) Cost *Accounting Department:* (i) Operating budgets to reflect the several management decisions. (ii) Standard costs for all products based on these decisions.

Various Types : Based upon tightness, looseness and period of operation, standards have been classified in the following categories:

Based on Period of Operations : (1) Current standards. (2) Basic standards. (3) Normal standards.

Based on Tightness and Looseness : (4) Ideal standards. (5) Expected or attainable standards.

Current Standards: Current standards are established giving specific regard to current conditions, in which standards are used. These standards (a) outline what cost should be under current conditions; (b) call for periodical review and frequent revisions; (c) require to be changed with changes in method of production and price level; and (d) hold good for related accounting period. These standards are easily understood and have proved most useful for managerial control. There are two main advantages of the use of current standards : (i) These standards provide definite goals for short periods, which employees can usually be expected to reach. They also appear to be fair bases with which the current performance is measured. Current standards are set at a level which is high yet attainable with reasonably diligent efforts and attention to the correct method of doing the job. These standards may be effective for stimulating efficiency. (ii) Use of current standards, which closely represent expected actual performance, is economical. Such attainable standards can be used in planning, budgeting and control processes. Where standards are not close to expected actual performance, they may be applicable for control purposes, but are not realistic for planning and budgeting use.

Basic Standards : These are referred to with different names, like bogey standards, static standards and fixed standards. These standards : (a) are established for an unaltered use for a long period of time; (b) allow consistent comparison with same base line; (c) may not stand in harmony with current conditions; (d) do not specify level of efficiency required; (e) represent a special class of standards of a statistical nature; (f) are used in the same way as the statisticians use commodity price indices; (g) serve as a yardstick with which actual performance is compared; and (h) are not revised unless the products or the manufacturing operations or processes are changed. The main advantage of the basic standard is that it minimises the number of revisions which would be required due to change in cost of materials and labour.

When basic standard is used, no change is required other than a computation of the cost relationships between the basic period and the current period. This computation is used in adjusting the standard costs before making comparison with the actual costs. To illustrate this point, the year 1984 is assumed to be the basis for comparison and calculation. The material used by the firm is copper sheet, which is Rs. 40 per kg. This figure is used to represent 100 per cent as base figure. In the year 1994, the average price of copper is Rs. 80 per kg. The basic standards for the copper material to be used must first be adjusted by 200 per cent before a comparison with the actual costs can be made. These standards can be used in industries, where routines and operations are well established and working conditions do not normally change for a long time. These standards may be good to spotlight trends, but they cannot form basis to gauge efficiency.

Normal Standards : These standards are based on past averages adjusted to anticipated future changes. These standards are prepared for relatively longer period covering a trade cycle. In formation of these standards, allowance is given to normal waste and scrap, normal fatigue and breaks, normal machine breakdown and maintenance and normal mistakes in production. These standards represent the cost performance which should normally be attained. While these standards are very likely attainable, they are difficult to compute, because of probable errors in predicting the extent and duration of cyclical effects. A good performance is more than an ordinary performance. A standard should not be very high to cause frustration, but still it should be high enough to expect a reasonably diligent effort for its accomplishment. The normal standard may be good for long-term planning and decision-making, but their utility in efficiency appraisal is limited.

Ideal Standards : Under these standards, attention is focused on perfection. These standards aim at absolutely minimum cost, which is attainable only in perfect operating conditions. These standards provide no scrap, no idle time, no rest period and no breakdown. In the long run, it is impossible to attain these standards. Ideal standards have also been referred to as theoretical standards. These standards are rarely attained in practice. Where ideal standards are used, the accounts reveal unfavourable variances as regular feature. This results in a depressing feeling among the staff members. Ideal standards can also be used for a long time without change or adjustment. These standards can also be used as engineering standards in highly mechanised industry. After these standards are once set, they are rarely changed, unless radical changes are made in the product or in the manufacturing processes. One Professor told his students *"ideal standards are like dreams of Sophia Lorens—distant, desirable but rarely attainable."*

Expected or Attainable Standards : It is a compromise between extremes of ideal standard and normal standard. These standards: (a) are set providing for operating inefficiencies, which are unavoidable; (b) take into account prevailing conditions in the period for which standards are used; (c) are very realistic in nature and provide best criterion for evaluation of performance; (d) have got the maximum usage because they fulfil all the requirements of good standards, *i.e.*, they are consistent, realistic, capable of attainment and provide incentive for improvement. In these standards, level of performance expected is higher than level of performance expected in normal standard. But this level is higher enough to expect reasonably diligent effort for accomplishment. It is capable of fulfilment. These standards are very useful for cost control purposes.

Setting of Standards : Determination of standards for various elements of cost is an exercise, that requires skill, imagination and experience. For setting standards, routines and process of working conditions are thoroughly studied and motion studies are conducted and different tests are carried out to ensure that standards are realistic and conform to management's view of efficient operations and relevant expenditure. This job of setting the standards is done by a group, which is represented by Engineering Department, Production Department, Purchase Department, Personnel Department and Cost Accounts Department. Setting of standards can be divided in two categories :

(i) Determination of quantity standards; and

(ii) Determination of price standards.

Quantity standards are pre-determined expressing in physical terms the relationship between a unit produced and resources consumed. Price standards are pre-determined measures expressing in money terms the cost per unit of resources consumed. Quantity standards are developed by representatives of Engineering Department in liaison with representatives of Purchase Department. Wage rate standards are developed by Personnel Department. Accounts Department works in advisory capacity supplying the information based on historical costing.

Setting of standards for various elements of cost has been taken up in detail in the following discussion :

Direct Material Cost Standards : The establishment of standard cost of material involves : (i) Determination of standard quantity of materials, and (ii) Determination of standard price of materials.

Determination of Standard Quantity of Materials : For determination of standard quantity of materials following information per unit of output is obtained : (a) Material contents of product; (b) Standard composition of mix; and (c) Quantity of wastage.

It is comparatively simple to ascertain the quantity of material to be used in the manufacture of a product. These quantity standards are established from records of past experience, from test runs, from mathematical or scientific computations or through use of standard bill of materials. Material quantity standards are primarily based on the estimates of engineers, who design the product and determine the processes through which the material passes. After processes are thoroughly studied and working conditions are satisfactorily analysed, the type and standard quantity of each raw material is specified in the form known as standard bill of materials. Various mechanical, and chemical tests are carried out to ensure that materials used will suit product design and quality. These are primarily engineers who lay down the standard composition of material mix. Many trial runs are made to ascertain normal spoilage which will include shrinkage, wastage and scrap. This is most important but exclusive area in determination of standard quantity of material. Too often this factor is overlooked or only partially included in determination of standard material quantity of product, because it cannot be seen. Waste, scrap and shrinkage have been referred to as the prime thieves of profits. Difficulty arises in determining standards for waste because of disinclination of management to recognise its presence. Too often, the attitude is that waste does not constitute an important factor. It is necessary that realistic standards should be set for waste, scrap, etc., for the purpose of : (a) Management guidance; and (b) Determining adequate and fairly stated product cost.

Material quantity standards are developed by representatives of-Engineering Department in liaison with representatives of Production Department to ensure that standards are truly realistic and representative.

Determination of Standards Price of Material : Determination of price standard presents a lot of difficulties because prices are susceptible to wide range of fluctuations. Purchase Department is ultimately responsible for development of these standards. A detailed study of market conditions of each material precedes determination of price standards. On the basis of management's policy, decision is taken whether price standards will be based on recent past averages, current prices of expected prices. Statistical methods can be used to ascertain the market trends, which are adjusted according to anticipated changes in future. Discounts and rebates available for different kinds of materials are taken into consideration. Methods of treatment of related costs like freight, material handling, inspection, receiving and storing are different in different organisations. If these costs form part of direct material, these costs are included in standard cost of material. Standard material cost of a product is determined by multiplying standard material quantity of a unit by standard price per unit of material.

Direct Wages Standards : Human element makes determination of standard labour cost a difficult job. These standards often remain sources of conflict between workers and management. For this reason, compliance to the following points should precede to determination of standard labour cost: (1) Working conditions should be studied. Plant layout, production method, material flow, material handling and material setting should be thoroughly gone through. (2) Standard specifications should be prepared for all jobs. Workers should be under instructions to adhere to these specifications. These specifications will show complete description of work, operations to be performed and time allowed for each operation. (3) All workers do not work with the same efficiency. They should be graded preferably by a specialised time observer on the basis of their skill and effort. It is a highly technical job and calls for an exceptional judgement on the part of time study specialist.

After the preliminaries are complied with, standard cost for labour is established. The exercise is divided in two categories: (a) Determination of standard time, and (b) Determination of standard rate.

Determination of Time Standards : These are also referred to as labour efficiency or labour performance standards. A standard time is specified for each activity or operation. Time standard is based on the following :

(1) Time study, (2) Motion study, (3) Average of past performance, (4) Test runs, and (5) Work sampling.

For developing time standard, the industrial engineers divide the job in different operations and a sequence likely to lead to maximum production is suggested after eliminating the unnecessary activities. Time and motion study is performed by industrial engineers to determine the standard hours required for an average worker to do a specified job (standard hour represents the amount of work, which should be done in one hour under specified conditions). For developing time standards, allowance is made for rest time, fatigue, machine breakdown and preventive maintenance, etc.

These days another term "work sampling" is also being used for developing time standards. Under this technique, performance of an activity is observed at random moments and data for a reasonably long period is collected. It helps to develop statistically valid conclusions relating to time required for an activity. In brief "work sampling" constitutes application of statistical methods for collection of basic data for development of time standards. The defect of this technique is that it reflects "What it is" and it has to be adjusted to establish "What it ought to be".

Determination of Standard Rate : It is very difficult to generalise the procedure for developing standard rate for labour. Each situation requires special study and regard to the factors involved. Standard rates are developed on the basis of collective bargaining agreements with unions and ruling of Government bodies. These agreements clearly mention hourly wages, piece rates and bonus differentials. In non-unionised organisations, these rates are determined on the basis of negotiations between employees and Personnel Manager or Departmental Manager. If modern wage incentive system is in vogue, the determination of standard rate is very simple. Job evaluation provides a basic rate, which is increased according to merit rating of employees plus adjustment of bonus and fringe benefits according to policy of management.

It is pertinent to discuss here the treatment of bonus, overtime and fringe benefits for fixing standard rate.

Bonus : Where bonus is a regular feature, it becomes a part of wages and hence it is logical to include it in setting standard rate. (The opinions differ whether bonus should be included or not for determination of standard labour rate.) Where bonus is paid as an ex-gratia payment, it should be treated as an overhead for that period.

Overtime : When regular overtime is worked, because it is not possible to meet the demand in regular hours, overtime should be included in setting standard rate. If overtime is paid occasionally, it should be treated as an overhead for that period.

Fringe Benefits : Sometimes fringe benefits constitute up to 30% or more of wages. These fringe benefits include payroll taxes, workmen's compensation, insurance, employer's contribution to pension, employer's contribution to group insurance, etc. Sometimes, these benefits are a straight percentage of wages and sometimes these benefits do not bear a constant proportion to wages. In other words, fringe benefits may be fixed or variable. Fringe benefits, which bear a constant ratio to wages, should be considered for computation of standard rate, fringe benefits, which are fixed in nature, should be considered as overhead. For example, payment to LIC for group insurance of employees should be considered overhead for the period under consideration.

Thus; after time standard and rate standard have been established, the standard labour cost for an operation is obtained by multiplying standard hours allowed by standard rate set for the operation.

Factory Overhead Standards : From control point of view, determination of standard for factory overhead is not important, because neither incurrence nor use of facilities is at the discretion of operating level. Standard for factory overhead is developed for product costing and product planning. Fixation of standard for factory overhead involves following steps :

Determination of Level of Production : This is the starting point for determination of standard overhead rate. Overheads, especially fixed overheads, are estimated for a particular level of production or activity. Level of activity can be determined with reference to any of the capacities such as maximum capacity, practical capacity, normal capacity and budgeted capacity. (The budgets are prepared expecting utilization of a particular capacity, which is referred to as budgeted capacity.) Level of activity can be expressed in terms of direct labour hours, direct labour cost, machine hours and units produced. It serves as the denominator by which standard overhead estimate is divided to arrive at the standard rate of overhead.

Determination of Standard Overhead Estimate: Overheads are controlled by budgets. The budgets are based on past experience and cannot be automatically considered as standard. Considerable amount of time and energy is spent to ascertain that budget represents "what cost ought to be". If there is a variation between "what cost ought to be" and budgets, suitable adjustments are carried out to arrive at the standard overhead estimate. This standard overhead estimate is divided by budgeted capacity to arrive at the standard overhead rate.

Classification of Overheads in Two Categories i.e., Fixed Overhead and Variable Overhead : That cost can be divided into two categories, i.e., fixed and variable, is the hypothesis of overhead control. For developing standard overhead rates also, separate rates are developed for fixed overhead and variable overhead. Thus, classification of overhead broadly in these two categories precedes determination of standard overhead rate for each of these categories.

Standard Factory Overhead Rate : This is the end result of the effort directed for determination of factory overhead standard. First, standard rate is arrived at separately for fixed overhead and variable overhead as follows .

(a) Standard fixed overhead rate = Standard fixed overhead of budget period ÷ Standard base for budget period, i.e., level of activity expressed in hours or units.

(b) Standard variable overhead rate = Standard variable overhead for the budget period ÷ Standard base for budget period, i.e., level of activity expressed in hours or units.

After standard fixed overhead rate and variable overhead rate are determined, a total standard factory overhead rate is developed.

Standard Cost Sheet : After the standards for various elements of cost have been set, these are recorded in a form, which is referred to as standard cost sheet. It contains quantity and price of each class of material used, grade of labour, labour rate and time and overhead rate for each product. Standard cost sheet also shows total of each element of cost for each department. One cost sheet is prepared for each product manufactured. The information is arranged in standard cost sheet in such a way that the cost of even a partly finished unit can also be quickly determined. These standard cost sheets are of great use in making quotations and finding out variances. The number and complexity of standard cost sheets or cards depend upon the size and characteristics of the business. A plant producing thousands of different articles naturally has need for many more cards than one producing a single article. In some firms, a large number of small parts must first be manufactured before the main product can be assembled. In the production of sewing machines, vacuum cleaners, pianos, washing machines and various motors, a separate standard cost sheet or card must be used for each part manufactured. Then, finally an assembly standard cost sheet for final product is prepared. Manufacturing process of pianos require more than four hundred different parts and for each part, there is standard cost sheet. In these situations, an assembly standard cost sheet for final product is prepared in the end.

Revision of Standards : Standards are always set for a particular period. Decision to change or not to change the standards rests entirely on circumstances. The revision of standard is a costly exercise involving a lot of labour and expenditure. At the same time obsolete standards lead to wrong conclusions and frustration. Minor changes can be taken care of by variance analysis, but major changes in method of production may necessitate prompt revision. A review of standards should be made at a specific interval according to decision of management, but revision should be attempted only when compelling unusual conditions come to prevail. A revision may be attempted in the following circumstances : 1. It has been proved that standards set were fundamentally wrong. 2. Changes in price level may compel to revise standards. Only unforeseen, substantial and apparently permanent price rise makes a case for revision of standards. 3.There is change in material specification. 4. Basic wage rates have changed substantially and almost permanently.

The guiding factor for changing the standard is, whether or not conditions have so changed that standards as set no longer reflect what was in mind at the time of their determination. The standards should be changed only when underlying conditions change. In many cases mania for revising the standards, when they ought not to be changed, has led to the weakening of effectiveness of standard costing in operation.

Some companies believe that standard should be changed each year. If fundamental concepts of standard costing are kept in mind, there is neither reason nor logic for this argument. The passage of time has nothing to do with the question of revising the standard. The standards should be changed only when they reflect something which no longer exists. Since basic standards are used fairly for a long time like index numbers for a particular base year, they should be changed only under the following circumstances: (i) Change in the method of manufacture. (ii) Change in the plant capacity. (iii) Disparity between base standard and actual performance is so substantial that standards lose their significance.

Factors Interfering with the Successful use of Standard Costing: Some of the factors, which tend to interfere with the successful use of standard costing, are summarised below: 1. Some companies have well developed standard cost plans for product costing. Still they make little use of standard costing for managerial purposes. One valve manufacturing concern had been collecting labour cost variances by departments for several years and yet they did not know what to do with them. When a discussion of these variances took place with the foreman of the department in which the variances occurred, the cost accountant could not believe that he had ignored these variances for control purposes. 2. Some standards are out-of-date or unreliable. They are not, therefore, taken seriously. 3. Reports are not made in terms which management understands. Using technical cost accounting terminology will not help executives having a production or sales background. 4. Changing conditions made it necessary to revise standards more often. Many firms do not do this. 5. Sometimes it is difficult for management to make effective use of standards, since it is difficult to determine the sources of variances. When these sources are eventually discovered, so much time has elapsed since they occurred that the managerial effectiveness of control is lost.

Special Use of Standard Costing : The use of standard costing is fast growing as an effective technique of cost accountancy. Its special uses are discussed under following headings:

Adds to Managerial Effectiveness and Efficiency : It is not enough for a manager to be effective. He has to be efficient as well. Performance of a manager should be both effective and efficient, i.e., desired objective should be accomplished with minimum input resources. The use of standard costing provides media to specify these objectives of effectiveness and efficiency. It also provides framework to measure the degree of attainment of effectiveness and efficiency.

Aids Inventory Costing : Valuation of inventory at standard cost simplifies the pricing of inventory. It enables the company to follow a consistent practice. All operating gains and losses are charged off to accounting period in which they arise. This enables executives to analyse the variances by type, causes and locations. When standard costing is used, a unit standard cost is available for inventory valuation and pricing of store issues. It avoids the need to compute a new average unit price with each input entry, as is the case, when perpetual inventory records are kept at actual cost.

Help in Product Pricing : The knowledge of standard cost of product can be useful as one of many factors to be taken into account for pricing. The standard cost of a product is a useful starting point in pricing. It provides a warning that unless this amount and something more for profit is recovered in the selling price, the product will not be really profitable. The knowledge gained in setting standard cost provides the entire cost picture of the product ranging from its out-of-pocket cost to full costs. With all this information, it becomes possible to ascertain the extent to which an available price will cover out-of-pocket costs and contribute to recovery of fixed costs. The standard cost provides one of the many factors that should be considered in pricing.

Reduce Clerical Record Keeping and Aids Cost Reduction : Standard costs may result in reduction of clerical work. For example, under actual cost system, each item of each material requisition must be costed separtely, when *LIFO* of *FIFO* method is used. In a large company, this is an enourmous task, since thousands of requisitions may be issued. Under a standard costing system, all the issues of a particular type have to be multiplied once by the standard cost. Under standard costing, only quantities have to be maintained on stores records. This saving is, of course, partially offset by the added cost of establishing and revising standards.

Aids in Budgetary Planning and Control : The use of standard costs and knowledge of relationship gained through establishment of standards are useful in budgetary planning and control. The standard costs developed for each product can be used to convert the sales estimates into projections of material, labour and overhead. In situations where a large variety of products are involved, it is possible to select and use the standard costs on a few products representative of large groups. Standard costs can also be used to develop representative proportion of material, labour and overhead by product group. Thus, the knowledge gained through studies for establishment of standard cost can be extremely effective and useful for planning and control.

Variance Analysis

The comparison of actual performance with standard performance reveals the variances. A variance represents a deviation of the actual result from the standard result. There can be cost variances, profit variances, sales value and operational and planning variances. *Whether a variance is favourable or unfavourable, is ultimately determined with reference its impact on profit.* For example, a cost variance will be adverse, if the actual cost exceeds the standard cost or *vice versa.* Profit variance will be favourable, if actual profit exceeds standard profit or *vice versa.* Variance analysis is an exercise, which involves efforts to isolate the causes of variances in order to report to management those situations which can be corrected and controlled by timely action. The extent to which the causes of variances are established, depends upon the amount of time effort and money, that a company is willing to spend in accumulating data, as the variances occur. In variance analysis, a point is reached where incremental information is not worth its incremental cost. This point indicates the limit of variance analysis and this point is determined by judgement in the light of individual circumstances. Variance analysis must be devised to suit to the conditions prevailing within a particular enterprise. Analysis of variances must be followed by intelligent and factual interpretation. Computation, classification and reporting of variances is a vital feature of standard costing. Variance analysis should be a continuous process for following reasons : 1. Labour rates, salary levels etc., changes due to union negotiations, policy decisions or changes in composition of the work force. 2. Selling prices change. 3. In a multi-product company, product mix changes and different lines have different margins, the overall profit position will change. 4. Improvement in systems can bring about reduction in costs. 5. Change in level of efforts of operators, supervisors, management and clerical staff can affect the existing cost levels. 6. Investment in new capital equipment and scrapping of old equipment/ processes/methods can affect the operating cost levels (*i.e.*, direct labour cost and direct material cost). These decisions, which are frequently taken in an organisation, can affect overhead items such as depreciation charges and insurance premium. 7. The prices of bought-out material may vary. 8. Changes in product design may change cost-inputs. 9. Policy decisions of various kinds, for example, changes in organisational structure, may affect cost levels. 10. The amount of idle time may change due to holdups, strikes lockouts and power failure.

Model Steps : Model steps approach has been adopted for computation of variances. These model steps have been arranged in a logical sequence which should be necessarily adhered to for arriving at the correct inferences. *For cost variances,* if the value of preceding step is more than the value of following step, it will be a case of adverse or unfavourable variance or *vice-versa. For Sales Variances,* if the value of preceding step is more than the value of following step it will be a case of favourable variance or *vice-versa. Whether a variance is favourable or unfavourable is ultimately determined* *with reference to its impact on profit.* It is important to remember this rule. Each model step represents existence of a particular value. If in a particular case, value of preceding step is zero then value of the step preceding immediately to preceding step will be considered for calculation of variances. For example, if a particular variance is the difference between M_4 and M_3 and the value of M_3 is zero then automatically difference of M_4 and M_2 will be taken for the purpose. This point is applicable to all variances.

Classification and computation of variances. For the purpose of classification and computation, variances can be discussed under the following headings :

(i) Cost variance, (ii) Sales margin variance. (iii) Sales value variance.

Cost Variance : 'Cost variance' represents the difference between the costs actually incurred for production and the costs specified for the same. It is the sum total of following variances :

(a) Direct material cost variance. (b) Direct wage variance. (c) Variable overhead variance. (d) Fixed overhead variance.

Each of these will be dealt with in detail.

Material Cost Variance : Material cost variance and its sub-divisions are summarised in the flow chart given below :

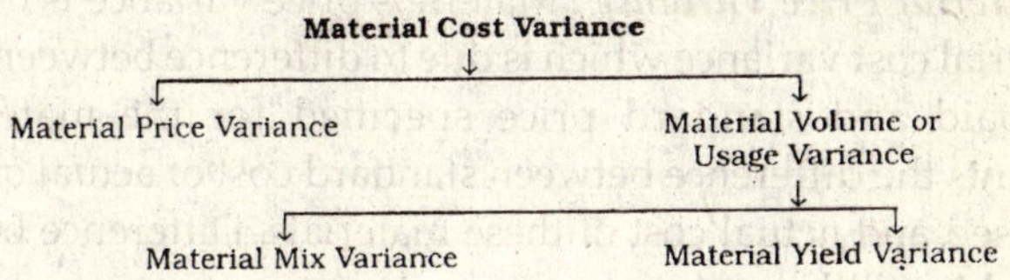

For finding out the material cost variances, four model steps are given below:

M_1—**Actual cost of material used** : (Actual quantity of materials used x Actual rate).

M_2—**Standard cost of material used** : (Actual quantity of material used x Standard rate specified for the material).

M_3— **Standard cost of material used, if it had been used in the standard proportion.** Standard engineering specifications may lay down that standard mix will include material A 4 kg. @ Rs. 3.00 per kg., material B 6 kg. @ Rs. 5.00 per kg. Actual mix may include material A 2 kg. @ Rs. 4.00 per kg. and material *B* 8 kg. @ Rs. 6.00 per kg. The value of step 3 will be worked out as follows :

Material A	4 kg. x Rs. 3.00	= Rs. 12.00
Materials	6 kg. x Rs. 5.00	= Rs. 30.00
	10 kg.	= Rs. 42.00

Note that actual ratio of consumption, *i.e.*, 2 : 8 had been disregarded for model step M_3

M_4—**Standard material cost of output** (Standard quantity of material required for the specified output x Standard rate).

The material cost variances have been taken up in detail in the following discussion:

Material Cost Variance : It represents the difference between actual cost of material used and standard cost of material specified for output achieved. Material cost variance arises due to variation in prices and usage of materials. Difference between M_1 and M_4 will be material cost variance.

Material Price Variance : Materials price variance is that part of material cost variance which is due to difference between actual price paid and standard price specified for the material. It represents the difference between standard cost of actual quantity purchased and actual cost of these materials. Difference between M_1 and M_2 will be material price variance.

Although the material price variance may not be controllable, it provides management with important information for purposes of planning and decision-making. The knowledge of this variance may prompt the management to increase product price, use substitute materials or find other offsetting sources of cost reduction.

Material Usage or Volume Variance : It is also referred to as quantity variance. It is that part of material cost variance which is due to difference between actual quantity used and standard quantity specified for output. This indicates whether or not material was properly utilized. A debit balance of material usage variance indicates that material used was in excess of standard requirements. A credit balance or materials usage variance will indicate saving in the use of material. Difference between M_2 and M_4 will be material usage or volume variance.

Material usage variance consists of: (a) Material mix variance, and (b) Material yield variance.

It cannot be automatically assumed that the material usage variance is controllable by the departmental supervisor. It is also not necessary that favourable material usage variance is advantageous to the company. There may be interrelationship between variances. For example, a favourable material usage variance may be related to an unfavourable labour efficiency variance, i.e., labour may have conserved material by operating more carefully at a lower output rate.

Material Mix Variance : This variance is that part of material usage variance which is due to difference between actual composition of mix and standard composition of mixing the different types of materials. Short supply of a particular material is, often the most common reason for material mix variance. Difference between M_2 and M_3 will be material mix variance.

Material Yield Variance : In certain industries, it is possible to lay down that output will be a particular percentage of total input of material. In a particular situation, it may be given that normal loss in production will be 20% of input of material. In a case like this, 80% of the total input of material will be the expected output. If actual yield obtained happens to be different from the standard yield specified, there will be a yield variance. Thus material yield variance is that portion of material usage variance, which is due to difference between actual yield obtained and standard yield specified. Difference between M_3 and M_4 will be material yield variance.

Direct Wage Variance : It represents difference between actual wages paid and standard wages specified for the production.

Standard wages specified for the production represents the wages which should have been paid according to standard specification for production achieved. Standard wages specified for production can be determined by multiplying standard labour cost per unit and units produced. Difference between L_1 and L_5 will be Direct Wage Variance.

Direct Wage Rate Variance : Direct Wage Rate Variance is that portion of Direct Wage Variance which is due to difference between actual wage rate paid and standard wage rate specified. It represents difference between : (i) Actual payment to worker for actual hours worked, and *(ii)* Payment involved, if worker had been paid at standard rate.

For computational purposes, actual payment to workers for actual hours worked will be referred to as L_1. L_2 will represent payment involved, if the workers had been paid at standard rate.

Direct Wage Efficiency Variance : It is that part of wage variance which is due to difference between actual hours paid and standard hours allowed for output achieved :

It represents difference between :

(i) Payment involved, if workers had been paid at standard rate, and (ii) Standard labour cost for output achieved. Difference between L_2 and L_5 will be Direct Wage Efficiency Variance. Direct Wage Efficiency Variance is the sum total of Labour Gang Variance, Labour Idle Time Variance and Labour Yield Variance.

Direct Wage Gang Variance : It is that portion of Direct Wage Efficiency variance which is due to difference between actual composition of gang used and standard composition specified for a gang. A need to change the composition of a gang may arise due to shortage of a particular grade of labour.

It may be mentioned in standard specifications that class A and class *B* workers will make 50%: 50% contribution to produce article Z. In actual working class A and class B workers might have been used in the ratio of 75% : 25% respectively. When actual composition of a gang is different from standard composition specified for a gang, it will give rise to Labour Gang Variance or Labour Mix Variance.

When composition of labour mix is changed, it will change the efficiency of that group. If workers in new labour gang are less skilled than the skill level planned in establishing standards for labour, it will adversely affect the output of the gang. On the other hand, if workers in the new gang are more skilled than the skill level planned in establishing standards for labour, it will favourably affect the output of the gang. Thus, mix variance should be considered part of labour efficiency variance only.

Labour Gang Variance represents difference between: (i) Payment involved, if workers had been paid at standard rate, and (ii) Payment involved, if workers had been used according to proportion of standard gang and payment had been made at standard rate. Difference between L_2 and L_3 will be Direct Wage Gang Variance.

Labour Idle Time Variance : It is that part of Wage Efficiency Variance, which is due to difference between labour hours applied and labour hours utilized. In practical life, there are sometimes abnormal circumstance like strike, lockout and power failure, which prevent utilization of an labour hours being paid for, *i.e.,* labour hours applied. Idle Time Variance represents difference between: *(i)* Payment involved, if workers had been used according to proportion of standard gang and payment had been made at standard rate, and (ii) Standard labour cost of labour hours utilized. Difference between L_3 and L_4 will be Labour Idle Time Variance.

Standard labour cost for labour hours utilized can be found out in two ways:

(1) Deduct from value of step L_3 the standard labour cost of labour hours not utilized, i.e., standard labour cost of idle time.

(2) Find out directly the standard labour cost of labour hours utilized. The idle time variance will be attempted only when there is a difference between labour hours applied and labour hours utilized.

Labour Yield Variance : It is that part of labour efficiency variance which is due to difference between actual output of worker and standard output of worker specified. There will be no difference between labour efficiency variance and labour yield variance, if efficiency variance had been exclusively due to difference between : (i) Actual level of performance of workers, and (ii) Standard level of performance of workers.

Method of computing yield variance can be divided in two parts :

(a) When there is idle time variance.

(b) When there is no idle time variance.

When there is Idle Time Variance : Yield variance will be the difference between :

(i) Standard labour cost of labour hours utilised, and

(ii) Standard labour cost of output achieved.

Difference between L_4 and L_5 will be labour yield variance.

When there is no Idle Time Variance : If there is nothing in the question to show that hours utilized were different from hours available, there will be no idle variance and L_4 will be taken to have zero value for computational purposes. The yield variance will then be the difference between the value of step L_3 and value of step L_5. Following example will illustrate computation of labour yield variance, when there is no labour idle time variance.

Variable Overhead Variance : Variable overhead per unit remains the same. It varies with output in total. Variable overhead variance and its sub-divisions can be summarised in a flow chart given below :

Variable Overhead Variance

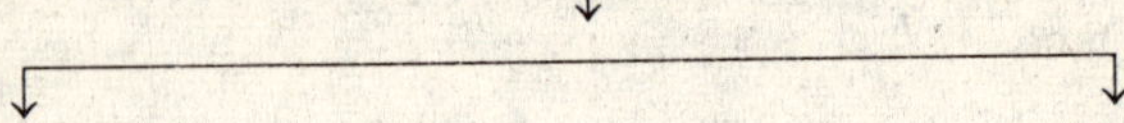

Variable Overhead Expenditure Variance Variable Overhead Efficiency Variance

For finding out the variable cost variance, three model steps are given below:

VO_1—Actual overhead incurred. (It is normally given)

VO_2—Actual hours worked at standard variable overhead

rate. (Standard variable overhead rate per hour x Actual hours worked).

VO_3—Standard variable overhead for the production. (Standard/Budgeted variable overhead per unit x Actual production).

All these variable overhead variances are discussed below :

Variable Overhead Variance : It represents difference between: (i) Actual overhead incurred during the period, and (ii) Standard variable overhead for production. Difference between VO_1 and VO_3 is variable overhead variance. This variance can also be determined by taking the aggregate of variable overhead expenditure variance and variable overhead efficiency variance.

Variable Overhead Expenditure Variance : Variable overhead expenditure variance is that portion of variable overhead variance which arises due to difference between actual variable overhead and standard variable overhead appropriate to the level of activity attempted. It will represent the difference between actual variable overhead incurred during the period and actual hours worked at standard variable overhead rate. Difference between VO_2 and VO_3 will be variable overhead expenditure variance.

Variable Overhead Efficiency Variance : Some accountants try to determine variable overhead efficiency variance like labour efficiency variance. This variance will be the difference between: (i) Actual hours worked at standard variable overhead rate, and (ii) Standard variable overhead for production. Difference between VO_2 and VO_3 will be variable overhead efficiency variance.

Fixed Overhead Variance : Fixed overhead variance and its sub-divisions are summarised in a flow chart given below :

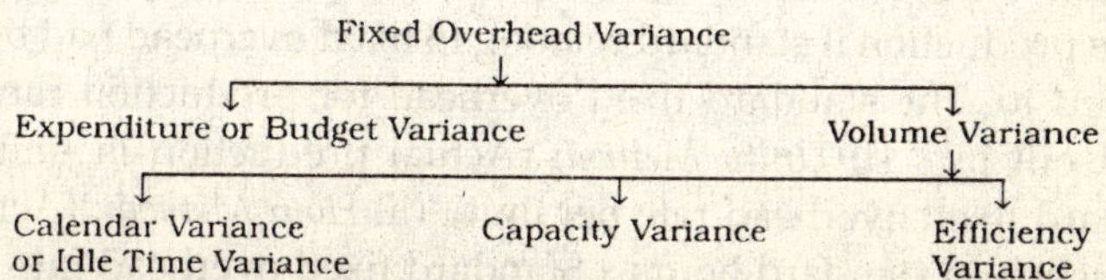

Fixed overhead variance arises when a company uses

absorption standard costing system. Under this system, a standard rate is developed for fixed overhead by dividing the total fixed overhead by a suitable base like labour/machine hours/ number of units, etc. Fixed overhead incurred differs from standard allowance for fixed overhead or standard fixed overhead for production for various reasons, which gives rise to different kinds of fixed overhead variances. For finding out the fixed overhead variances, five model steps are given below:

FO_1— Actual fixed overhead incurred.

***FO_2*—Budgeted fixed overhead for the period or standard fixed overhead allowance.** It represents the amount of fixed overhead which should be spent according to budget or standard during the period. The amount is pre-determined for finding out the fixed overhead rate for the related period. The amount of standard allowance for fixed overhead does not change due to change in volume.

FO_3—Fixed overhead for the days/hours available at standard rate during the period. The related period may be given in terms of days/hours. The value of this step is found out by multiplying days/ hours available and standard overhead rate.

***FO_4*—Fixed overhead for actual hours worked at standard rate.** In actual working conditions, hours worked and hours available during the period may be different due to strike, lockout, etc. Therefore, value of *FO_4* can be determined by multiplying actual hours worked and standard rate.

FO_5—Standard fixed overhead for production. It is different from budgeted fixed overhead for the period or standard fixed overhead allowance (refer to step 2). It is arrived at by multiplying the actual production and standard rate. Standard and fixed for production denotes the amount which should have been incurred for the production if standard relating to fixed overhead had been adhered to. The standard fixed overhead for production can be found out by : (i) *Unity Method*: (Actual production in units x Standard fixed overhead rate per unit), (ii) *Hour Method* : (Actual production in standard hours x Standard fixed overhead rate per hour).

Fixed Overhead Variance : It represents the difference between actual fixed overhead incurred and standard cost of fixed overhead absorbed. It can also be referred to as the difference between actual fixed overhead incurred and standard fixed overhead for production. Difference between FO_1 and FO_5 will be fixed overhead variance.

Fixed Overhead Expenditure Variance : It is that part of fixed overhead variance, which is due to difference between actual fixed overhead incurred and budgeted fixed overhead or the standard allowance for fixed overhead. This variance indicates difference between actual fixed overhead incurred and budgetary estimates of what should have been spent. It highlights how far the budgeted overhead for the period has been taken care of. It is also referred to as budget variance. Difference between FO_1 and FO_2 will be fixed overhead expenditure variance.

Fixed Overhead Volume Variance : It is that part of fixed overhead variance which is due to difference between budgeted fixed overhead for the period (or standard fixed overhead allowance for the period) and standard fixed overhead for actual production. This variance indicates how far the plant and facilities have been under/ overutilized compared to budgeted level of operation. The difference between level of activity attempted and level of activity budgeted gives rise to fixed overhead volume. For computational purposes, it is the difference between FO_2 and FO_5. Fixed overhead variance consists of following variances :

(a) Calendar variance/idle time variance,

(b) Capacity variance, and

(c) Efficiency variance

These variances are taken up in detail in the following discussion.

Calendar Variance or Idle Time Variance : Calendar variance is that part of fixed overhead volume which is due to difference between budgeted fixed overhead and fixed overhead for days available during the period at standard rate. This variance arises due to difference between days in budgets and days actually available during the related period. Calendar variance represents difference between:

(a) budgeted fixed overhead, and

(b) fixed overhead for days available during the period at standard rate. For computational purposes, budgeted fixed overhead for the period will be referred to asFO_2- FO_3 will represent fixed overhead for days available during the period at standard rate.

Idle Time Variance : Idle time variance is determined almost on the line of calendar variance. It is that part of volume variance which is due to difference between budgeted fixed overhead and fixed overhead for hours available during the period at standard rate. This variance arises due to difference between hours as per budget and hours available in the period, to which budget is applied.

It is necessary to understand the difference between calendar variance and idle time variance. For computational purposes, both will represent the difference between FO_2 and FO_3. The difference between FO_2 and FO_3*will* be calendar variance, when there is a difference between number of days as per budget and days actually available during the period. The difference between FO_2 and FO_3 will be idle time variance, when there is a difference in hours as per budget and hours actually available during the period.

Capacity Variance : It is that part of fixed overhead variance which arises due to difference between capacity utilized and planned capacity or available capacity. It represents difference between : (a) Budgeted fixed overhead or standard fixed overhead for days/hours available at standard rate, and (b) Fixed overhead for actual hours worked at standard rate.

It should be remembered that difference between budgeted capacity and capacity available gives rise to capacity variance. An adverse capacity variance indicates that available capacity has not been fully utilized. It will lead unobserved balance of fixed overhead. Favourable capacity variance indicates that production has exceeded standard capacity. It will mean that fixed overhead costs are over-absorbed. Capacity variance represents difference between FO_3 and FO_4.

Efficiency Variance : Fixed overhead efficiency variance is that portion of volume variance which reflects increased or reduced output arising from efficiency being above or below standard. In other words, it is that portion of fixed overhead volume variance which is due to difference between budgeted or standard efficiency and actual efficiency in utilization of fixed common facilities. A supervisor is responsible for the efficient utilization of space, equipment and fixed overhead facilities. If he is able to utilize the facilities more than expected in standard, the result will be a favourable efficiency variance. Unfavourable fixed overhead efficiency variance will result, if utilization of fixed facilities is poorer than expected in standard. It is a barometer by which management comes to know how efficiently or inefficiently fixed indirect facilities or services are being used. It represents difference between FO_4 and FO_5.

Total Sales Margin Variance : Sales margin variance and its sub-divisions are summarised in a flow-chart given below.

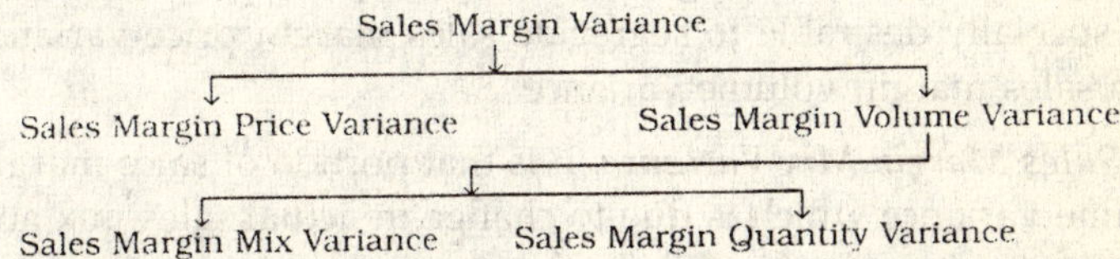

For finding out the Sales Margin Variances, four model steps are given below:

SM_1-Actual sales margin on actual sale effected. Actual sales margin represents difference between realisation from actual sales and standard cost.

SM_2 Standard sales margin in actual sales effected.

SM_3 Standard sales margin, if actual sales effected had been in the ratio of standard mix.

SM_4- Standard sales margin on standard sales mix or budgeted sales margin for sales as per budget or standard.

Sales Margin Variance represents the difference between: (a) Actual margin (difference between standard cost and the realisation from actual sales), and *(b)* Standard margin appropriate to the quantity of sales budgeted. Difference between SM_1 and SM_4 will be total sales margin variance.

For determining whether variances are adverse or favourable, the approach will be exactly the opposite of what it was in the case of cost variances. In Sales Margin Variances if the preceding step is less than the following step, it will be a case of adverse variance. Alternatively, if the preceding step is more than following step, it will be a case of favourable variance. Logic is simple. For favourable sales margin variances, actual sales margin should be more than sales margin as per budget. This point should be carefully remembered to avoid confusion . This will hold good for Sale Value Variances also.

Sales Margin Price Variance. It is that portion of sales margin variance which is due to difference between actual price and standard price of actual sales effected. Difference between SM1 and SM_2 will be Sales Margin Price Variance. Sometimes ,it is necessary to adapt the selling price of the product to changing market condition by raising or lowering the prices. In these cases, it is specially desirable to segregate sales margin price variance from sales margin volume variance.

Sales Margin Mix Variance. It is that portion of sales margin volume variance which is due to change in actual sales mix and budgeted sales mix. It arises because actual sales mix does not always remain constant. It has to be changed due to changing market conditions, i.e., national or internal conditions or management policies. Difference between SM_2 and SM_3 will be the sales margin mix variance.

Sales Margin Quantity Variance. It is that portion of sales margin volume variance is due to difference between: (i) standard sales margin on actual sales effected, if these sales had been in the ratio of standard mix, and (ii) standard sales margin on standard sales mix or budgeted sales margin for the sales as per budget.

Difference between SM_3 and SM_4 will be Sales Margin Quantity Variance. SM_3 will represent standard sales margin on actual sales effected, if these sales had been in the ratio of standard mix. SM_4 will represent standard sales margin on standard sales mix.

Sales Value Variance : Since management is primarily interested in the analysis of profit variations, sales value method is not frequently used in practice. However, the sales value variances are useful for sales manager in determining the effect of changes in different factors on sales value. Following diagram gives an overall idea of sales value variance.

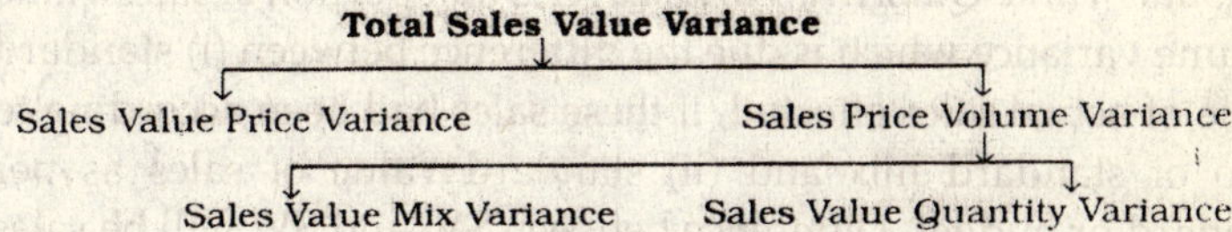

For finding out the sales value variances, four model steps are given below:

SV_1—Actual value of sales realised.

SV_2— Standard value of actual sales.

(Actual sales quantity x Standard sales price)

SV_3—Standard value of actual sales if these sales had been effected according to the ratio of standard sales mix.

SV_4— Standard value of sales as per standard or budget.

Total Sales Value Variance : It represents the difference between (i) Sales value realised and *(ii)* Standard value of sales as per standard or budgeted. Differences between SV_1 and SV_4 will be total sales value variance.

Sales Value Price Variance : It is that portion of total sales value variance which is due to difference between actual sales price realised and budgeted sales price. Difference between SV_1 and SV_2 will be sales value price variance.

Sales Value Volume Variance : It is that portion of total sales value variance which is due to difference between standard value of actual sales effected and standard value of sales as per standard or budget. Difference between SV_2 and SV_4 will be sales value volume variance. This variance can also be found out by taking aggregate of sales value mix variance and sales value quantity variance.

Sales Value Mix Variance : It is that portion of sales value volume variance which is due to the difference between (i) standard value of actual sales effected, and (ii) standard value of actual sales effected, if these sales had been according to the ratio of standard mix. Difference between SV_2 and SV_3 will be sales value mix variance.

Sales Value Quantity Variance : It is that portion of sales value volume variance which is due the difference between (i) standard value of actual sales effected, if these sales had been according to ratio of standard mix and (ii) standard value of sales as per standard or budget. Difference between SV_3 and SV_4 will be sales value quantity variance.

Two-Variance, Three-Variance and Four-Variance Methods of Analysis: The variance analysis has already been discussed in detail. The terms "Two-Variance", "Three-Variance" and "Four-variance" methods are not separate methods of variance analysis. These terms simply indicate the extent to which variances are being analysed in a particular organisation. Following discussion will indicate what these terms convey with reference to "Material Cost Variance" and "Overhead Variance". This thinking on the same lines can be extended to labour variance, sales variance and profit variance.

Material Cost Variances "Two-Variance": The term 'Two-Variance" indicates that analysis is being confined to highlight the interplay of two factors, *i.e.*, price and quality only. Diagrammatically, it can be presented as follows :

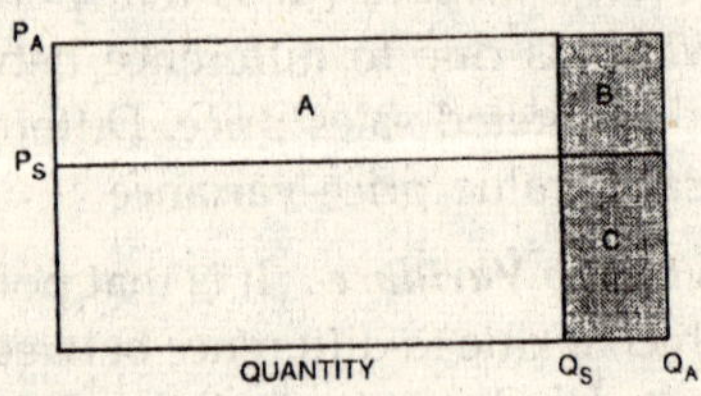

Fig. Two-Variance Analysis.

where P_A—Actual price; Q_A—Actual quantity

P_s—Standard price;

Q_s—Standard quantity

Actual cost = $P_A 9_A$ Standard cost = $P_s Q_A$

Total Variance = Actual cost - Standard cost = $P_A Q_A$ - $P_S Q_S$ If "two variance" approach is adopted to material cost variance, then only material price variance and material quantity variance will be determined.

"Three-Variance" : This approach takes variance a little further and total material cost variance, *i.e.,* P_AQ_A-P_sQ_s is taken to be equal *toA + B + Cin* Fig. This is very simple. In three variance analysis witn regard to material cost variance, following variances will be attempted :

(a) Material Price Variance

(b) Material Mix Variance

(c) Material uantity Variance.

"Four Variance" : The "four-variance" approach takes the analysis still further. The area represented by A + *B* + C in figure will be divided according to causes under following heads :

(a) Material Price Variance

(b) Material Mix Variance

(c) Material Sub-usage Variance

(d) Material Efficiency Variance.

Thus, the terms Two-Variance", "Three-Variance" and "Four-Variance" only indicate the extent to which variances are being analysed in an organisation. It is difficult to lay down hard and fast rules in this connection. An organisation has to decide the extent of variance analysis to suit to its specific requirements.

Overhead Variance and "Two-Variance", Three-Variance", and "Four-Variance" Approach : Overhead variance is the result of numerous contributory factors. The knowledge of overhead variance can be effective only when it is further analysed according to reasons. Following discussion will explain, what these terms, i.e. 'Two-Variance", Three-Variance" and "Four-Variance" mean with reference to overhead variance analysis.

Two-Variance Approach : Under this approach, only expenditure variance or budget variance and volume variance are attempted. Some authors refer to budget variance as controllable variance.

Three-Variance Approach : Some managers hold the view that two-variance approach is inefficient for control purposes of management. They recommend "three-variance" approach. Under this approach following three variance will be determined:

(a) Expenditure variance or budget variance

(b) Capacity variance

(c) Efficiency variance.

Four-Variance Approach : Under this approach, analysis of variances is stretched a little further than three-variance approach. All variances are throughly analysed. Following variances are attempted under "four-variance" approach.

(a) Expenditure variance (b) Calendar variance

(c) Capacity variance (d) Efficiency variance.

The foregoing discussion sufficiently explains how various variances are determined under "Two-Variance", "Three-Variance" and "Four-Variance" approaches. The readers should attempt the variance according to normal practice of "Model Steps" and then according to requirements of"Two-Variance", Three-Variance" and "Four-Variance" approach, results should be presented. An example on overhead variance analysis will illustrate the idea.

Non-Conventional Variance Analysis : Conventional variance analysis suffers from some recognised disadvantages. When environment changes, then mere routine comparison of actual performance with standard performance will not reflect the desired result. For this reason, Joel Demski and Bromwich have advocated ex-post variance analysis. Variance analysis must take into account changes in original plan. Following new headings are relevant for discussion:

Operating and Planning Variances : Following factors invalidate the conventional variance analysis and necessitate the use of operating and planning variances: (a) Internal factors such as technological and organisational changes arise with the organisation. These are controllable variances. They are normally known and planned for in advance. (b) Extraneous factors such as inflation arise outside the organisation. These factors are likely to be uncontrollable and usually necessitate changes in plan at fairly short notice.

The basic idea of the operating and planning variances is to analyse variances into variances due to operational factors (hence controllable) and variances due to planning errors (some of which might have been avoidable and some entirely unavoidable, i.e., unforeseeable price changes). The difference between the original budget and (ex-ante budget) and revised (ex-post) budget represents the planning variances. It is analysed into avoidable and unavoidable elements. This enables management to appraise the efficiency of its planning methods with a view to improve future planning.

As per the Chartered Institute of Management Accountants, London, Operating and Planning Variances are subsets of material total variance replacing traditional usage and price variances. These variances are used to isolate variances caused by (i) unforeseen circumstances, i.e., planning variance, and (ii) operational variance, which reflects non-standard performance. This approach may also apply to labour and overhead. CIMA has defined these variances as under:

Operational/Planning Variance. Subsets of direct material total variance replacing traditional usage and price variances, used to isolate variance caused by unforeseen circumstances (planning variance) leaving operational variances that better reflect cost of non-standard performance. May also apply to labour or overhead.

Operational Price Variance. (Actual materials used or purchased x Revised standard price) - (Actual materials used *or* purchased x Actual price)

Operational Usage Variance. (Standard materials used x Revised standard price) - (Actual material used x Revised standard price)

Planning Price Variance. (Standard material cost) - (Revised standard material cost). The revised standard is an efficient buying price, determined at the period end.

An example will fully illustrate these recent concepts:

Quality Cost Variance : It represents difference between (a) actual quality cost, and *(b)* budgeted quality cost. In this era of technological changes and acute competition, this variance attracts extra attention. It is not a part of pyramid of inter-related variance, because quality cost is incurred within various functions.

Market Share Variance : It represents the difference between (a) actual sales units at standard contribution per unit, and (b) sales units representing the budgeted share of actual market at standard contribution per unit. Actually, it is a subset of sales volume contribution variance. It is applicable when actual size of a product or product group is known. It indicates how well market share has been maintained.

Market Size Variance : It represents the difference between (a) sales units representing the budgeted share of actual market at standard contribution per unit, and (b) budgeted contribution.

It should be particularly noted that step (b) in preceding variance becomes step (a) in this variance and this also represents the difference between the two.

Market Cost Variance : It represents the difference between (a) actual marketing cost, and (b) budgeted marketing cost. Where marketing cost is variable and fixed, approach can be adapted accordingly.

Revision Variance : It is a common experience that the standard becomes outdated very quickly. Mostly it is due to the change in circumstances and inflation is the main factor contributing to this need. Other factors, which invalidate the existing standard are : (a) Technological changes such as changes in production methods, changes in design of products and changes in office equipment. (b) Organisational changes such as different sales mix, changes in warehousing and distribution methods, changes in management, new agreements, changes in remuneration methods, new health and safety provision. (c) hanges in fiscal policy. (d) Changes in economic environment. (e) Exchanges rate variations.

The CIMA Terminology defines revision variance as "the difference between an original and a revised standard cost. It arises when on an interim adjustment of a standard cost is made without adjusting the budget and is revised to allow full analysis of the difference between budgeted and actual profit. The variance can be further analysed to reflect revisions due to price of materials, labour and overhead rates and changes in methods."

For a complete, analysis, a statement can be prepared reconciling actual and budgeted profit for a particular period incorporating revision variance where appropriate. The main objective in computing revision variance is to eliminate known factors from analysis. Thus areas needing investigation and remedial action get highlighted.

For quick computation, it is the difference between : (a) standard cost and (b) revised standard cost.

A method variance is one form of revision variance.

A Relevant Cost Approach to Variance Analysis : Traditional approach to variance analysis is to calculate variance based on acquisition costs and the standard prices for the acquisition of the resources. This is misleading, when scarce resources exist. Failure to use scare resource efficiently leads not only to increased acquisition cost but also to a lost contribution. Therefore meaningful approach would be to incorporate the lost contribution in variance analysis. For example, if scarce material is used excessively, it will cause material costs to be greater and in addition there will be lost contribution, which should be attacked to material usage variance. When this approach is used, price or expenditure variances are not affected. Quantity variances are affected by how efficiently scarce resources are being used.

Causes of Variances : A large number of reasons are at play in causing variances. The measurement of variances is a mechanical task, that has no importance in itself. The value of variances comes from an analysis of significant variances, the identification of their causes and the correction of these causes. Therefore, the purpose of variance analysis will be defeated, if the causes of deviations are not promptly communicated to management. The delay in reporting these causes may render the variance analysis useless, because by the time the reports are made, it may be too late to take the remedial measures. Further discussion deals with causes of different variances:

Material price variances

(i) Change in market price.

(ii) Loss of discount.

(iii) Incorrect shipping instructions.

(iv) Emergency purchases.

(v) Acceptance of orders requiring special purchases, high transportation cost.

(vi) Changes in taxes and duties,

(vii) Inefficient purchase system.

(viii) Failure to take advantage of seasonal purchases,

(ix) Use of substitute material of different prices,

(x) Uneconomic size of purchase order.

Material usage variance

(i) Poor quality of material.

(ii) Changes in mix.

(iii) Changes in production method.

(iv) Changes in design.

(v) Careless handling.

(vi) Faulty machine processing,

(vii) Improperly set standards.

(viii) Poor inspection.

(ix) Labour inefficiency.

(x) Improper engineering specification.

(xi) Pilferage of material.

(xii) Substitution by non-standard material

Direct wage rate variance

(i) Use of defective grading of employees.

(ii) Payment of wages at higher rates to carry on emergency operations.

(iii) Revision of pay scales due to national awards.

(iv) Establishment of incorrect standards by Personnel Department.

(v) Change in philosophy of management leading to a change in method of remuneration.

(vi) New workers not being allowed full wage rate.

Direct labour efficiency variance

(i) Poor working conditions.

(ii) Poor supervision of workers.

(iii) Poor scheduling of production processes.

(iv) Poor maintenance and repair of machines.

(v) Use of sub-standard materials.

(vi) Use of employee with low competence.

(vii) Frequent power failures.

(viii) Go-slow techniques of employees,

(ix) Incorrect recording of performance.

(x) Increase in labour turnover.

Overhead expenditure variance

(i) Seasonal conditions.

(ii) Improper use of available facilities.

(iii) Use of efficient tools, tackles and construction equipment.

(iv) Improperly set standards.

Overhead capacity variance

(i) Chance in scheduling of production process.

(ii) Power failures.

(iii) Labour troubles.

(iv) Lockout.

(v) Shortage of materials.

(vi) Machine break-down.

(vii) Slump in customers' demand.

Overhead efficiency variance

(i) Poor working conditions.

(ii) Poor supervision.

(iii) Poor scheduling of production processes.

(iv) Frequent power failures.

(v) Improperly set standards.

Disposition of Variances : A wide divergence of opinion exists among accountants regarding disposition of variances . It is very difficult to lay down hard and fast rules to be followed for this purpose. It is commonly recognised that disposition of variances is a very important decision area, which affects both inventory valuation and measurement of income. Following are the important considerations relevant to this decision: (i) Materiality of variance; (ii) Cost of inefficiency; and (iii) Cost of product.

The choice of disposal method depends on the following points: (a) Type of variances, *i.e.*, material, labour and overhead variances, (b) Size of variances, (e) Past experience of using standard costing system, (d) Causes of variances, and (e) Timing of variances, *i.e.*, unusual variance can be caused by seasonal variations.

Following are the three disposal methods of variances: (1) Transferring them to the profit and loss account. (2) Prorating them over cost of sales and closing inventory of work-in progress and finished goods. (3) Writing off the controllable variances to profit and loss account and uncontrollable variances to be prorated over cost of sales and closing inventory of work-in-progress and finished goods. (4) Setting up as reserve.

Transfer to Profit and Loss Account : When this method is used, all variances are written off against income for the period. Hence, cost of sales and closing inventory of work-in-progress and finished goods are all stated at standard cost. Unfavourable variances (debit) are deducted from gross profit calculated at standard cost. Favourable variances (credit) are added to gross profit computed at standard cost. All variances shown in profit and loss account are supported by variance analysis report. No variance is treated as an increase or decreasing manufacturing cost. On the other hand, variances are taken as deviations from standard cost due to inactivity, inefficiency, extravagance, or other changes in business condition. If this method is followed, inventories are valued at standard cost and, therefore, financial statements can be prepared at an early date. If there are reasons to believe that variances are from efficiency factor that could have been controlled, transferring the variances to profit and loss account will appear to be most feasible practice. Following reasons are often advanced in favour of this method of disposing of variances: (i) Standard cost represents the normal cost of production. Variance from standard cost represents changes which should not form part of product cost, (ii) If inventories are valued at standard cost, the loss of time at final account closing is reduced. (iii) When variances are transferred to profit and loss account with complete details, the variance analysis will attract managerial attention.

Prorating Variances Over Cost of Sales and Closing Inventories: When this method is followed, cost variances are distributed to cost of sales and inventories of work-in-progress and finished goods. This proportion may be attempted on any reasonable basis like units or values, etc. Under this method, cost of goods sold and inventories are all shown at actual cost. Following arguments are advanced in favour of this method: (a) Actual cost is a fact and it is logical that actual cost should be used in financial statements irrespective of their effects. (b) For ascertaining income for the year, the auditors are generally interested in actual profits and not to standard profits . (c) If variances are transferred to profit and loss account, it will distort the figure of profit. Therefore, it seems logical that variances should be distributed between sales and inventories of work-in-progress and finished goods. (d) The value of inventories will not be truly depicted, if appropriate share of variances is not assigned.

This method is very simple and logical. If price-changes beyond the control of management have taken place, these should be depicted in inventories and cost of sales.

Writing off the Controllable Variances to Profit and Loss Account and Uncontrollable Variances Prorated Over Cost of Sales and Closing Inventories This step constitutes writing off the controllable variances to the profit and loss account and uncontrollable variances to be prorated over cost of sales and inventories of work-in-progress and finished goods. This method presents a compromise between the two extremes referred to above.

If variances arise due to efficiency factors within the control of management, they should be closed to profit and loss account. On the other hand, if variances are due to reasons beyond the control of management, these should form part of cost of sales and inventories.

Setting up Reserves : Certain accountants hold the view that variances should be set up as reserves, until they are setoff. When this method is followed, variances debit or credit balances will be carried forward unless they are mutually set off. The variance balance, which may be either debit or credit due to inefficiency or efficiency, is shown in the profit and loss account.

The foregoing discussion reveals that disposition of variances is an area, in which accountants are not entirely in agreement. The common view is that variances resulting from incorrect standards or conditions beyond the control of management, i.e., increase in wage rate due to an award of some Wage Tribunal and price rise, etc., should be distributed to cost of sales and inventories of finished goods and work-in progress. On the other hand, variances due to efficiency or inefficiency factors, which might have been influenced by management, should be transferred to profit and loss account.

Reporting of Variances

Variances are not ends in themselves. They communicate signals for further analysis, investigation and action. Variance analysis will lose its utility and objective, if variance reports are not promptly made to appropriate level of management. The report on variance analysis should be made assuming three levels of management, i.e., Top Management, Middle Management and Operating Management. These levels of management have been discussed in detail elsewhere. 'Variance report" should be made keeping in view the ultimate use of the report and the periodicity of reports. The cost accountant should make vivid reports highlighting: (a) Essential cost deviations, and (b) Possibilities for improvement.

The variance report should be prepared with due regard to the following points: (i) The executive concerned should be informed about, what the cost performance should have been. (ii) How close actual cost performance was with reference to standard cost performance. (iii) The analysis of causes of variances to enable the control action to be taken appropriately. (iv) Reporting activity should be guided by principle of "Management by Exception". Based on this principle, a cost accountant communicates to appropriate level of management only essential facts from the great mass of his cost data. (v) The magnitude of variances.

Reporting of Variances through Ratio Analysis : Cost control efforts can be aided considerably by using ratio analysis technique. The rationale behind ratio analysis is that mangement must take greater interest in relative term as opposed to absolute figures in order to control costs. The management can compute a number of ratios pertaining to liquidity, profitability and capital structure, etc., but this discussion is concerned with only operating cost ratio. Variances expressed in terms of absolute figures do not convey the true picture very effectively. Absolute figures of variances are also not very useful when comparison of two different periods is to be made. Variance are also not very useful when comparison of two different periods and highlighting the abnormal situations which are of interest to management. Following variances ratios are commonly used:

Eficiency Ratio : Efficiency ratio summarises the rationaship between output expressed in standard hours and actual hours spent for that output. Following formula is used for determining the Efficiency Ratio :

$$\text{Efficiency ratio} = \frac{\text{Output expressed in terms of standard hours}}{\text{Actual hours spent for producing that output}} \times 100$$

In other words, efficiency ratio reveals the input-output relationship. Input is available in terms of hours worked. Output is converted into standard hours to determine the relationship of input and output. It is a very important ratio and it reveals the extent of efficiency or inefficiency of production during the related period. (The reader should bear in mind that standard hour is the media of expressing output in terms of hours.) It can be referred to as a hypothetical hour which measures the amount of work which should be performed in one hour according to standard.

Activity Ratio : This ratio refers to the relationship between output expressed in terms of standard hours and the budgeted standard hours. In other words, following three steps are involved in determining this ratio : (a) actual output should be expressed in terms of standard hours. (b) budgeted output should be expressed in standard hours. (c) percentage relationship of (a) and (b) should be expressed.

In other words, this ratio highlights the actual level of activity in comparison to budgeted activity level. This ratio reveals how effecively or ineffectively actual efforts were made in comparison to budgeted estimates. Activity ratio is expressed as under :

$$\text{Activity ratio} = \frac{\text{Actual output in standard hours}}{\text{Budgeted output in standard hours}} \times 100$$

Calendar Ratio : It refers to the relationship between actual number of working days in a period and the number of working days in the related budget period:

$$\text{Calendar ratio} = \frac{\text{Actual No. of working days in a period}}{\text{No. of working days in related budgeted period}} \times 100$$

Actual Capacity usage Ratio : This ratio refers to the relationship between actual number of working hours and the maximum possible number of working hours in a period as per budget:

$$\text{Actual Capacity Usage Ratio} = \frac{\text{Actual hours worked}}{\text{Maximum possible working hours}} \times 100$$

Actual usage of Budgeted Capacity ratio. This ratio refers to the relationship between actual number of working hours and the budgeted number of working hours for that period. While actual capacity usage ratio refers to the utilisation of available capacity, actual usage of budgeted capacity ratio stresses the utilisation of budgeted capacity only:

$$\text{Actual usage of budgeted capacity ratio} = \frac{\text{Actual working hours}}{\text{Budgeted Hours}} \times 100$$

Standard Capacity usage Ratio. This ratio refers to the relationship between budgeted hours and maximum possible working hours in a budget period.

$$\text{Standard Capacity Usage Ratio} = \frac{\text{Budgeted Hours}}{\text{Maximurn possible no. of working hours}}$$

Decision to Investigate variances : Variances focus attention on deviations, but all deviations cannot be taken as "out-of-control" situations. Therefore, a cost accountant is often faced with a problem of determining "out of control" situations, which are significant enough to warrant management's attention and further investigative efforts. The investigative effors should be directed towards a particular "out of control" situation, when incremental benefits promise to increase the incremental costs. This means that there exists reason to determine tolerance limits or range. If any variance falls within this range, it can be considered acceptable or normal. If the variance falls beyond "tolerance limits" an investigation should be made provided the benefits of investigation justify the cost. Varnaces falling beyond these boundaries, are assumed to be abnormal or significant. These deviations call for thorough investigation.

A control charge appears as shown in the figure given below. As long as the data relating to variances fall within the control limits, variances will not be taken as significant. The data falling beyond the lower and upper control limits demand special managerial attention and extra investigaive efforts.

Following three methods of accounting of standard costs are commonly used: (i) Partial Plan or Output Plan, (ii) Single Plan, and (iii) Dual Plan.

Partial Plan : It is also called Output Method. The features of partial plan are given below: (i) Work-in-progress account is debited with actual cost of material, actual cost of labour and actual overhead. (ii) Work-in-progress account is credited with standard cost of finished goods. (iii) At the end of accounting period work-in-progress account is credited with standard cost of unfinished goods. (iv) After entering at above is passed, debit and credit sides of work-in-progress account are compared and difference in transferred to cost variance, which is further analysed for reporting to management on the basis of additional information not recorded in accounts.

Single Plan. The features of single plan are summarised below: (i) Work-in-progress account is debited with standard cost, (ii) Work-in-progress account is credited with standard cost. (iii)

Inventory is valued at standard cost. (iv) All variances are computed at any stage before debiting work-in-progress account.

Some companies compute rate and expenditure variances at the inception. Quantity/efficiency variances are calculated at the time of crediting control accounts.

Dual Plan. Under this method all cost ledgers are maintained at actual cost. Standard cost is used in subsidiary records to give statistical information to management for purpose of control. For paucity of space, detailed discussion on accounting method has not been attempted here.

5

Marginal Costing

Even a school-going student knows that profit is a balancing figure of sales over costs, i.e.. Sales - Cost = Profit. This knowledge is not sufficient for management for discharging the functions of planning and control, etc. The cost is further divided according to its behaviour, i.e., fixed cost and variable cost. The age-old equation can be written as :

Sales - Cost = Profit *or* Sales - (Fixed cost + Variable Cost) = Profit.

The relevance of segregating costs according to variability can be understood by a very simple example of a shoe-maker, whose cost data for a particular period is given below :

(a) Rent of shop is Rs. 1,200 for the period under consideration.

(b) Selling price per pair is Rs. 55.

(c) Input material required for making one pair is Rs. 50.

(d) He is producing 1000 pairs during period under consideration.

In this data, only two types of costs are mentioned — rent of shop and cost of input materials. The rent of shop will not change, if he produces more than 1,000 pairs or less than 1,000 pairs. This cost is, therefore, referred to as fixed cost. The cost of input material will change according to the number of pairs produced. This is variable cost. Thus, both the costs do not have the same behaviour. This knowledge about the changes in behaviour of costs can yield wonderful results for the shoe-maker in decision-making. Based on these changes in behaviour of costs, a very effective cost accounting technique emerges. It is known as marginal costing. Marginal Costing is a management technique of dealing with cost data. It is based primarily on the behavioural study of cost.

Absorption costing, i.e., the costing technique, which does not recognise the difference between fixed costs and variable costs does not adequately cater to the needs of management. The statements prepared under absorption costing do elaborately explain past profit, past losses and the costs incurred in past, but these statements do not help when it comes to predict about tomorrow's result. A conventional income statement cannot tell what the profit or loss will be, if the volume is increased or decreased. These days, there is a cut-throat competition in market and management has got to know its cost structure thoroughly. Marginal costing provides this vital information to management and it helps in the discharge of its functions like cost control, profit planning, performance evaluation and decision-making. Marginal costing plays its key role in decision making. First of all various terms related to this chapter and methodology are discussed below :

Marginal Cost : CIMA defines marginal costing as *"the cost of one unit of product or service which would be avoided if that unit were not produced or provided."*

Simple Calculation of Marginal Cost : Suppose following cost data is given :

Variable cost = Rs. 5 per unit

Fixed cost for a specific period = Rs. 2,000 and

Present activity level = 200 units.

In this case total cost of producing 200 units will be found out as follows :

Fixed cost + (Variable cost per unit x Present production) = Total cost

= Rs. 2,000 + (Rs. 5 x 200) = Rs. 3,000

If activity level becomes 201 units aggregate cost will be

= Rs. 2000+ (5x201)

= Rs. 2,000 + 1,005 = Rs. 3,005

It means marginal cost is Rs. 5 because change in activity level by one unit leads to a change in aggregate cost by Rs. 5.

Marginal Costing : CIMA defines marginal costing as *"the accounting system in which variable costs are charged to the cost units and fixed costs of the period are written-off in full against the aggregate contribution. Its special value is in decision-making"*. Marginal costing is not a distinct method of costing like job costing or process costing. It is a technique which provides presentation of cost data in such a way that true cost-volume-profit relationship is revealed. Under this technique, it is presumed that costs can be divided in two categories, *i.e.,* fixed cost and variable cost. Fixed cost is charged to contribution ofthe period in which it is incurred and is considered period cost.

Certain readers vainly try to find out difference between marginal costing and direct costing. In accounting literature marginal costing and direct costing are basically one and the same thing. Actually, what has been called direct costing in the United States has been referred to as marginal costing in Great Britain. Still certain authors hold the view that there is a difference between these two terms. Contribution costing and variable costing are other synonyms of marginal costing. The terms differential costing and incremental costing are somewhat like marginal costing. These have been taken up in detail separately in the discussion ahead.

Process of Marginal Costing : Under marginal costing, the difference between sales and marginal cost of sales is found out. This difference is technically called contribution. Contribution provides for fixed cost and profit. Excess of contribution over fixed cost is profit or net margin. Emphasis remains here on increasing total contribution.

Variable Cost : Variable cost is that part of total cost, which changes directly in proportion with volume. Total variable cost changes with change in volume of output. Increase in output will lead to increase in total variable cost and decrease in output will lead to reduction in total variable cost. However, variable cost per unit of production remains the same irrespective of increase or decrease in volume of production. Variable cost includes cost of direct material, direct labour, direct expenses, etc. Variable cost per unit is arrived at by dividing total variable cost by units produced. Variable cost per unit has also been referred to as variable cost ratio. Variable cost can be arrived at by dividing change in cost by change in activity.

Variable costs are very sensitive in nature and are influenced by a variety of factors. Main aim of'marginal costing' is to help management in controlling variable cost because this is an area of cost which lends itself to control by management.

Fixed Cost : It represents the cost which is incurred for a period, and which, within certain output and turnover limits tends to be unaffected by fluctuations in the levels of activity (output or turnover). Examples are rent, rates, insurance and executive salaries.

Break-even Point : Break-even point is the point of sale at which company makes neither profit nor loss. The marginal costing technique is based on the idea that difference of sales and variable cost of sales provides for a fund, which is referred to as contribution. Contribution provides for fixed cost and profit. At break-even point, the contribution is just enough to provide for fixed cost. If actual sales level is above break-even point, the company will make profit. If actual sales is below break-even point the company will incur loss. When cost-volume-profit relationship is presented graphically, the point, at which total cost line and total sales line intersect each other will be the break-even point.

Contribution : Marginal costing analysis depends a lot on the idea of contribution. In this technique, efforts are directed to increase total contribution only. Contribution is the difference between sales and variable cost, i.e., marginal cost. It can be expressed as follows :

Contribution = Sales - Variable cost of sales.

Suppose sales is Rs. 1000 and variable cost of sales is Rs. 800. The contribution will be Rs. 200, *I.e.,* Rs. 1000 - Rs. 800.

Key Factor or Limiting Factor : There are always factors that do not lend themselves to managerial control. For example, if at a particular point of time there is a Government restriction on the import of a material, which forms the principal ingredient of company's product, company cannot produce, as it wishes. It has to plan production taking into consideration this limiting factor. However, its efforts will be directed for maximum utilization of available sources. Thus, limiting factor is a factor which influences the volume of output of an organisation at a given point of time.

Key factor is the factor whose influence must be first ascertained to ensure that there is maximum utilization of resources. Gearing the production process in the light of key factor's influences will lead to maximisation of profit. Key factor constrains managerial action and limits output of company. Generally sales is the limiting factor, but any of the following factors can be a limiting factor:

(a) Material

(b) Labour

(c) Plant capacity

(d) Power

(e) Government action.

When a limiting factor is in operation and a decision is to be taken regarding relative profitability of different products, contribution for each product is divided by key factor to select the most profitable alternative.

The choice of management rests with the products or projects, which show more contribution per unit of key factor. Thus, if sale is the key factor, contribution to sales ratio should be considered. If management is facing labour shortage, contribution per labour hour should be considered. Suppose sales of products *A* and Bare Rs. 100 and Rs. 110 arid variable cost of sales are Rs. 30 and Rs. 23 respectively. The labour hours (key factor) required for these products are 2 hours and 3 hours respectively. The contribution will be: Products, Rs. 100 - Rs. 30 = 70 per unit or Rs. 35 per hour;

Product—B, Rs. 110 - Rs. 23 = Rs. 87 per unit or Rs. 29 per hour. In this situation *P/* V ratio of product *A* (79%) is better thanP/V ratio of products (70%) and normal conclusion should be to produce product B. Here, time is the key factor. Contribution per hour is better in product *A* than in B. Therefore, during labour shortage, product *A* is more profitable than product B.

Basic Marginal Cost Equation

We know that : Sales - Cost = Profit

or Sales - (Fixed costs + Variable costs) = Profit

or Sales - Variable costs = Fixed costs + Profit

This is known as marginal equation ana it is also expressed as follows : S-*V*=*F*+*P*

Where S = Sales, *V* = Variable costs of sales

F = Fixed costs and P = Profit

The reader is advised to discourage the use of formulae. All problems on marginal costing should be attempted by use of this basic relationship, as far as possible.

Profit/Volume Ratio : When the contribution from sales is expressed as a percentage of sales value, it is known as profit/ volume ratio (or P/V ratio). It expresses relationship between contribution and sales. Better P/V ratio is an index of sound 'financial health' of a company's product. This ratio reflects change in profit due to change in volume. Broadly speaking, it shows how large the contribution will appear, if it is expressed on equal footing with sales. The statement that P/V ratio is 40% means that contribution is Rs. 40, if size of the sale is Rs. 100. One important characteristic of P/V ratio is that it remains the same at all levels of output. P/V ratio is particularly useful, when it is considered in conjunction with margin of safety. The other terms being used to refer to P/V ratio are : (a) marginal income ratio, (b) contribution to sales ratio, and (c) variable profit ratio.

P/V ratio may be expressed as :

P/V ratio = (Sales - Marginal cost of sales)/Sales

or = Contribution/Sales

or = Change in contribution/Change in sales

or = Change in profit/Change in sales

Suppose sales price and marginal cost of product are Rs. 20 and Rs. 12 respectively.

The *P/V* ratio will be (Rs. 20 - Rs. 12/20 = (8 ÷ 20) x 100 = 40%

P/V ratio remains constant at different levels of operations. A change in fixed cost does not result in change in *P/V* ratio since P/V ratio expresses relationship between contribution and sales.

Advantages of P/V Ratio

(i) It helps in determining the break-even point.

(ii) It helps in determining profit at various sales levels.

(iii) It helps to find out the sales volume to earn a desired quantum of profit.

(iv) It helps to determine relative profitability of different products, processes and departments.

Improvement of P/VRatio : *P/V* ratio can be improved, if contribution is improved. Contribution can be improved by any of the following steps :

(i) Increase in sale price.

(ii) Reducing marginal cost by efficient utilization of men, material and machines.

(iii) Concentrating on the sale of products with relatively better *P/Vratio.* This will help to improve overall *P/V* ratio.

Limitations of P/VRatio. There is a growing trend among companies to use the profit-volume-ratio in deciding the product-worthy additional sale efforts and productive capacity. and host of other managerial exercises. Following are the limitations of the use of P/V Ratio :

1. P/V ratio heavily leans on excess of revenues over variable cost.
2. The P/V ratio fails to take into consideration the capital

outlays required by the additional productive capacity and the additional fixed costs, that are added.

3. Inspection of P/V ratio of products can suggest profitable product lines, that might be emphasized and unprofitable lines, that may be re-evaluated or eliminated. Mere inspection of P/V ratio will not help to take final decision. For this purpose, analysis has to be broadened to take into consideration differential cost of the decision and opportunity costs, etc. Thus, it indicates only the area to be probed.
4. The *P/V* ratios has been referred to as the questionable device for decision-making because it only gives an indication of the relative profitability of the products/ product lines, that too, if other things are equal. P/V ratio is good for forming impression and not for making decision.

The above points highlight that P/V ratio should not be used inconsiderately. Its limitations should be alive in the mind of user.

Margin of Safety : Margin of safety represents the difference between sales at a given activity and sales at break-even point. (B.E.P. is the point of sales where company makes neither profit nor loss). Consequently, it indicates the extent to which a fall in demand could be absorbed, before company begins to sustain losses. The margin of safety is expressed as percentage of sale. The validity of safety always depends on the accuracy of cost estimates. The wide margin of safety is advantageous for the company. Margin of safety depends on level of fixed cost, rate of contribution and level of sales. The relationship of margin of safety with sales can be expressed as follows :

Sales - Sales at B.E.P = Margin of safety.

Thus, soundness of a business can be measured by margin of safety. This knowledge is very useful in taking policy decision like reduction in price to face the competitors. Margin of safety indicates how much present sales are able to keep business away from the crucial point, where business will earn neither profit nor loss. Its relationship with P/V ratio and profit can be expressed as follows:

Basic marginal cost equation is *S- V= F+ P*

By multiplying and dividing *L.H.S.* by S, we get,

S(S-V)/S = F+P

or S x *P/V*Ratio = *F+ P*

or (B.E.S. + margin of safety) x *P/V* Ratio = *F+ P*

(Total sales = B.E'.S. + Margin of safety)

or (Sales at B.E.P. x *P/V* Ratio + Margin of Safety x P/V Ratio)

=*F*+*P* (i)

But we know that sales at B.E.P. x *P/V* Ratio = Fixed Cost at B.E.P. contribution is just sufficient to meet fixed cost)

By deducting *(BEP* × *P/* V Ratio) from *L.H.S.* and Ffrom *R.H.S.* in we get Margin of Safety × *P/V* Ratio = Profit

The algebraic treatment of margin of safety can be illustrated by an example given below :

Improvement in the Margin of Safety : The margin of safety can be improved by adopting the following steps :

1. *Increase in sales volume.* It widens the difference between sales at activity level and sales at break-even point.
2. *Increase in selling price.* If it is not possible to increase sales volume, selling price is increased to improve the margin of safety.
3. *Change in product mix thereby increasing contribution.* This will lead to improvement in margin of safety, because it widens the gap of sales at specified activity level and sales at break-even point.
4. *Lowering fixed cost.* It increases margin of a safety, because break-even sales go down by lowering fixed cost.
5. *Lowering variable overhead.* It increase margin of safety by improvement in *P/V* ratio.

Angle of Incidence : The angle which the sales line makes with the total cost lines, is known as the angle of incidence. This angle gives the pictorial relationship between profit and sales. This angle indicates the profit earning capacity of a company over the break-even point. A large angle of incidence will indicate earning of high margin of profit. Small angle of incidence will indicate earning of low margin of profit. Low angle of incidence indicates that variable costs form a major part of cost of sales. Normally, margin of safety and angle of incidence are considered together. For example, a high margin of safety with a large angle of Incidence will indicate the most favourable conditions of a company. Under such situation, the company is monopolising in the market.

Main features of marginal costing

(1) Costs are divided into two categories, i.e., fixed costs and variable costs.

(2) Fixed cost is considered period cost and remains out of consideration for determination of product cost and value of inventories.

(3) Prices are determined with reference to marginal cost and contribution margin.

(4) profitability of departments and products is determined with reference to their contribution margin.

(5) In presentation of cost data, display of contribution assumes dominant role.

(6) Closing stock is valued on marginal cost.

Effect of Opening and Closing Stock on Profit. Following points should be noted when income statements under absorption costing and marginal costing are compared :

(1) When sales and production coincide i.e., there is neither opening stock nor closing stock, the results under both the methods will be same.

(2) When closing stock is more than the opening stock, profit under absorption costing will be more than the profit under marginal costing. This is because, under absorption costing, a portion of fixed overhead is charged to the

closing stock and carried over to the next period instead of being charged to the current period.

(3) When closing stock is less than the opening stock, the profit shown under absorption costing will be lower than the profit shown under marginal costing. This is because, under absorption costing a portion of fixed cost relating to the previous year is charged to current period.

Reconciliation of Results of Absorption Costing and Marginal Costing : When results of absorption costing and marginal costing are compared, it is necessary to make adjustments for under-absorbed and/or over-absorbed overheads. Under absorption costing, fixed overhead rate is predetermined based on normal level of activity. When actual activity level is different from normal activity level, a situation of under-absorption and/or over-absorption of fixed overhead arises.

(i) Under-absorbed fixed over = Excess of normal activity level actual overhead activity level x Fixed overhead rate per unit.

The profit under absorption costing should be reduced with under-absorbed fixed overheads before comparison with profit as per marginal costing, if there is under-absorption. Alternatively, the same objective can be achieved by adding the under-absorbed fixed overhead to cost of production.

(ii) Overabsorbed fixed overhead = Excess of actual level over normal activity level x Fixed overhead rate per unit.

The profit under absorption costing should be increased with over-absorbed fixed overheads before comparison with profit as per marginal costing, if there is over-absorption. Alternatively, the same objective can be achieved by reducing the over-absorbed fixed overhead from the cost of production.

Presentation of Data : The table given below summarises the difference of presenting the data under absorption costing and marginal costing.

Absorption Costing			Marginal Costing		
Sales :		XXX	Sales :		XXX
Less :	Manufacturing cost of goods		Less : Variable cost		
	sold (Including fixed manufacturing overheads)	XXX	Manufacturing	XX	
			Administration	XX	
		XXX	Selling	XX	XXX
Less :	Administration and		Contribution		XXX
	Selling Expenses	XXX	Less : Fixed cost		
	Profit	XXX	Manufacturing	XX	
			Administration	XX	
			Selling	XX	XXX
			Profit		XXX

Note : If there are opening and closing inventories, profit figures under the two methods will be different.

Limitations of Absorption Costing

1. In practice, this method employs highly arbitrary method of apportionment of overhead. This reduces the practical utility of cost data for control purposes.
2. Under absorption costing, fixed cost relating to closing stock is carried forward to the next year. Similarly, fixed cost relating to opening stock is charged to current year instead of previous year. Thus, under this method, all the fixed cost is not charged against the revenue of the year in which they are incurred. It is an unsound practice.
3. Under absorption costing collection and presentation of cost data is not very useful for decision-making, because process of assigning product cost a reasonable share of fixed overhead obscures cost-volume-profit relationship.
4. Under absorption costing, behavioural pattern of costs is not highlighted and thus many situations, which can be utilized under marginal costing, are likely to go unnoticed in absorption costing.

Criticism of Marginal Costing

In recent years, there has been a widespread interest in marginal costing. Still very few have adopted it as method of accounting for cost. Main points of criticism are :

1. It is not proper to disregard fixed cost for product cost determination and inventory valuation.
2. Marginal costing is specially useful in short-run profit planning and decision-making. For decision of far-reaching importance, one is interested in special purpose cost rather than variability of costs.
3. Marginal costing technique disregards the use of recovering fixed cost through product pricing. For long-run continuity of business it is not good. Assets have to be recovered in the long run.
4. Establishing variability of costs is not an easy task. In real life situations, variable costs are rarely completely variable and fixed costs are rarely completely fixed.
5. Exclusion of fixed cost from inventory valuation does not conform to accepted accounting practice.
6. The income-tax authorities do not recognize the marginal cost for inventory valuation. This necessitates keeping of separate books for separate purposes.

Determination of Marginal Cost : Determination of marginal cost is first practical step in the introduction of 'Marginal Costing'. It is not a simple problem. Studying the trend of data relating to cost and dividing it in two categories, i.e., fixed and variable, requires a lot of labour, skill and experience. Methods frequently used for analysis of cost according to variability are :

(1) Comparison of level of activity,

(2) Range or high and low method,

(3) Analytical method,

(4) Scatter Graph Method, and

(5) Least Square Method.

Measurement of Volume : Marginal costing is primarily used to analyse the cost behaviour in relation to volume. This presents a difficulty of selecting a base for measuring volume. A number of bases can be used for expressing volume such as (i) Physical units manufactured or sold, (ii) Volume of goods produced or sold, or (iii) Productive or actual hours, which may be either machine hours or labour hours. Selecting a unit to express volume is a complex exercise requiring a lot of experience. In different situations, different bases will be selected for expressing volume. Unless everything that is sold in a given period comes from the production of that period, sales do not measure production. Nor does production provide a measure of sales activity. Similarly, labour hours are a measure of time and not of output. They are affected by efficiency. The idea is that different bases can be used for measuring volume and selection has to be with reference to a particular situation. Importance of selecting proper measure of volume should not be ignored. Tests should be applied to ensure that there is a correlation between the basis of volume and cost. Points that merit attention in the selection of a measure for volume or activity are (a) the base should be representative of the activity, (b) it should be easily understood, (c) base should be capable of being used unaltered to facilitate adequate control, and (d) where it is possible to express production in terms of common physical units like tonnes, kg. litres, cubic feet and barrels, the volume should be expressed in terms of these units only.

Selling at or below Marginal Cost : Conditions in business are always changing. Sometimes it is sellers market, while at other times it may be difficult to sell the goods even at cost. These situations may justify to sell the goods at or even below marginal cost for a short while. Selling the goods at or even below marginal cost cannot be resorted to as a matter of routine. But this step may help the organisation to overcome the situations under which recovery of even full cost appears a difficult proposition. This step cannot continue for a long time and should be resorted to after very careful consideration. Selling the goods at or even below marginal cost may be necessary for the following reasons :

(i) To keep machinery and factory in running condition so

that it remains in readiness to go 'full steam ahead', when the temporary difficult period is over.

(ii) To keep the employees occupied.

(iii) To dispose of the perishable goods.

(iv) To drive the weak competitors out of market.

(v) To popularise the new products—This step may be temporarily resorted to so that the new product may gain recognition in the market.

(vi) To prevent loss of trade — If new products are likely to eliminate the company's product and there exists a possibility of loss of trade, it may be necessary to temporarily reduce the price to marginal cost or even below that.

(vii) To overcome the period of depressing prices — Sometimes a trend of depressing prices sets in and company finds no alternative but to follow suit in order to remain in business.

(viii) To maintain the sale of joint products — There are situations in which production of one product is necessarily associated with the production of other product. For example, A and B may be the joint products. A may find a very poor response in market, while B may continue to sell very well in the market. In this situation, the company may have to sell the product A at marginal cost or even below that, to maintain the production of B. In this situation, losses in one product may be offset by the profit of other product. Sometimes, this step is used to maintain the level of production of joint products only.

Selling the product at marginal cost or even below that is a very difficult decision. This step should be taken for a short while to overcome a temporary difficult situation, where recovery of even full cost may not be possible. This step may lead to a landslide in price, which may permanently damage the market position of the product. For this reason, this step should be taken exceptionally after very careful consideration. It should be kept in mind that the subject of pricing is exceedingly complex and cost price relationship represents only a part of the problem. A cost accountant should ensure the following two points :

(i) Selling price equal to marginal cost or even below it has not been through ignorance.

(ii) There is cost consciousness in the organisation and cost offers resistance point to the lowering of prices. This cannot be done, if cost is not known or ignored.

Application of Marginal Costing Technique : Marginal cost is essentially a technique of decision-making. Following discussion will reveal how it is used in solution of managerial problems.

Profit Planning : Normally, a company carries on its activities for the year long and at the end of the year an exercise of accounts closing is carried out to compute profit for the year. Under profit planning this order is reversed. Profit planning involves forecasting activity level in order to gain or maintain specified amount of profit. Under profit planning start is made from the end result. Profit figure is planned and activity level necessary for yielding that profit is attempted. It should be noted that determination of required activity level will involve working out how that level will yield specified profit. In this exercise, 16,000 sale, cost and production activities are all reviewed in harmony with each other to determine how they will yield the desired profit figure. Marginal costing technique helps in profit planning, because it is based on behavioural study of cost.

Presentation of Cost Data for Control Purposes : Marginal costing can be called a distinctly fine method of cost analysis and cost presentation. Under marginal costing, cost data is presented in such a way that it conforms to all the requirements of management to effect control. Data presentation is based on the behavioural study of cost. This leads the management to exercise relatively better control over cost. An effort has been made to illustrate this point by the following example. Readers should note how marginal costing helps the management to grasp the actual state of affairs by better presentation. Under absorption costing, cost data may be misleading for the purpose of decision-making.

Statement No. 2

Marginal Costing Method

	Period I	*Period II*
Sales	Rs. 70,000	Rs 80,000
Marginal cost :		
Opening stock	—	9,000
Goods manufactured	51,000	42,000
Less : Closing stock	9,000	3,000
Cost of goods sold	42,000	48,000
Contribution Margin	28,000	32,000
Less : Fixed cost Profit	15,000	15,000
	13,000	17,000

Following points should be noted from Statements 1 and 2.

1. Statement 1 shows that profit figure is going down by Rs. 1,000 despite increase in sale by Rs. 10,000.
2. Statement 2 shows that with increase in sale by Rs. 10,000 profit figure is also increasing by Rs. 4,000.
3. Reasons for difference :
   (a) Under period I, Absorption Costing shows a profit of Rs. 16,000, while under marginal costing profit figure is Rs. 13,000. The reason is that fixed cost relating to 3,000units (closing stock) has not been charged under absorption costing. It has been carried over to the next period. For this reason, profit under absorption costing is more than profit under marginal costing by Rs. 3,000.

   (b) Under period *II*, Marginal Costing shows more profit than absorption costing.Profit figure by marginal costing method is Rs. 17,000, while profit figure by absorption costing is Rs. 15,000. Closing stock is less than opening stock. For this reason, the fixed cost relating to units produced in period *I* has been charged in period *II* under absorption costing. The amount of difference can be explained as follows :

(Opening stock - Closing stock) x Fixed cost per unit (i.e., 3,000 - 1,000) x I = Rs. 2,000.

The difference between profit under two methods In period *II* Is also Rs. 2,000.

This example shows the fallacy of absorption costing. Despite the increase in sales from period *I* to period *II*, the profit figure is decreasing. Marginal costing analysis presents the data in the manner that suits the requirements of management.

Make or Buy Decision : Sometimes, a company has to decide, whether it should make the component of its product or it should buy it from the market. On the face of it, decision to make or buy should involve comparison of seller's price with marginal cost of that component. But this approach will lead to wrong conclusion. When a component is produced, a part of plant capacity is utilized, i.e., some contribution is earned. If a company is running at its full capacity the contribution thus earned will be lost by not manufacturing the component. Of course, if company is not working at its full capacity the question of lost contribution will become irrelevant. Thus this "lost contribution" becomes another factor of consideration in taking decision, whether to manufacture a component or to buy it from outside. This factor of'lost contribution' will assume importance only when the company is running at its full capacity. Following points will be the main considerations in deciding whether company should manufacture the component of its product or it should buy it from market:

(i) Seller's price.

(ii) Marginal cost of producing the component.

(iii) *Lost contribution.* This point will gain importance only when company is running at full capacity. It will not be out of place to mention here that in a make-or-buy decision certain other factors sometimes gain importance.

(a) Company may not like to depend on contractor for

supply of component. In a situation like this, company will only like to make the component.

(b) Government policy etc., may influence the decision of the company.

Additional Remarks : This decision has been taken on the assumption that machine No. 001 is working at full capacity and by taking over the production of component S, the contribution presently being earned by production of H will be lost. If the machine had not been working at its full capacity, there would not have been any lost contribution. In that case it would have been economical to make than to buy.

Optimising Product Mix : When a concern manufactures a number of products, a problem arises as to which product or sale mix will yield maximum profit. Such a problem can be solved by marginal contribution analysis. Product mix, which gives the maximum contribution, will be the optimum mix. Following example will illustrate the point:

Alternative use of Production Facilities : When an alternative method of manufacturing a product or alternative is available, marginal contribution analysis should be made to arrive at the decision. The alternative yielding the highest contribution will be selected.

Evaluation of Performance : A company may have different departments or product lines. All these departments and product lines may have different revenue earning potential. A company always concentrates on the departments or the product-lines which yield more contribution than others. The relative performance of each department or product is studied by marginal contribution analysis. This analysis will help the company to take decision that will maximise the profits. Following example will explain how relative profitability of different departments is studied.

Cost-volume-profit Relationship

Profit is always a matter of primary concern to management. The volume of sale never remains constant. It fluctuates up and down and income also goes up and down with fluctuations in volume. Profit is actually the result of interplay of different factors like cost, volume and selling price. Effectiveness of a manager depends on his capability to make right predictions about future profits. This can be done when correct relationship existing between cost, volume and profit is known. For this reason, knowledge of relationship among cost, volume and profit is of immense help to management. This knowledge of cost-volume profit relationship helps management to find out right solution for such problems as are given below:

(i) What should be the volume to be attempted for obtaining a desired profit?

(ii) How will the change in selling price affect the profit position of the company?

(iii) How will the change in cost affect profit?

(iv) What should be the optimum mix of the company?

These basic questions present themselves to management for solution in different forms. The conventional income and expenditure statement does not provide any answer to all these questions. The answer to all these questions is sought by analysis of cost-volume-profit relationship. Cost-Volume-Profit Analysis spotlights the relationship existing among factors like cost, volume and profit.

Use of Cost-Volume-Profit Analysis

1. This relationship enables management to predict profit over a wide range of volume. This knowledge is very useful in preparing flexible budget.
2. In a lean business season, company has to determine the price of the products very carefully. It becomes necessary sometimes to bring down the price to boost the sale of a product. For all decisions like this, management must determine, by cost-volume-profit analysis, what impact this reduction in price is going to have on profit position of a company.
3. Analysis of cost-volume-profit relationship helps in decision-making. There are situations when management

has to decide whether it should add to its capacity or not. With the knowledge of cost-volume-profit analysis, a manager can easily take decision showing, in its report how utilization of available capacity will lead to increase in profit. The following example will illustrate the point:

Cost-Volume Profit : Cost-Volume Profit analysis helps in profit planning. Under profit planning, company first declares the profit that it wants to make during the ensuing year. Thereafter, sales level necessary to yield that profit is attempted. Cost-volume-profit analysis helps in profit planning in the following ways.

(a) It helps in estimating income at a particular sales level.

(b) It helps to determine change in profit due to change in sales volume.

(c) It helps to execute the idea of profit planning. In other words, we arrive at the sales level to be attempted for a desired profit by the knowledge of relationship existing between cost, volume and profit.

(d) It helps to find out the sales required to meet proposed expenditure.

The Knowledge of Cost : Volume-profit relationship can be of substantial help in pricing. The studies based on cost-volume-profit relationship make it possible to visualise the probable results of proposed or expected changes on cost, volume or price. Companies are often tempted to reduce prices on existing products in an effort to increase volume. This is done to spread fixed costs over a larger volume of production. For taking any decision for reduction of prices the management should know the relationship between decrease in price and increase in volume. Any price decision has to take into account short-run and long-run considerations, i.e., possibility of spoiling the market and the probable action of competitors.

Presentation of Cost-Volume-Profit Relationship : The result of analysis of cost-volume-profit relationship can be presented in any of the following manners :

(i) Algebraical formulae

(ii) Reports/Statements,

(iii) Graphic Charts.

(i) *Algebraical formulae.* Presentation of cost volume-proflt analysis by algebraical formulae has been taken up in detail elsewhere in this chapter. It involves finding out different values by use of basic marginal cost equation.

(ii) *Reports and statements.* A statement showing how the relationship is presented through statement is being given below.

Forecast of Cost-Volume-Profit Analysis at Different Activity Levels

Plant Capacity	*70%*	80%	*90%*	*100%*
Sales (in units)	7,000	8,000	9,000	10,000
Price per unit (Re.)	1.00	1.00	0.90	0.80
Sales value	Rs. 7,000	Rs. 8,000	Rs. 8,100	Rs. 8,000
Variable Costs				
Direct labour	700	800	900	1,000
Direct material	1,400	1,600	1,800	2,000
Factory overhead	700	800	900	1,000
Admn. and selling overhead	350	400	450	500
Total variable costs	3,150	3,600	4,050	4,500
Contribution Margin	3,850	4,400	4,050	3,500
Fixed Factory Overhead	1,000	1,000	1,000	1,000
Admins, and Selling Overhead	500	500	500	500
Total Fixed Cost	1,500	1,500	1,500	1,500
Profit	2,350	2,900	2,550	2,000
P/V Ratio (Contribution/Sales)	0.55	0.55	0.50	0.44
Return on Sales (Profit/Sales)	0.34	0.36	0.31	0.25
Capital employed	20,000	21,000	22,000	25,000
Return on capital	11.75%	13.81%	11.59%	8.00%
Turnover Ratio (Sales/Capital employed)	35%	38%	37%	32%

Graphic Presentation of Cost-Volume-Profit Relationship : Graphic charts furnish an effective means of presenting cost-volume-profit relationship. In graphic presentation, a diagram of the relationship among various factors, like cost, volume and profit is presented. This pictorial presentation makes this relationship easy to understand. Following are the important charts for portraying this relationship : 1. Break-even Charts, 2. Profit/ Volume Charts and 3. Sequential Profit graph.

Break-even Charts : Pictorial expression of cost-volume-profit relationship by means of break-even chart is invaluable in making inferences in determining how costs respond to a variety of influences. Break-even chart gives an overview of cost-volume-profit relationship. This chart demonstrates, more than any thing else, importance of fixed cost in the operations of an undertaking. Following are important break-even charts :

(a) Simple break-even charts.

(b) Elaborate break-even charts.

(c) Cash break-even charts.

(d) Control break-even charts.

Simple Break-even Charts : These charts present only the basic relationship of cost, volume and profit. These charts are easy to understand. They show not only the break-even point but also the profit or loss, that may be expected at different levels of activity. The effect of change in selling price and cost can also be presented by drawing a new set of lines preferably with different colours. Primarily, a simple break-even chart contains three lines — sales line, fixed cost line and total cost line. Cost data to be presented is summarised in the form of a statement. This data includes sales and total costs for different levels of activity.

Elaborate Break-even Charts : These charts are also called Revenue Analysis charts or Fantail charts. One limitation of simple break-even charts is that they show only basic relationship of cost, profit and volume by pointing out break-even point and margin of safety. Break-even charts can be prepared exhibiting relatively more details regarding cost and profit.

For this purpose available area is broadly divided into three categories i.e., profit, variable cost and fixed cost. The wedge for profit can be divided into different sections to show income before tax or after tax. Similarly, it can contain appropriation of profit to taxes, dividend and reserves. It can also show preference dividend, ordinary material, direct labour, variable factory overhead, variable administration overhead and variable distribution overhead. Area for fixed cost can be divided in different sections to show out-of-pocket cost or depreciation, etc.

Cash Break-even Chart : In this chart, attempt is made to show that, if a particular activity level is attempted, enough cash will be received from sale to meet all cash expenses like payment of loan, interest, taxes, preference share dividend, etc. In preparation of this, fixed costs requiring cash flow are considered. Book adjustments like depreciation and deferred expenses for which immediate payment is not required, are not considered at all for the purpose of drawing this chart.

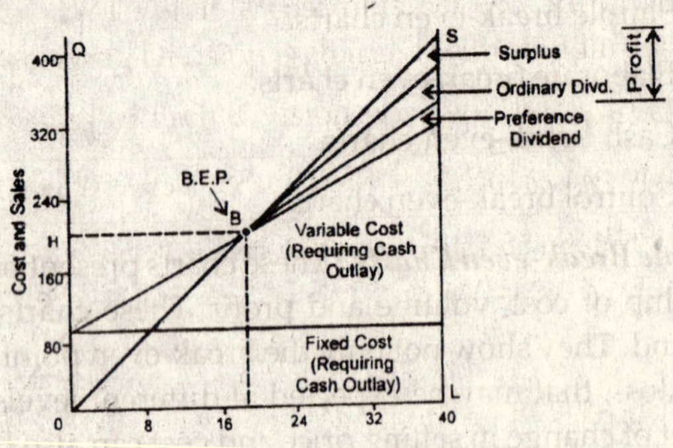

Fig. Cash Break-even Chart.

Control Break-even-chart : Control break-even charts are constructed to depict how much actual performance has deviated from budgeted performance. As may be clear from the title of this chart, it shows : (i) Actual cost in comparison to budgeted cost. (ii) Actual profit in comparison to budgeted profit.

In preparation of these charts, preferably two inks should be used. Actual total cost line and actual sales line should be in one ink and budgeted total cost line and budgeted sales line should be in different ink. The main advantage of this chart is that actual profit and profit variances can be read from the chart. This chart presents a very good mental picture of difference between actual profit and budgeted profit. The procedure involved is very simple. First of all, actual total cost line and actual sales line should be drawn following usual procedure for simple break-even chart. Thereafter, budgeted total cost line and sales line should be drawn on the same basis. An example will illustrate the point.

The control break-even indicates :

(a) Actual profit is equal to *FG, i.e.,* Rs. 200.

(b) Budgeted profit for budgeted activity is equal to *RQ,* i.e., Rs. 200.

(c) Budgeted profit for actual activity is equal to *FH,* i.e., Rs. 400.

(d) Actual break-even point happens to be at a sale level of 133 units or a sale of Rs. 1,330.

(e) Budgeted break-even point occurs at a sales level of 100 units or a sale of Rs. 1,000.

Profit-Volume Chart **:** Profit-volume chart prominently exhibits the relationship between profit and sales volume. The normal break-even charts suffer from one limitation. Profit cannot be read directly from the chart. It is essential to deduct total cost from sale to know the profit figure. The profit graph overcomes the difficulty by plotting profit directly against an activity. These charts are easy tounderstand and their preparation involves drawing sales curve and profit curve. The point at which profit line cuts the sales line is called break-even point. Taking the methods and objects under consideration, the profit-volume chart can be further divided into following categories. i.e., (a) simple profit-volume chart, and (b) profit-volume chart showing break-even point at different price levels.

(a) *Simple Profit-Volume Chart* : Its preparation involves the following steps:

(i) Finding out profit at any two levels of activity.

(ii) Drawing sales line.

(iii) Drawing profit line.

Sequential Profit Graph **:** Sometimes, a company manufactures more than one product of varying profitability. A change in the profitability of one product will lead to a change in the profitability of group as a whole. Profit-volume chart can be prepared for a group also. This chart shows relative profitability of different products. It is also called profit-volume graph for a group of products, sequential profit graph or profit path chart. Its main advantage is that it exhibits the relative profitability of different products at a glance.

Method of drawing "Profit Path" : In sequential profit graph or profit path chart for a group of products, a line "profit path" is drawn in order to draw total profit line. For drawing profit path, a statement is prepared showing cumulative sale and cumulative profit. The line 'profit path' is drawn with the aid of columns for cumulative sale and cumulative profit.

Assumptions of Cost-Volume-Profit Analysis

1. This analysis presumes that costs can be reliably divided into-fixed and variable category. This is very difficult in practice.
2. This analysis presumes an ability to predict cost at different activity volumes. In practice, a lot of experience may be required to reliably develop this ability.
3. A series of break-even charts may be necessary where alternative pricing policies are under consideration. Therefore, differential price policy makes break- even analysis a difficult exercise.
4. It assumes that variable cost fluctuates with volume proportionally, while in practical life the situation may be different.
5. This analysis presumes that efficiency and productivity remain unchanged. In other words, this analysis presents a static picture of a dynamic situation.
6. The break-even analysis either covers a single product or presumes that product mix will not change. A change in mix may significantly change the results.
7. This analysis disregards that selling prices are not constant at all levels of sales. A high level of sales may only be

obtained by offering substantial discounts, depending on the competition in the market.

8. This analysis presumes that volume is the only relevant factor affecting cost. In real life situations, other factors also affect cost and sales profoundly. Break-even analysis becomes over-simplified presentation of facts, where other factors are unjustifiably ignored. Technological methods, efficiency and cost control continuously influence different variables and any analysis which completely disregards these over changing factors will be only of limited practical value.
9. This analysis presumes that fixed cost remains constant over a given volume range. It is true that fixed costs are fixed only in respect of a given capacity, but each fixed cost has its own capacity. This factor is completely disregarded in the break-even-analysis. While factory rent may not increase, supervision may increase with each additional shift.
10. This analysis presumes that influence of managerial policies, technological methods and efficiency of men, materials and machines will remain constant and cost control will be neither strengthened nor weakened.
11. This analysis presumes that production and sales will be synchronised at all points of time or, in other words, changes in beginning and ending inventory levels will remain insignificant in amount.
12. The analysis also presumes that prices of input factors will remain constant.

Cost-profit-volume analysis is based on the above-mentioned limitations. Attempts to draw inferences disregarding these limitations will lead to formation of wrong conclusions. The application of cost-volume-profit relationship is restricted by the assumptions on which it is based. Therefore, cost-volume-profit analysis cannot be used indiscriminately.

Curvilinear Cost-volume-profit Analysis : Certain critics are of the opinion that traditional cost-volume-profit analysis (CVP) is only of theoretical importance due to its assumptions stated earlier. The views of accountants contradict with the views of economists, who hold that:

(i) based on the phenomenon of diminishing marginal productivity, total cost line will not be a straight line. It will be of curvilinear shape.

(ii) in real life situation, additional units can be sold only by lowering the price. Therefore, sales line will not be a straight line. It will be a concave to the base, *i.e.*, sales line will be curvilinear.

(iii) the decreasing rate of sales line and behaviour of cost line provided two break-even points. Behaviour of cost line is influenced by such factors as :

(a) fixed cost is not fixed throughout; and (b) variable cost is not the same throughout. It will decline initially as long as there are increasing returns. It will remain constant as long as average physical product per unit of input is constant. It will eventulally increase after the point of decreasing average return has been reached. This causes the total cost line to behave as in figure above. When the total cost line and total sales line of economist are plotted on graph paper, they appear as in Figure. A. The points A_1 and A_2 are two break-even points. A_1 is at a relatively lower level of output and A_2 is at a higher level. The area between A_1, and A_2 (shaded area) represents profit area. One of the benefits of this analysis is that it identifies the optimum level of output. Profit will be maximum at the point where there is maximum vertical distance between total revenue and total cost curves. Traditional cost-volume-profit analysis is of limited advantage only within a narrow range of activity. Certain authors have gone to the extent of asking whether traditional break-even chart has any operationally significant meaning at all. The divergence in the views of the accountants and the economists based on assumptions relating to traditional CVP analysis. Recent analysis of industrial CVP experience also confirms that a more sensitive and segmentised approach (incorporating the above refinement and based on micro-economic approach) should be made to provide management with better base for decision making.

Stochastic Cost-Volume-Profit Analysis : In traditional cost-volume-profit analysis realism is sacrified in order to render the analysis and presentation of results more understandable. These days use of computers is fast growing and efforts are being directed to make cost-volume-profit analysis more realisitc through use of simulation. Simulation takes advantage of computer's capability to randomly select factor values based on parameters given by experts. The computer uses specified parameters to randomly select selling price per unit for thousands of iteration. For each iteration profit is determined. This approach brings CVP analysis close to reality. Kattas and Lau have, used the term Stochastic cost-volume-profit analysis to describe the cost-volume-profit analysis, that uses factor estimates based on statistical parameters. The authors have also held the view that simulation is most powerful, inexpensive and accurate approach to Stochastic CVP Analysis. Suppose it is given that in a normal probability distribution, mean variance cost is Rs. 22.00 and standard deviation is Rs. 2.00. Based on properties of normal distribution, it is expected that there is only 15.87% (50.00% - 34.13%) chance that variable cost should be more than Rs. 24.00 (the mean plus one standard deviation). Stochastic cost-volume-profit analysis presents the difficulty of selecting appropriate probability distribution. The situation gets complicated when factors being considered do not have normal probability distribution. For paucity of space it is assumed that readers know how to calculate these values based on knowledge of statistics.

6

Costing and Management

Activity-based Costing

These days the term 'Activity-based Costing' is growingly used. It is necessary to view this term in the context of job costing and process costing. Job costing and process costing are two basic methods of cost accounting. Activity-based costing is not a distinct method of costing like 'job costing' and 'process costing'. It is only a new practice or intermediate change in the process of attribution of costs to jobs or processes. Earlier costs were first collected for production departments and service departments and finally the costs of production departments were absorbed by jobs or processes. Now in the context of activity-based costing, the costs are collected according to activities such as material ordering, material handling, quality testing, machine set-ups, customer support service, etc. and jobs and processes for which cost collection is being attempted are loaded with costs of these activities rationally.

Traditionally costing systems always use volume-related measures, such as direct labour hours or machine hours to allocate overheads to products. Many organisational resources exist for activities that are unrelated to physical volume. Now volume-related activities consist of support activities such as material handling, material procurement, performing set-ups, production scheduling and first item inspection activities. Traditional product cost systems, which assume that products consume all resources in proportion to their production volumes, thus report distorted product costs.

Traditional costing systems were designed decades ago when most companies manufactured a narrow range of products and direct labour and direct material were dominant factory costs. Overhead costs were small and thus inappropriate overheads allocations were insignificant. Since information processing costs were higher, it was difficult to justify more sophisticated overhead allocation method.

In the present era, companies produce wide range of products and direct labour represents only a small percentage of total costs. The intense global competition has made decision errors due to poor cost information more probable and more costly. These changes contributed to advent of 'Activity-based Costing'.

Given below are the two charts outlining how activity-based costing is different from conventional cost allocation:

Service departments

Production departments

Factors Prompting the Development of Activity-based Costing System Include:

(i) Growing overhead costs because of increasingly automated production.

(ii) Decreasing costs of information processing because of continual improvements, and increasing application of information technology.

(iii) Increasing market competition, which necessitated more accurate product costs.

(iv) Increasing product diversity to secure economies of scope and increased market share.

(v) Traditional costing fails to capture cause and effect relationship.

(vi) Traditional costing often fails to highlight inter-relationship among activities in different departments.

(vii) Growing dissatisfaction among the working executives regarding traditional costing, which is based on averages and estimates.

(viii) Traditional costing systems are driven by the need to value stocks rather than to provide meaningful product cost.

(ix) Direct labour has shrunk as percentage of total cost for majority of manufacturing companies.

(x) Overhead costs are no long a mere burden to be minimised. Overhead functions such as product design, quality control, customer service, production planning and sales order processing are as important to customer as physical processes on the shop floor.

(xi) Availability of computer has enhanced requirement for improvement in information gathering technology.

Activity-based Cost System

Activity-based costing emphasises the need to obtain a better understanding of the behaviour of overhead costs and thus it seeks to ascertain (i) what causes costs, and (ii) how they relate to product or services. ABC recognises that in the long run most costs are not fixed and seeks to understand the forces that cause overhead costs to change over time.

Activity-based costing is a system that focuses on activities, as the activities cause costs. ABC systems assume that cash outflows are incurred to acquire a supply of resources (i.e., labour, material and resources), which are consumed by activities. In other words, activities cause cost and products create demand for activities. A link is made between activities and products by assigning costs to products based on individual product's consumption or demand for each activity. Therefore, ABC system is based on understanding of the following:

(i) identifying major activities that take place in an organisation.

(ii) creating a cost pool/cost centre for each activity or costing activities.

(iii) determining cost driver for each major activity.

(iv) assigning cost of activities to products based on product's consumption or demand for activities.

Identifying Activities : The first stage is to identify the major activities in the organisation. Examples of activities include machine-related activities (i.e., machining cost centre), direct labour-related activities (i.e., assembly departments) and various support activities such as ordering, receiving, material handling, parts administration, production scheduling, packing and despatching. This step requires the management accountant to acquire a familiarity with what is happening in the indirect areas of the organisation. This has to be done systematically and involves examining physical plans of the work place (to identify how all space is being used) and payroll listings (to ensue all relevant personnel have been taken into account). This examination normally has to be supplemented by the observation of work and particularly by a series of interviews with staff involved. A number of criteria underlie the choice of activities. The activities should be at a reasonable level of aggregation. To break down activities into actions and tasks (*i.e.,* filing an order, photocopying a document) is usually too detailed for product costing. Such actions and tasks are normally combined into large purpose-oriented activities. For example, activities may be listed as follows:

— Production schedule changes

— Customer liaison

— Purchasing

— Production process set-up

— Quality control

— Material handling

— Maintenance

Final choice of activities (i.e., aggregation of actions and tasks) will be judgemental in any organisation. In the beginning at the time of introduction of ABC, activity cost pools ran into hundreds. Now-a-days it is felt that 20 to 30 cost pools have become common. The choice is between information details and cost of setting up and operating the system. For example, an activity such as quality control can be sub-divided into appraisal activity and prevention activity. The benefit of this would be more detailed profits of cost reported to management and a possible increase in the homogeneity of the costs in each activity cost pool.

Creating a Cost pool/Cost Centre for Each Activity or Costing the Specific Activities : The second stage requires that a cost centre (also called a cost pool) be created for each activity. For example, the total cost of all set-ups might constitute one cost centre for all set-up related costs. In other words, after establishing the activity structure for the system, it is necessary to identify the resources consumed by each individual activity during the relevant period. This provides a basis for identifying level of costs in each pool. Both allocation (where particular individuals, suppliers or pieces of equipment are identified as having a full-time commitment to a specific activity) and apportionment (where labour and equipment resources are shared by two or more activities) will be involved at this stage. In the absence of time records, labour and equipment usage will have to be identified in broad terms by observation and interviews. For other costs, such as occupancy, the most appropriate available measures of resource consumption (i.e., space occupied) should be used. Thus some amount of approximation and estimation is inherent in even ABC systems. The activity cost information generated on this pattern is very useful. It represents what is often called, a novel profiling of overhead cost for management rather than analysing cost in terms of inputs (labour, supplies, equipment depreciation). It indicates how resources have been applied in the business. For example, cost of specific activities under customer-order processing can be attempted as follows:

Customer Order Processing
(Rs. in lakhs)

Specific activities	Indirect labour	Occupancy costs	Depreciation	Consumables	Total
Pricing	0.25	0.18	0.02	0.08	0.53
Draw-up agreements	0.42	0.23	0.03	0.10	0.78
Customer vetting	0.22	0.11	0.03	0.09	0.45
Customer liaison	0.95	0.69	0.14	0.11	1.89
Problem resolution	0.34	0.04	0.02	0.03	0.43
Expedite delivery	0.12	0.22	0.01	0.02	0.37
Adm. / Secretariate	0.10	0.33	0.05	0.07	0.55
	2.40	1.80	0.30	0.50	5.00

This type of analysis gives a particular visibility to overheads incurrence. It details why and how overheads nave been incurred. It allows an assessment of relative magnitude and will permit time-periods and inter-plant comparison at a detailed level. In addition, supplementary analysis of activities into value-added/ non-value-added categories or core support activities can assist management in designing policies aimed at cost containment or cost reduction.

Determining the Cost drivers for each activity. Next step is to identify the factors, that influence the cost of a particular activity. The term 'cost driver' has been used to describe the events or forces, that are significant determinants of the cost of activities. If production scheduling cost is generated by the number of production runs, that each production generates, then number of set-ups would represent the cost driver for production scheduling. A *cost driver is a variable, which determines the work volume or work load of a particular activity.* It will provide the justification for amount of resources consumed by an activity and hence its cost. Due to this causal relationship it will be a significant measure of activity cost variation. To permit its practical application in an ABC system, it must be conveniently measurable and readily attributable to individual products. Most cost drivers will reflect the transactions, which underlie the activity under consideration. Hence the number of purchase orders processed, number of customer orders processed, number of inspections undertaken and number of set-ups achieved all represent a volume of transactions related to an activity. Sometimes characteristics chosen represent factors, which primarily determine the number of activities undertaken and for this reason they are used as cost drivers. For example, number of customers, number of suppliers and number of component parts have all been used as cost drivers. These are all situational factors, which one would expect to influence the volume of transactions and hence the cost respectively, of the customer order processing, procurement and scheduling activities. Then special attention should be directed towards cost causality in determining cost drivers. The ascertainment of cost drivers will normally involve repeat interviews with personnel involved in the specific activities. The focus remains on identifying what causes a particular activity to consume resources and so incur cost. Some typical questions aimed at bringing out the cost drivers are given below :

- What is the number of staff working on a particular activity?
- Why are X numbers of staff needed ?
- Is there sufficient staff ? If not, why ?
- What might cause the need for more or less staff ?
- What is it, that determines the amount of time spent on a particular activity ?
- Why is overtime worked ?
- Why does the idle time occur ?

The end result of this type of questioning will be a typical set of cost drivers for each sub-activity. Given below is a list of cost drivers identified for different activities under customer-order processing: (This is to show a pattern of how cost drivers are identified.)

Customer Order Processing

Activities	*Cost drivers*
Pricing	• Number of orders
	• Number of customers
	• Complexity of orders
Setting Agreements	• Location of customers
	• Number of orders
Customer Vetting	• Number of customers
	• Number of customers
	• Size of orders
	• Location of customers
Customer Liaison	• Order book position
	• Number of customers
	• Number of orders
	• Location of customers
Problem Resolution	• Delivery performance
	• Product quality
	• Number of orders
	• Number of customers
	• Location of customers
Expediting Delivery	• Location of customers
	• Production hold-ups
	• Number of orders
Adm. / Secretarial	• Number of orders
	• Number of problems
	• Number of staff.

Therefore in order to link activity costs to product or service output, a cost driver has to be identified with each cost pool. As historical data are sometimes not available to undertake statistical testing of the relationship between the cost driver and the behaviour of cost in the cost pool, the choice of cost driver may require the exercise of judgement. In practice, four alternative types of cost driver are to be found:

Pure volume Cost Drivers : Pure volume cost drivers are most common and represent a reasonable homogeneous measure of the output of the activity concerned. Number of customers or number of inspections or number of call-outs are pure volume cost drivers.

Weighted Volumes Cost Drivers : These cost drivers are used, where the output of activity is clearly non-homogeneous. If purchasing were an activity pool and purchase orders were made both domestically and overseas, the overseas orders may involve considerable more administrative work. In this situation it may be advantageous to weigh the overseas orders *vis-a-vis* the home orders. Based on the assessment of work undertaken to make respective orders, it may be decided that each overseas order be weighted by 1.5 before determining the total weighted volume of cost driver to be used in calculating the appropriate rate.

Situational Cost Drivers : Sometimes a situational characteristics of the activity can be important in determining its work load and thus hold credence as its cost driver. For example, the number of suppliers pertaining to a particular purchasing activity could be used as the cost driver. In other words, the number of suppliers is not an output measure of the activity but may be a convenient surrogate for a pure volume cost driver such as the number of purchase orders. Further, some of the purchasing cost may relate to vetting and liaisoning with individual suppliers.

Motivational Cost Drivers : These cost drivers are used when the intention is to motivate cost-conscious behaviour rather than produce product cost information in the most accurate manner. This type of cost driver may lack some of the qualities mentioned above but its selection may give prominence to one particular aspect of operations and influence managerial behaviour in a desired manner. For example, in Japan, element of direct labour hour has remained a popular cost driver, despite its inherent flaws, because it makes labour a costly resource and prompts designer to attempt optimum utilisation of labour hours.

Cost Driver Analysis : Companies engage in many activities that consume resources and thus cost cause to be incurred. All activities have cost drivers, i.e., the factors having direct-cause effect relationship to a cost. Cost drivers can be volume-related (such as machine hours or labour hours) and non-volume related, which generally reflect the incurrence of specific transactions (such as set-ups, work orders or distance travelled). There is a tendency to identify greater number of cost drivers than can be used for cost accumulation or activity elimination. It is an important function of management to ensure that cost drivers selected are limited to a reasonable number. Care should also be taken to ascertain that the cost of measuring the driver does not exceed the benefit of using it. A cost driver should be easy to understand, directly related to activity being performed and appropriate to performance measurement. Cost have been traditionally accumulated into one or two cost pools (total factory overhead or variable or fixed factory overhead and one or two cost drivers (direct labour hours and/ or machine hours) have been used to assign costs to products. However, the use of single cost pools and single drivers many produce illogical products or services cost for internal management use in complex production (or service) environment. The accounting system must first recognise that costs are created and incurred at the following different levels:

Unit-level Cost : Traditionally, cost drivers were viewed only at the unit level, for example, one may try to find out how many hours of labour or machine time was taken to produce a product or render a service. These drivers create unit-level costs meaning that they are caused by the production or acquisition of a single unit of product or the delivery of a single unit of service.

Batch-level Cost : Costs that are caused by a group of things being made, handled or processed at a single time are referred to as batch-level costs. Using a batch-level perspective indicates the commonality of the cost to the units within the batch is more indicating of the relationship between the activity (set-up) and the driver (different production runs).

Product-level (Process-level) Cost : A cost caused by the development, production, or acquisition of different items is called a product-level (or process-level) cost. These costs may include engineering change orders (E.C.Os.), equipment maintenance, product development and scrap, if related to product design.

Facility-level Cost : Some costs cannot be related^) a particular product line. These are, instead, related to providing a facility. For example, cost of maintaining building or plant security or advertisement promoting the organisation. These costs and cost bases are extensively used in traditional cost analysis.

Organisational-level Cost : Certain costs are incurred at organisation level for the single purpose of supporting continuing facility operations. These organisational level costs common to many different activities and products and services can be prorated among services and products on an arbitry basis only. Organisational level costs are not product-related. Thus, they should be subtracted in total from net product revenues instead of an arbitry and illogical apportionment

Assigning Cost of Activities to Products based on Product's Consumption or Demand for Activities : The last step involves tracing the cost of the activities to products according to product's demand (using cost driver as measure of demand) for these activities during the production process. A product demand for the activities is measured by the number of transactions it generates for the cost driver. The best way to complete the final step is to apply cost driven rate to individual products. Here it is important to state that if a cost driver rate is to be practical the variable chosen must be measurable in a way which permits its identification with individual products. For example, the number of parts associated with each product must be known, if products are to be individually costed. The requirement may represent one of the significant costs of ABC, especially where a new system has to be established to collect the cost driver information, both in total and for each product. The ability of a cost driver to meet this requirement should, therefore, be considered, when the cost driver is being chosen.

Given below is a representative list to show how activities drivers should be listed for specific types of costs :

Cost Type	*Related Activity Driver*
Accounting costs	Number of billings
	Number of cash receipts
	Number of check payments
	Number of general ledger entries
	Number of reports issued
Administration costs	Hours charged to law suits
	Number of stock-holder contacts
Engineering costs	Hours charged to design work
	Hours charged to process planning
	Hours charged to tool design
	Number of engineering change orders
Facility costs	Amount of space utilization
	Human resources costs
	Employee head count
	Number of benefit changes
	Number of insurance claims
	Number of pension changes
	Number of recruiting contacts
	Number of training hours
Manufacturing costs	Number of direct labour hours
	Number of field support visits
	Number of jobs scheduled
	Number of machine hours
	Number of machine set-ups
	Number of maintenance work orders
	Number of parts in product
	Number of parts in stock
	Number of price negotiations
	Number of purchase orders
	Number of scheduling changes
	Number of shipments
Marketing and sales costs	Number of customer service contacts
	Number of orders processed
	Number of sales contacts made
Quality control costs	Number of inspections
	Number of supplier reviews
Storage time *(e.g.,* depreciation,	Inventory turnover
taxes) Storage transactions	Number of times handled
(e.g. receiving)	

Outgrowth of ABC : The original reason for implementing ABC systems was to correct over-or under-costing through more accurate assignment of indirect cost. The introduction, however, results into some important benefits, which can be termed as valuable outgrowth of ABC systems

Non-value Added Activities : The identification of non-value-added (NVA) activities was an important additional benefit of introduction of activity-based costing system. An NVA activity represents the work, that is not valued by external or internal customer. NVA activities do not improve the quality or function of a product or service but they can adversely affect costs and prices. Moving materials and machine set-up for a production run are examples of NVA activities. Identification of such activities can instigate efforts to eliminate or reduce NVA activities. It should be kept in view that even if an activity is classified as NVA, it is not necessarily completely non-essential. For example, given the current state of technological development in a particular field, it may be impossible to reduce set-up time to zero, activity is judged to be or contain non-essential actions, that do not contribute to customer value or the organisation's needs. The implementation of ABC analysis can also point out non-essential components of so-called value added activity, which can be classified an NVA, for example, unnecessary materials costs and production time caused by excessive components in a product design. The organisations should be on the watch to :

(a) identify activities or efforts not required at all or can be eliminated;

(b) ineffectively accomplished and can thus be reduced or redesigned; and

(c) identify the activities required to sustain the organisation and, therefore, cannot be eliminated (i.e., provide plant capacity).

Process Improvements : ABC primarily focuses on costing activities. The initial intention was to improve the assignment of costs to products or services. Later, the identification of activities and their cost drivers was recognised as valuable for organisations that were trying to continuously improve processes and not just activities within departments. For example, material handling is likely to cross departmental boundaries. One of the cost drivers of material handling (an NVA activity) is distance travelled between operations. The reduction of such distance, say, through machine reconfigurations, should reduce materials handling costs. *Process Value Analysis (PVA)* has been developed to complement ABC in cost management endeavours. PVA has been defined as a methodology for reducing costs and improving processes by identifying resource consumption within a process and the underlying root causes of cost, i. e., cost drivers. PVA is a systematic way to identify VA and NVA activities. PVA supports ABC by seeking to improve the identification of activity cost pools, the casual factors of activities. PVA steps include :

(a) Prepare flow chart to document the activities in the processes of organisations.

(b) Define activities as VA and NVA.

(c) Identify the cost drivers and the casual factors of each activity.

(d) Identify improvement possibilities based on PVA and ABC information.

Uses of Activity-based Costing

Points a Way to Increase Shareholder Value : When an ABC system is combined with a review of investment costs for various tactical or strategic options, one can determine the return on investment to be expected for each investment option.

Effectively Appraises a Distribution Channel Cost : An ABC system can accumulate all the costs associated with a particular distribution method, which allows manager to compare this cost to the profit margin earned on sales of products sold through it. One can then determine, if the distribution channel should be reconfigured or eliminated in order to improve overall levels of profitability.

Effectively Compares inter-plant Performance : An ABC analysis itemises the costs of each plant and correctly allocates these costs to the activities conducted within them, which allow a company to determine which plants are more efficient than others.

Provides Reliable Data for Such Decision-making as Make or Buy : An ABC analysis includes all activity's costs associated with a manufactured item providing a comprehensive view of all costs associated with it and can then be more easily compared to the cost of a similar item that is purchased.

Helps to Collect Benchmark Costs : By using internal ABC analysis to determine the costs of various activities, a company can create a benchmark for these costs in potential acquision targets.

Determines the Cost of Each Activity : An ABC analysis can reveal the cost of each activity within an organisation. The system is really designed to trace the costs of only the most significant activities; but its design can be altered to itemise the costs of many more activities.

Helps to Charge Optimum Price : An ABC analysis serves all costs associated with a product and thus it is useful in determining the minimum price that can be charged. The actual price charged may be much higher, since it may be driven by the ability of the market to absorb a higher price rather than the underlying cost of the product.

Helps to Make Right Products to be Sold : An ABC analysis can be combined with product prices to yield a list of margins for each product sold. When the information collected is sorted by market, product line, or customer, it is easy to determing which products have low or negative returns or yield such low margin volumes that they are not worth keeping.

Identification of Non-value Added Costs : An ABC analysis can reveal which activities contribute to the completion of products and which do not. By focussing on those non-value-added activities that do not create value, a company can create significant improvements in its profitability.

Helps to Identify Area to Reduce Costs : An ABC analysis reveals the cost of anything a management team needs to know about activities, products or customers, which can afterwards be sorted out to see where highest cost-items are located combining this with value analysis, one can determine what costs return the lowest value and structure a cost reduction programme accordingly.

Helps to Identify Most Profitable Customers : An ABC analysis can itemise the costs specific to each customer such as special customer service or packaging as well as increases in warranty claims or product returns. When combined with margins on products sold to customers, this analysis reveals, which customers are the most profitable, after all costs are considered.

In brief it helps managers to :

(a) identify and mention significant technological cost,

(b) trace many technology costs directly to products,

(c) promote achievement of market share through use of target costing,

(d) understand the impact of new technologies on all elements ofperformance,

(e) translate company goals into activity goals,

(f) analyse the performance of activities across business functions,

(g) promote standards of excellence,

(h) helps to introduce business process re-engineering (BPR), which is a method of improving, replacing complex processes that already exist. BPR finds and implements radical changes in the way things are made or the way tasks are performed to achieve cost, service or time reductions.

Actually, the number of uses to which ABC system can be put is limited by the imagination of the user. It is necessary to address this is one, before system is installed.

Implementing an Activity-based Costing System. Given below is a list of standard implementation steps for ABC system.

Obtain high-level Support : An ABC project involves the procurement of funding and dealing with multiple departments. To make these chores easier, it is necessary that there should be a high-level supporter of the project on the management team, who can give enough 'push' through the corporate bureaucracy to ensure that project is completed in time.

Obtain a Project Schedule and Budget : The project team leader should work with the high-level project sponsor to obtain a project schedule and funding that is sufficient for completion of the project.

Assemble the ABC Team : In view of the wide array of knowledge required to formulate an ABC system, it should include employees from the engineering, marketing, materials management, computer services and production departments.

Train the Team : Many team members may have heard of ABC before and they may be having only a passing familiarity with it. An in-house expert or a consultant can be brought in to conduct an intensive review session with the team.

Gather Information : The project team requires to collect data to identify activities, costs, relationships between activities and costs and types of cost drivers. The best information is usually obtained through interviews. Additional sources of information are the general ledger, financial statements and a detailed review of all costs. The project team can also obtain general operational information by observing operations in action.

Conduct Modelling and Analysis : With all information in hand, the team should use flow charting to determine how activities occur and flow through departments. It is at this point that resource drivers, cost pools and activities are identified and documented.

Select and Purchase a Software Package : It may be necessary to purchase a third-party ABC software package, which typically makes it easier to conduct analysis and ad hoc enquires. It also makes it easier to control the systems since all ABC-related files are kept in one place.

Create a Software Linkage : It may be possible to create automated linkages between ABC system and other systems such as general ledger that allows one to save time by streamlining the flow of information into the ABC system. The interfaces should be carefully tested to ensure dependability.

Test the Software : The team should create a set of sample ABC transactions and run them through the ABC software. This step is designed not just to see if the software works as advertised, but also to ensure that the team understands how the ABC system works.

Design Reports : An ABC system usually requires an entirely new set of reports. These may be constructed with ABC package's report writer or customerised or written with the aid of a third party's software package. The team should create sample reports with test transactions to be certain that reports function as planned.

Design Policies and Procedures : Once the software is determined to be acceptable, the team must prepare a set of policies and procedures to integrate the operation of the ABC system and software into existing operations of the accounting department. These should be tested with the people who will be using the system and retested after the system has been installed to ensure that they are constructed correctly.

Implement the System : The team should co-ordinate the training of all ABC system users just prior to the "go line" date, be present on the date the system is made operational. Even for several weeks after this date, a help desk should be made available to users to answer all questions.

Follow-up on the Installations : An ABC system or so to say any system rarely works exactly as expected. It is common to come across problems, caused by improper or inadequate training, missing procedures or faulty analysis. These problems can be documented and corrected by proper follow-up. Further reviews can be spread out over longer periods as the new system gradually 'settle down'. These steps only form a rough guide for the implementation of ABC system. Steps can be added to or subtracted from this list to arrive at the most functional set of activities for a particular ABC installation.

Criticism of Activity-based Costing : Activity-based costing typically provides better information than traditional overhead allocation process. Still it is not the presence for all managerial problems. Following criticism has been levelled against ABC system :

1. ABC system implementation requires significant amount of time and cost to implement.

2. An environment of change must be created for implementation of ABC system. It requires overcoming a variety of individuals, organisational and environmental barriers as follows:
   (a) fear of unknown and shift in status quo,
   (b) potential loss of status,
   (c) a necessity to learn new skill.

To overcome these barriers, a firm must recognise that these barriers exist. The causes of the barriers should be investigated. Then organisation should communicate information about, 'what', 'why' and 'how' of ABC to all concerned parties. It presents limitations of ABC system.

3. Top management must be involved and support the implementation process. Lack of commitment or involvement of top management will make any meaningful progress slow and difficult.
4. Employees and managers must be educated in some non-traditional techniques, that include new terminology, concepts and performance measurements.
5. Additional time will be required to analyse the activities taking place in the activity centers, trace cost to those activities and determing the cost drivers.
6. Another problem with ABC is that it does not conform to Generally Accepted Accounting Principle (GAAP). ABC would suggest that some non- product cost (such as those in research and development) be allocated to products whereas certain traditionally designated product cost (such as factory building depreciation) may not be allocated to products. Therefore, most companies have used ABC for internal reporting while continuing to main their general and subsidiary ledger accounts and prepare their external financial statements on the basis of traditional system.
7. One final criticism levelled against ABC is that it does not promote Total Quality Management (TOM) and continuous

improvement. Activity-based prescriptions for improved competitiveness usually entails steps that lead to selling more or doing less what should not have been done in the first place. It does not make company a long-term global competitor.

ABC and the Service Sector : The ABC approach is just as applicable to service industry as manufacturing. The design of ABC system for service organisations typically involves basically the same steps. The work carried out by staff and equipment should be arranged into activities. This is normally achieved by a combination of interview and self-analysis by staff and management involved. The output when measured will provide the cost driver which can be used to associate the cost with a cost object. This will mean end services (the ultimate source of demand for activities) will have the cost of activities traced to them. Each activity's output should be traceable to the source of the demand for it. Where the object is to cost a service provided to external customer then tracing the output directly to this object will best meet this aim. However, it should be realised that direct link of this type might not always exist, where, for example, one activity is providing the service for another service rather than for end service. In a situation like this a across-activity charging system may have to be instituted in order to obtain a cost system, which reflect how resources are actually being used. A chart given below shows how cross-activity charging takes place.

ABC and Variance Analysis : Traditional budgeting and standard costing produce overhead variances, which have been subject to major criticism. First, the computation of variances in conventional costing systems is based upon the use of volume-related over-head absorption bases such as labour hours or machine hours. Flexing the budget on the basis of these variables produces relatively meaningless values for what cost 'should be' and hence renders the resultant variances of questionable utility. Second, the computation of total standard cost of fixed overhead involves treating these fixed costs as if they were variable and again results in a devaluation of the worth of cost variances. When ABC is applied in this area, it provides a methodology, which can contribute to the rectification of these difficulties. The use of range of cost drivers provides a refinement, which when applied to a series of appropriate standard cost driver rates will generate a more accurate measure of the expected overhead cost. The following example will clarify the point:

Role of the Cost Accountant in an ABC System : The Cost Accountant is positioned squarely in the centre of any ABC system purchase, installation and operation. This is because purpose of ABC is to obtain better costing information, which is the business of a cost accountant. A cost accountant plays a key role in the selection of software, because it is the cost accountant, who gives the requirements definition — a listing of all the features needed in the software packages to be reviewed. The cost accountant gains this knowledge of the requirements by interviewing other employees to see what they need, as well as from their theoretical knowledge of cost accounting, knowledge of how other companies use ABC and what the company's strategy requires in the way of costing information. This information is assembled on a checklist which the cost accountant uses to review all prospective software options. The best approach is to design a sample transaction that tests the presence of each requirement and then run the transaction through the sample software to see if it functions as per the itemised requirements. Because of this detailed review process, the opinion of cost accountant is frequently the deciding factor in determining which ABC package is purchased.

It is cost accountant who structures the flow of cost through the ABC system. This involves determining what costs are to be consolidated into which cost pools and how they are to be allocated to various activities. The cost accountant has the best knowledge of this and he deals with this every day. A cost accountant should determine what will (and will not) be included in ABC system so that it measures only what is needed and does so within the cost budgeted for the system

Once the system is installed, the cost accountant is the chief user. He determine whether any allocation requires alteration, what reports it should issue, how the information is used. What employees receive information and how this information can support strategic and tactical decisions. Since these activities nearly match a cost accountant's job description, it is evident that he must become its most expert user in order to complete his job. The ABC system and the cost accountant are actually intertwined.

Activity-based Management : The early adopters of Activity-Based Costing (ABC) used it to produce more accurate product (or service) costs but it soon became apparent to the users that it could be extended beyond purety product costing to a range of cost management applications. The terms activity-based management (ABM) or activity-based cost management are used to describe the cost management application of ABC. Activity-based management is a discipline, that focusses on the management of activities as the route to improving the value received by the customer and the profit achieved by providing this value. This discipline includes cost driver analysis, activity analysis, and performance measurement. Activity-based management draws on activity-based costing as its major source of information.

For continuous improvement, activity-based management attempts following analyses:

Cost Driver Analysis : The factors that cause activities to be performed need to be identified in order to manage activity costs. Cost driver analysis identifies these casual factors. For example, a cost driver analysis study might determine that slow processing of customer invoices results largely from lack of training of the customer invoice associates. This lack of training is thus a cost driver of the customer invoice processing activity. It is one of the factors causing this activity to take place (in this case inefficiently). Managers have to address this cost driver to correct the root cause of the slow processing problem. To accomplish this task managers might decide that an internal training programme for customer invoice associates should be designed and implemented to increase the speed of customer invoice processing. The time-saving from improved saving may lead to reduction in the number of customer invoice associates and thus lower cost for 'customer invoice processing' activity. The tangible cost savings and intangible benefits from the customer invoice processing improvements should be compared with the tangible and intangible costs of the new training programme in a cost-benefit analysis. This hypothetical customer invoice processing example shows that the identification and analysis of cost drivers (casual factors) is a necessary first step towards improving the cost effectiveness of activities and cost management through ABM.

Activity Analysis : Activity analysis in ABC identifies the activities of an organisation and the activity centres (or activity cost pools) that should be used in an ABC system. Activity analysis also identifies value added and non- value added activities. The degree to which activities are grouped together into activity centres depends on the costs and benefits of the alternatives. The number of activity centres is likely to change over time as organisational needs for activity information evolve. Identification and follow-up of non-value-added activities can tremendously improve the activity-based management.

Performance Analysis : Performance analysis involves the identification of appropriate measures to report the performance of activity centers or other organisational units consistent with each units goals and objectives.

Performance analysis aims to identify the best ways to measure the performance of factors that are important to organisations in order to stimulate continuous improvement.

Difference between ABC and ABM : Activity-based costing is logical distribution of overhead, *i.e.*, overhead should be distributed on the consumption of resources consumed by products and services. It helps to avoid distorted product/service cost. Activity-based management, on the other hand, is a discipline that focuses on efficient and effective management of activities as the route to improve the value received by customers and profits received by providing this value. This discipline of focussing on activities is being effectively used in cost reduction, business process re-engineering, benchmarking and performance measurement, etc. ABM brings about a change in viewing at the objective by incorporation of financial perspective, internal business perspective, innovation and learning perspective and customer perspective.

Activity-based Budgeting (ABB) : A budget is a financial expression of a plan. Traditional budgeting focusses on planning resources for an organisational unit. The budgeting process starts with the senior executive's announcing budget goals. Many managers respond by looking at last year's numbers and increasing their budget for the year based on inflation and/or the amount of the increase in revenues. For example, if revenue increases 10 per cent, the various department managers might increase the budgets for their departments by 10 per cent. The problem with traditional approach is that last year's inefficiencies are incorporated into this year's budget and often little attention is paid to improvements in each department. Finally, little incentive is incorporated into the budgeting process for continuous improvement. Changing work load for each department often is not considered. Senior managers, during budgeting, often make arbitrary cuts across the board. A potentially negative consequence is that the better managed departments may have already cut the majority of waste and now may have to cut into necessary resources. Budgets in traditional environment become wrestling matches in which those who are the best presenters are given larger budgets. The theory goes that the best at presenting the reasons for the larger budget deserves the larger budget. Traditional budgeting does not support excellence.

Activity-based Budgeting—Definition : Activity-based Budgeting (ABB) is the process of planning and controlling the expected activities of the organisation to derive a cost-effective budget, that meets forecast workload and agreed strategic goals. *Activity-based budgeting is a quantitative expression of the expected activities of the organisation reflecting management forecast of workload and financial and non-financial requirements to meet agreed strategic goals and planned changes to improve performance.* The three key elements of 'Activity-based Budgeting' are as follows:

(i) Type of work to be done,

(ii) Quantity of work to be done, and

(iii) Cost of work to be done.

Principles of Activity-based Budgeting : Activity-based Budgeting must reflect, what is done, *i.e.*, the activities or business process not cost elements. Resources required (cost elements) must be derived from the expected activities or business processes and workload. Workload is simply the number of units of an activity, that are required. For example, in the human resource department, the workload for the activity 'hire employees' might be to hire 25 employees. The cost elements to perform that activity might be the wages and benefits of the recruiter, travel, advertising, testing supplies and occupancy costs for the space occupied by the recruiter and for interviewing. If hiring freeze occurs, the workload for this activity would be zero. Budgets must be based on future workload in order to meet:

(i) Customer requirements,

(ii) Organisational/departmental goals and strategies,

(iii) New/changed services and service mix,

(iv) Changes in business process,

(v) Improvements in efficiency and effectiveness,

(vi) Quality, flexibility and cycle-time, and

(vii) Goals changes in service level.

The final budget must reflect the changes in resource cost levels and foreign exchange fluctuations. As a part of the activity-based budgeting process, it is important to highlight continuous improvement. Each department should identify the activities or business processes to be improved, the amount of improvement and how it plans to achieve its improvement targets.

Requirements for Successful Activity-based Budgeting : The organisation must be committed to excellence. If the organisation does not have this commitment, resources will be wasted on data analysis activities, that will never be implemented.

Process Management Approach : The organisation must use a process management approach to improvement. This requires defending each activity as part of a repeatable robust business process, that can be continuously improved and variability removed. Activities defined in this way can use various techniques to decrease time, improve quality and reduce the cost of those activities. Process management is crucial to excellence because high levels of performance are possible only when activities are done to best practices, the unused capacity is minimal, the best practices are continuously made better and the activities are executed perfectly.

Culture Encourages Sustaining Benefits : The organisational culture should encourage sustaining benefits. These benefits should not be something that lasts for only a short while, after which every one goes back to the old way. Organisation must overcome the cultural barriers.

Commitment to Excellence : Many organisations take a short-term approach to improving operations. Costs are easy to control if one simply stops spending. This approach is, however, like crash dieting. Business process performance must be tied to the balanced score-card and strategy.

Activity-based Budgeting Process : The ABB process begins with the customer. The organisation must determine who the customer is and what the customer wants. It must look to competitors. The organisation must develop a strategy to meet customer needs. Then the organisation should forecast workload. Planning guidelines must be articulated to each manager to establish the specific activity-level targets within a business process context. Inter-departmental projects should be identified. This improvement must tie into strategy. Activity-based investment analysis consists of defining improvement projects, evaluating those projects and then using committees to select projects that will meet the organisational goals and meet customer's needs. It involves following:

Customer Survey : One of the first steps in the strategic management process is to perform customer survey. Based on this survey, organisation should start with factors most important to the customer and determine whether it is satisfying the customers on those factors of performance. Activity or business process and investment preference must be given to those activities or business processes that the customer feels are important.

Core Competence Analysis : An organisation starts by asking what activities or business processes are critical to its industry. These activities or business processes become the core competencies of that industry. Then the organisation can ask from themselves which activities or business processes they perform well. Organisations need to compare themselves with external benchmarks and determine where there is core competence gap. Then the organisations can set budget targets in terms of cost, quality and time.

Benchmarking : The benchmarking process compares performance to other organisations either internally or externally. Benchmarks may measure activities, business process, time, new service introduction, customer service, quality and cost. Comparisons should be made, where possible, across divisions, with competitors and with the best organisations in the world. For example, one telephone company can process a request for new phone service within 43 seconds. This is a speed few other organisations can duplicate and would serve as benchmark for the activity 'Process new customer's credit request.

Activity Function Deployment (AFD) : Activity function deployment (AFD) is a concept similar to quality function deployment (QFD), which originated in quality field and is applicable to activity budgeting. In AFD, the organisation compares the customer's requirements with the activities or business processes necessary to meet those requirements. For each activity or business process, a comparison is also made with the competitors to determine how the organisation is doing against the competition. Besides a correlation is made between activities to show which activities have a strong positive or strong negative correlation with meeting customer requirements. Some activities will have no correlation with each other. Finally, a correlation is made between various activities and customer requirements. With this knowledge the organisation can determine which activities are critical to greatest customer satisfaction. Customer requirements are ranked as part of this analysis. Suppose an airline is looking to increase market share by better satisfying its customers. Using AFD, the airline determines that quick turn around time is important in order to have an on-time departures. One way to improve in this area is to have two jet bridges to load customers instead of only one. There are two activities— "Move jet bridge" and "Maintain jet bridge" connected with second jet bridge. For the two activities data can be collected on following lines:

For the activities "move jet bridge" and maintain "jet bridge"

Activity	*Activity cost*	Salary	*Depreciation*	*Parts*	*Occupancy*
Move bridge	Rs. 6,40,000	Rs. 6.40,000	—	—	20,000
Maintain bridge	37,00.000	1,00,000	2,00,000	50,000	20.000
	43,40,000	7,40,000	2,00,000	50,000	40,000

The idea of this discussion is to show how budgeting process is focussed on activities.

Reverse Engineering : Reverse engineering involves studying competitors' services. In the beginning one gains the impression that reverse engineering is a concept that applies only to products. However, applying reverse engineering to a service and seeing how competitors perform the service is a useful tool. For example, consider a company, that has a regulatory affairs department, that must file with the Food and Drug Administration to get regulatory approval. The company's manager studied the competitor's process of filing for regulatory approval. The objective was to determine how to perform the process more effectively. For improving "the FDA Approval Process" the manager will determine the activity cost separately.

Cost for "Improving FDA Approval Process"

Total Cost	*Salaries*	*Travel*	*Supplies*	*Seminar*	*Occupancy*
Rs. 12,300	Rs. 5,000	Rs. 3,000	Rs. 600	Rs. 1,700	Rs. 2,000

Translate Strategy to Activities. Strategy must be translated to an activity lend to identify specific necessary changes:

Steps	*Example*
(a) Define mission statement with enterprise goals	Dominate the market and diversify where advantage can be applied.
(b) Establish critical factors	Grow market share : increase new service sales as percentage of total sales.
(c) Establish service target	Increase market share : Service 1 by 7%; Service 2 by 8%; Discontinue service 3.
(d) Establish service level target	Service 1 - Increase Sales by 5% ; Decrease Cost by 8% Deliver in 2 hours.

7

Price Control

Hitherto, discussion was confined to cost. Now it will extend to pricing, relationship of costs and prices and mechanism of price fixation. Pricing is a profit-planning exercise in which management searches out the alternatives in an effort to choose one alternative which promises to be the most advantageous. In the process of pricing, Cost Accountant plays a very significant role by assisting the management in the evaluation of profit arising out of various alternatives. It should also be made clear that cost is only one consideration in price determination. There may be other considerations which may influence price more than cost. Similarly, profit in not the only objective of pricing function. For example, penetration in a particular export market may be the objective of pricing function. Thus, it is a very complex game which is played with due regard to: (i) pricing policy laid down by the company; (ii) pricing objective, and (iii) external constraints like Government regulation, etc.

Related Terms

Single of Uniform Price : Here a single uniform price is fixed for all the producers irrespective of their cost of production. The general principle adopted here is that the price is fixed by Government on the basis of most efficient producers. Thus, a weighted average single price is worked out based on the price of efficient producers. Under such a pricing, low cost or efficient manufacturers are bound to gain. On the other hand, high-cost or inefficient manufacturers are compelled to go out of production or adopt cost reduction and cost control measures by higher capacity utilisation or efficient use of facilities. Consumers also get the products or services at a single or a uniform price. The reasons for adoption of single or uniform price are summarised below:

(a) It is simple to determine and easier to administer than the separate retention price for each producer.

(b) It recognises that the low cost manufacturers are entitled to a large margin of profit. In other words, it encourages efficiency.

(c) It compels inefficient producers to strive for cost reduction and cost control for survival.

The *drawbacks* of single or uniform price are: (i) It discourages future investment in the areas where heavy investment is called for; and (ii) Some of the existing units are compelled to curtail production or stop it altogether.

Dual Pricing : Dual pricing system is adopted when the intention of the Government or price fixing agency is to provide essential goods or services to the weaker sections of the society at subsidised prices. Here the manufacturers are compelled to sell a part of their production at controlled price and a part at market price. Sugar industry is an example where dual price system has been in operation for a number of years. The sugar factories are required to sell certain percentage of the production to Government at a levy price and remaining percentage production can be sold at market price. The objectives of dual pricing system in sugar industry are indicated below:

(a) *To safeguard the interest of weaker sections of the society.* This objective is achieved by making available levy sugar to the common man at controlled price.

(b) *To enable the industry to pay higher sugarcane price to farmers than the minimum.* This objective is met by charging higher price on sugar sold in the open market.

(c) *Minimum return allowed on levy sugar.* The goods and services sold to the common man should be at fair prices. Therefore, the price worked out for levy sugar includes the minimum rate of return.

While the dual pricing depends upon the market forces, government has followed a policy of releasing sugar in the free market to hold the open market prices down. In some cases, this hampered the industry to recover the full cost plus a reasonable profit margin on the free sale sugar.

Retention Price : Retention price system is adopted in those industries where a product is in short supply, *viz.*, fertilizers, steel, aluminium, etc. This method of pricing is used where there are wide variations in the cost of production of different manufacturers. Variations in cost of production of different units of the industry may be due to the following reasons:

(a) Size of the plant,

(b) Change in manufacturing technology,

(c) Age of the plant,

(d) Locational factors,

(e) Wage structure of the unit,

(f) Capacity utilisation,

(g) Use of own manufactured raw materials and service, and

(h) Other miscellaneous reasons.

If uniform pricing system is adopted in an industry, high cost units will not be able to recover the full cost and as such they may go out of production. In order to overcome this difficulty, a separate retention price is fixed for each unit or a group of units based on their cost of production after allowing return on capital invested or return on networth as the case may be. The manufacturers may get different retention prices, but based on retention prices a common sale price for the ultimate consumer is determined. The consumers get the goods or services at a uniform price. The surplus or deficit of the individual manufacturer is adjusted through a pool account which is operated by a central agency. The objectives of retention prices system are given below:

(a) It encourages the maximisation of production.

(b) Low cost and high cost producers are suitably compensated.

(c) It facilitates setting up of industries in backward areas where cost of production may be high due to some difficulty in availability of raw materials or other infrastructure.

Zonal Price System : Under this system, the units in an industry are divided into different zones based on geographical location and a separate price is fixed for each zone. A uniform price is allowed to all the manufacturers in a particular zone. However, a single price is charged from the customers throughout the country. For example, earlier our country was divided into five zones for the purpose of ex-factory price of sugar. Ex-factory price for each zone is fixed on the assumption of some common factors of production in a zone, *viz.*, recovery, cane price, labour cost, etc. However, in fixing the zonal price, no weightage is given to the size and the life of the plant which affects the cost of production substantially.

Leader Price. Leader prices are fixed by Government with reference to pharmaceutical industry. Leader price means a price fixed by Government for formulations (i.e., medicines) keeping in view the cost or efficiency or both of a major producers of such formulations. Such leader price shall operate as a ceiling price for other manufacturers of such formulations. In other words, after fixation of leader price of a product, other manufacturers cannot charge a price higher than the leader price. Leader price concept is also used under conditions of free market economy. Leader price means a reduction in the price of a product of well-known brand called "a leader product". The basic idea of reduction in the price of a 'leader' is that it will attract customers who are at present opt to purchase other merchandise. Such a pricing is called as leader pricing. If the price is reduced below cost, the product involved is usually termed as a "loss leader".

Import Parity Price : Import parity price is adopted in the early stages of indigenous production where the cost of production of manufacturing units in the country is abnormally very high. As such, indigenous manufacturers are not allowed to charge prices based on their own cost of production. In such a situation, a uniform selling price is fixed both for indigenous and imported products on the basis of landed cost of imports. Price policy based on import parity cannot be a long-term measure.

Differential Pricing : Under this pricing system, two or more buyers pay different prices to the same seller for an identical product or service. Differences in prices may be based on quantities purchased, terms of payment, status of the buyers, bargaining power of buyers, location of the buyers within the country or outside the country and the nature of competition that prevails in the industry. In certain exceptional cases. Government has fixed differential prices for the various manufacturers. Under this pricing system, each manufacturer is allowed a different price. Consumers are also charged different prices based on the price fixed for each manufacturer. This policy can be resorted to only when the number of manufacturers and direct customers are limited and the demand and supply position is more or less equal.

Skimming Price : This term is used in pricing a new product. Basically, there are two alternatives in pricing a new product. One, which calls for a relatively high price, is called "skimming price", and other, which calls for relatively low price, is called "penetration price". The product should have some special features involving drastic departure from accepted ways of performing the service. For example, Prestige Cooker was priced very high when it was first introduced in the country. The product is introduced with high price coupled with large promotional expenses in the early stages and lower prices at later stages. Skimming pricing provides funds for financing expansion scheme, early higher prices may safeguard profits at early stages, but it may prevent quick sales to many potential buyers on whom company's future depends. A policy of skimming pricing is adopted under conditions such as: (a) a new product is introduced in the market; (b) there are a few producers;(c) demand is inelastic; and (d) a sophisticated product for use of rich and affluent customers.

Penetration Pricing : It is the reverse of skimming pricing. Penetration price is a low price that is designed to penetrate mass market as quickly as possible. This method is also used initially. The company may not earn a profit at the initial stage. Later on, the price can be increased when the demand picks up. Penetration pricing policy can also be adopted at any stage in the product life cycle, for products whose market potential is good, heavy investment is made and the market is approached with low initial price. This will discourage the new entrepreneurs to enter the market. For this reason, the penetration pricing is also called "stay-out pricing". Penetration pricing policy can be adopted under the following conditions:

(1) High price elasticity of demand for the product.

(2) Volume of production is very high.

(3) The market will not accept high price.

(4) There is a strong threat of potential competitors.

Shadow Price : The relevance of this concept arises in the situation of scarce resource. This is an important by-product of the linear programming solution. Shadow price also known as dual price, represents the opportunity cost of a unit of constrained resource. It is the increase in the value of objective function, which would be achieved, if one more unit of the resource was available. For example, if one additional machine hour had been available in Department *A*, the additional possible production would have increased the contribution margin by Rs. 6. This is the shadow price. The shadow price quantifies the benefit the firm can expect from increasing capacity. These benefits should be compared with the cost of expanding capacity in arriving at a decision relating to capacity increases. Only a constrained resource has shadow price. Where resources are not fully utilised, shadow price is zero. This accords with common sense as there can be no benefit in increasing the amount of a resource of which there is already a surplus. The shadow price is the opportunity cost of one unit of resource for the decision maker. It is not the synonym of opportunity cost. The concept will be clear by following examples:

1. If every extra kilogram of alloy will increase contribution by Rs. 4, shadow price is Rs. 4.

2. If sales constraint of product *B* is lifted, every extra unit of product *B* sold would increase contribution by Rs. 5. Shadow price here is Rs. 5.

3. Suppose situation is such that if any unit of product *C* is manufactured, overall contribution will fall by Rs. 6. Here shadow price is Rs. 6 (i.e., impact of increase/decrease of one unit of objective function.)

Margin : It represents sales less the cost of sales expressed either as a value or a percentage. Since the margin may be calculated at different stages, the terms gross and net margin, also known as gross profit and net profit, are used to differentiate between the levels.

Target Costing Approach in Pricing : It is relevant here to mention that target costing approach can be used as a pricing guide. When a decision to enter a new market is being considered, the prices of the competitors of their products are important factor in making this decision. The estimated long-run cost of the product which will enable a company to enter or to remain in the market competing its competitors successfully is called target cost. The target cost concept which is often used in pricing these days has an external market focus as its starting point, *i.e.*, cost of competitors or price of competitors. The Japanese consumer product companies often use target cost in their pricing strategies. The readers should note that the concept of target costing and its effective utilization, which has its origin in Japan can contain extremely useful lesson in improvement strategies.

Objectives of Price Policy : Formulation of price policy begins with the clarification of basic objectives of the firm. Pricing objectives have to be in conformity with overall organisational objective. In most of the situations, profit maximisation is the main objective of price policy but it is only one objective. Following may be other objectives of price policy in an organisation:

1. Pricing the goods based on reasonable costs,

2. Increase in the market share or its growth rate at the expense of immediate profits,

3. Avoid adverse public reaction consequent on charging high price,

4. Ethical consideration not to reap high profits,
5. Immediate survival of the firm,
6. Charge reasonable prices so as to have good relations with Government and public at large,
7. Maximisation of prestige of the firm rather than profits, and
8. To safeguard against the emergence of new producers in the same line.

Although its importance varies from firm to firm, pricing is one of the tools that a firm has at its disposal in its attempt to reach the stated objective. In order to be meaningful and effective, the price policy adopted must be consistent with the overall objectives of the firm. Thus a firm, whose overall objective is to increase market share, may adopt a price policy of always charging prices that are below those of competitors in order to expand its market share.

Techniques of Pricing

Cost-plus price. Cost-plus price mechanism under which a fixed percentage of profit is added to the historical cost. This method of pricing is applied under the following conditions:

(a) It could be the only method possible when an enterprise is entering a new technological area, where the 'one-term cost' cannot be predicted accurately. The only rationale here is to cover the full cost of production plus a reasonable profit margin.

(b) Where the customer has no choice but to accept the cost-plus price. Government during World War II entered into cost-plus contracts with suppliers for Government supplies. In certain cases Government departments like the Department of Supplies and Disposals entered into such cost-plus contracts for bulk purchases.

Advantages

(i) Use of cost-plus price technique leads to prompt cost calculations, which are very much needed for billing purposes in an organisation.

(ii) It provides convenient base in risky ventures.

(iii) Assures the contractor of a reasonable profit margin.

(iv) It is easy to understand and thus it is commonly used in Government supplies.

The principal advantage of this method is that it assures total cost recovery and the earning of a planned profit margin. This is particularly important in long-run pricing. It tends to introduce a certain degree of price stability into the market.

Disadvantages

(1) There is no incentive to the manufacturers for bringing down cost, as profit is determined as a percentage of total cost.

(2) It encourages inefficiency. The manufacturer tries to burden as much cost as he can on the product to be supplied or sold.

(3) This technique is not based on any scientific basic. It introduces an artificial and arbitrary element.

(4) This technique does not differentiate between high technology and low technology. Uniform percentage of profit is, therefore, unrelated to efforts required to manufacture the product under two different conditions.

(5) This method tends to ignore the demand or market side of the pricing problem and concentrates instead on production or selling side of the problem.

(6) It does not facilitate advance budgeting, as the price to be paid is not known before hand.

Marginal Cost Pricing : Marginal cost is the change in total costs that results from production of additional unit of a product or service. In other words, it is the extra or additional cost incurred in the production of an additional unit. The marginal cost technique of pricing is adopted under the following conditions:

(a) In public utility services where social returns are more important than generation of profit.

(b) Organisations operating in conditions of excess installed capacity.

(c) There is a cut-throat competition.

(d) The demand is much less than the supply.

(e) Where there is no demand of the product at full cost. This situation may arise from wrong investment decisions.

(f) A company introduces a new product in the market.

Pricing at marginal cost is a short-run measure. The objective of an organisation is to earn a reasonable surplus on its products after meeting all fixed costs. So, it can be summed up that it is a temporary or short-run measure of pricing. Following points should be noted carefully in use of marginal cost pricing:

(1) Additional sales at reduced cost should not endanger relationship with regular customers.

(2) Idle capacity cannot be used otherwise.

(3) Excess reliance on this technique should be avoided.

While there are important advantages to be derived from the use of marginal costs as a guide to pricing, indiscriminate reliance upon this technique can be dangerous.

Discriminatory Price : Sometimes an organisation is compelled to sell its products at discriminating prices to the consumers, i.e., different prices are charged from different set of customers. It is adopted where discrimination becomes necessary under external pressure.

Import Parity Price : This method is employed where indigenous cost of production is much higher than the landed or international price. This technique has two variations:

Landed Cost Basis : Here, the pricing concept is that the consumer should not be burdened with high cost of production of indigenous producers arising out of inefficiencies or low capacity utilisation. The prices are so fixed as to be equal to landed cost of similar important products.

International Parity Price: Here indigenously manufactured product is priced on the basis of internationally prevailing selling price. The international parity price has one disadvantage. Sometimes, international price is so low that it can be extended to the local manufacturers, because it is less than the variable cost of indigenous production.

Administered Prices : Sometimes Government enforces price control on certain essential or basic products. The prices are administered by Government in order to safeguard the interest of consumers. On account of supply being less than the demand, the uncontrolled prices may go up substantially. Therefore, Government does not allow the market forces to play their part in pricing of such product. Under the administered prices, consumers are charged on single price on the one hand, and the producers may be paid retention prices. This arrangement is called single selling price to the consumers and retention price to the producers.

Return on Investment Pricing : In computing the selling prices under each of the method discussed earlier, no consideration has been given to the capital required to produce/sell the products. Return on investment is the ultimate measure of business efficiency. While computing the product price, it is necessary to add to total cost a certain percentage of capital employed as profit margin. This percentage varies from industry to industry depending upon its nature. Capital employed consists of the following two elements:

(a) New fixed assets employed for production, and

(b) Working capital.

This method of pricing is commonly employed because it recognises full cost of production plus reasonable return on investment. This is very useful for performance measurement.

Affecting Factors

In a country like India, price controls are enforced on a number of products like sugar, drugs and Pharmaceuticals etc. Recently, Government has withdrawn price distribution control on certain industries. These factors limit the role of manufacturers in price fixation. Price fixing authority, like the Bureau of Industrial Costs and Prices (Now Tariff Commission), recommend the products' prices whereas price control is enforced by administrative

Ministries. Government fixes the maximum price at which the product could be sold. The manufacturers are free to sell the products below the maximum selling price so fixed.

Price controls are not existing for all goods and services. When price controls are not existing, pricing function is influenced by numerous factors, some of which are summarised below:

(a) Internal factors or cost factors, and

(b) External factors or non-cost factors.

Internal Factors or Cost Factors : Internal factors for pricing includes price policy and product costs. Cost is one of the important factors that influences pricing decisions. The main reason of the importance of cost as a factor in pricing is that product price should not be less than its cost, if the price policy is to earn a reasonable profit. Thus, it implies that cost is the chief determinant of price. The relationship between cost and price is very complex and more difficult to understand than over simplification of saying such as "price must cover merely determining costs and adding a margin of profit."

Relation of Costs and Prices : From a Cost Accountants' point of view, costs should be used to establish a floor below which a firm will not price its products. The proper function of cost is to set the lower limits on the initial price charged for a product while value to consumers sets the upper limit. The job of management, entrusted with pricing function, is to pick the space between these two extremes. No company should charge prices below full costs unless such a policy appears necessary or expedient in the short period. In other words, unless market conditions, competition or other factors require that less than full cost price be charged, it is unwise to do so in terms of company's profit. To sum up, costs are just one of the several factors to be considered in a pricing decision, and for pricing purposes costs are best regarded as a floor below which a company will not normally price its products.

External Factors or Non-cost Factors Effecting Pricing Decision: Besides the above-mentioned internal factors, various external factors also influence pricing decisions in an organisation. Unlike the controllable internal factors, the external factors are largely out of the control of the company. External, uncontrollable or non-cost factors are discussed below:

Demand : The nature of demand for the product or service in question is one of the most important considerations in pricing decisions. The demand is determined by a number of factors, *viz.*,

(a) price, (b) availability of substitutes, (c) income of buyers, (d) tastes and preferences of buyers, (e) number and size of competitors in the industry, and (f) number and size of buyers, etc. In order to make the best decisions regarding product pricing, the pricing executive should clearly endeavour to learn about the characteristics of the demand. He must establish a relationship between demand and adjustments in prices both in short run and long run.

Degree of Competition : Market structure of the constituent units of the industry also influences the pricing decisions. The market structure consists of following basic elements:

(a) Number of competitors,

(b) Size of each competitor,

(c) Degree of product differentiation, and

(d) Easy entry into the industry by new competitors.

Market structure is influenced by:

(i) pure competition, (ii) pure monopoly, (iii) monopolistic competition, and (iv) oligopoly

Pure competition and pure monopoly is very rare in the real world. However, monopolistic competition is often found in business. Under this situation, there is room for some degree of price administration. In an oligopoly situation, there are small number of sellers, each of them can affect the pricing decisions of others. The prices of different firms tend to be uniform.

Age of the Industry: The age of the industry also influences pricing decisions. Prices in a new industry tend to be more flexible than in old and well-established industries. Downward price adjustments in a new industry can produce significant changes in sales.

Suppliers of Raw Materials: Suppliers of raw materials, where raw materials cost forms a sizable part of total cost of production, exert some pressure on pricing decisions. Thus, the company is compelled to increase the product price due to increase in the price of raw materials.

Type of Buyers : The types of buyers that buy the company's products also determine the product pricing. As a rule where there are more buyers, they exert less influence on prices. There is no resistance to price increase if the buyers belong to an affluent society.

Economic Conditions in the Market : The economic conditions in the market served by the company are also important in pricing. The economic conditions of the people may vary considerably from area to area. As a consequence, the company may wish to use differential pricing in a different area. This should be used very carefully.

Price Controls : Government decision to control the product prices is also an important external factor in pricing. Although the cost of a product may be high, Government may decide to fix the price substantially lower than the cost on import parity basis. In some cases Government directs the companies to manufacture a particular product to the levels of licensed capacity. All these decisions are external for pricing purposes.

Nature of the Product : The nature of product is an important factor in pricing. Price increases in essential consumer products are vehemently opposed by consumers as well as by Government. On the other hand, price increase in luxury or capital nature products may not face an opposition from purchasers, *i.e.*, in case of automobile industry.

Aims and Objectives

(1) To bring about a reasonable stability in prices.

(2) To ensure optimum production with due regard to the efficiency of the various sectors of the economy.

(3) To ensure availability of goods and services to consumers at fair prices.

(4) To ensure fair return to producers on funds invested.

(5) To discourage the producers and other intermediaries to reap high and disproportionate profits.

(6) To contain inflation.

(7) To protect the weaker sections of the society.

(8) To encourage growth and combat shortages.

The Impact

Impact of price controls on the various sections of the society is summarised below:

(1) *Government*. Government is primarily concerned with the implementation of price controls in order to safeguard the interest of the weaker sections of the society. Through price control, government protects consumers and ensures availability of goods and services at reasonable prices.

(2) *Industry*. The general complaint of the industry is the poor rate of return allowed by the Government. The main attack on the methodology adopted by price fixing body is regarding some special costs which are not taken into account in price fixation. It is complained that while the price of final product is controlled, there is no price control on major input materials. The Government takes considerable time for granting increase in product price due to escalation in the prices of raw materials and utilities.

(3) *Trade*. Wholesalers and retailers indulge in profiteering and black-marketing when the products are in short supply. This was very true in case of steel, where traders indulged in unfair practices. Before the commencement of dual pricing system in cement industry, traders were indulging in black-marketing. This situation has since been eased due to economic liberalisation, *i.e.*, price decontrols in most of the industries.

(4) *Consumers*. The main objective of price control is to provide the essential commodities to a common man at a most reasonable price. The properly regulated price control system helps the consumers by providing the necessities of life at fair prices. This is in conformity with the social

objective of a welfare State. But this objective is partly defeated when the economy is dogged by shortages.

(5) *Economy as a whole.* Price control leads to black-marketing in a number of commodities since the money generated through black-marketing cannot be made accountable. No tax is paid on this money. This results in loss of revenue to the exchequer.

The Mechanism

It has already been pointed out that price fixation is a key function in an organisation. This function will be discussed under the following two heads:

(A) Process of price fixation in general or process of privately administered prices; and (B) Process of price fixation under State regulation and control.

Process of Price Fixation in General : Pricing decisions are to be taken in almost all the organisation. Following procedure is generally adopted in price fixation by the organisations:

Pricing Objective : The objective of pricing should be clearly defined. The overall objectives of the firm should be articulated as clearly as possible since they are the proper guide to pricing. In order to be meaningful and effective, price policy and procedure must be consistent with overall objective of pricing.

Determining the Organisation for Pricing : Responsibility for the establishment of price policy and its implementation must be clearly assigned. In smaller companies and a few large companies where top executives are principal owners, the President or top executives (*e.g* .Vice-President, in charge of sales or general manager) make all the pricing decisions. In large companies, top management, (*e.g.,* President, Board of Directors, a committee of top executives) establish price policies generally and approve price lists and quotations on important orders. In large companies the task of day-to-day decisions on prices is delegated to the sales department as long as these decisions are within the scope of established policies. Some of the large companies designate a committee of executives from various functions (i.e., sales, manufacturing, accounting, general control), which formulate policies and approve price lists and prices on large orders. Pricing is not a no-man activity and proper organisation for pricing is, therefore, necessary.

Collection and Analysis of Information Required for Price Fixation: For price fixation, both cost factors, and non-cost factors, discussed elsewhere in this chapter are considered. The information for price fixation may be collected from company records, company personnel, outside consultants, research studies done in the field, suppliers and buyers.

Process of Price Fixation under State regulation and Control : The price fixation under State regulation and control will involve the following steps:

Selection of Product : When certain imbalances emerge in the economy, the whole price-cost relationship is disturbed. It becomes the paramount duty of the Government to check such imbalances by selection of products for price control. It is the responsibility of the Government to ensure that commodities are available to consumers at reasonable prices. This object is borne in mind while selecting commodities. Some of the commodities now under price control (full,or partial) are: sugar, drugs and Pharmaceuticals, fertilisers, etc.

Selection of Units : Sometimes there are a large number of units in an industry. It may not be possible for the price fixing body to study all the units. As such, representative units are selected for cost study. Samples may be selected each from small-scale, medium-scale and large-scale factories. The sample units selected should be of economic size. These should cover the regional dispersal of units in the industry and should be representative of the conditions of the different regions.

Choice of Agencies : The price fixing agencies in India are:

Bureau of Industrial Costs and Prices (B.I.C.P.) (now Tariff Commission): This is a permanent agency under the Ministry of Industry. It handles industry-wise cost studies referred to it by various Government Ministries/Departments. This agency is a purely recommendatory body.

Cost Accounts Branch, Ministry of Finance: It is one of the departments under the Ministry of Finance, Department of Expenditure. It is an expert organisation headed by Chief Adviser (Cost), who is head of the Indian Cost Account Service. It handles specific cases referred to it by various Government departments.

Agricultural Price Commission: It is a permanent agency under the Ministry of Agriculture. The agency enquires into costs of agricultural products and advises on the pricing policies thereof.

Ad hoc Committees: Sometimes *ad hoc* committees are also set up to go into the pricing problems of specific commodities. National Pharmaceuticals Pricing Authority, and Fertilisers Pricing Committee are some of the examples of *ad hoc* committees.

Special Committees : Joint Plant Committee is set up for steel price fixation within limited framework as well as for steel allotment. Another example is of Oil Coordination Committee which looks after pricing, distribution of oil products and maintenance of equalisation funds.

TariffCommission (since wound up): Tariff Commission was responsible for handling all price fixation cases pertaining to various industries. It was a statutory price fixation authority. Tariff Commission was wound up in 1972 and its work was transferred to B.I.C.P. It handled a large number of cases of industrywise price fixation. All the reports of Tariff Commission were published. The work of B.I.C.P. has since been transferred to the Tariff Commission.

Determinants of Items of Cost : While costs have a bearing in prices, the level of prices at a particular point of time is the resultant of many factors. Cost is only one of the many complex factors which together determine prices. The price fixing body critically scrutinises all the elements of cost which are discussed below:

Material Cost : In most cases, materials form major component of product cost. Therefore, material costs are thoroughly verified. Material cost consists of two components, *viz.*, quantity consumed and unit rate. Abnormal consumption and abnormal purchase rates of materials should not form part of material cost. Consumption norms of material vary from factory to factory depending upon stabilisation of production, life of plant, process technology and operational efficiencies. As regards prices of materials purchased, the rush or emergency purchases or expenditure incurred in air freight, etc., should not be considered as normal cost. Some companies use own manufactured materials while others use purchased ones. This gives rise to the variation in raw material costs of each unit.

Power and Fuel: Consumption of power and fuel and their rates have greater impact on cost. Power tariffs charged by different State Electricity Boards vary widely. Almost all the Indian industries are dogged by major power-cuts and short supply of furnace oil. Due to this reason, some companies have installed generators for uninterrupted supply of power. This gives rise to variations in power and fuel costs from industry to industry.

Conversion Cost: It is that part of cost which is incurred for converting the raw materials into finished product. Conversion cost includes direct salaries and wages, consumable stores, repairs and maintenance services, depreciation and factory overheads, etc.

In a capital-intensive industry, depreciation forms a major cost element. The quantum of depreciation differs from unit to unit in a industry depending upon size or age of the plant. Depreciation is worked out based on written-down value method or straight-line method.

Conversion cost mainly depends upon wage structure, plant life, technology adopted, capacity utilisation, etc. It also depends upon the size, *viz.*, small-scale, medium-scale, large-scale or multinational. In addition to conversion costs, other costs such as administrative overheads, packing cost and selling and distribution overheads are also included in arriving at the total cost of sales.

Bonus: Price fixing body now recognises the statutory minimum bonus. In support of this argument, it is argued that the amount of bonus in excess of statutory minimum should be paid out of profit margin only.

Items Not Considered as Cost Elements : The following items do not form part of cost:

(a) Bonus in excess of statutory minimum limit.

(b) Interest on borrowings, being non-operational charge. However, it is included as part of the element of profit for determining the price.

(c) Loss on sale of fixed assets.

(d) Litigation expenses.

(e) Donations and charities.

(f) Bad debts or reserve for bad and doubtful debts.

(g) Other non-operating and extraneous expenses.

(h) Extraneous income.

(i) Expenditure relating to previous year.

Selection of Pricing Period : First of all, actual cost for a specified period is worked out by the price fixing body. Actual cost being a historical cost serves as a base for fixation of estimated fair selling price. Such fair price will remain in vogue for specified pricing period which is normally three years. In some exceptional cases, the price period is limited to one year only.

Capacity Utilisation : Various industries in India operate below the installed capacity due to the following reasons:

(i) Shortage of raw materials.

(ii) Shortage of power and fuel.

(iii) Labour trouble.

(iv) Plant breakdown.

(v) Periodical maintenance.

(vi) Installation of plant of fairly large capacity than presently required.

(vii) Due to unfavourable prices fixed by Government.

(viii) Lack of demand.

In view of the above, it becomes necessary to determine the capacity at which plant is expected to work. The price fixing body considers the normal capacity which means total machine time available *less* reasonable allowance for breakdown, repairs, power cuts, and normal holidays. In addition, due care is taken about the demand factor by taking into account long-term sales forecast. The capacity utilisation normally ranges between 60% and 70% of the capacity depending upon various factors noted above.

Technical Parameters for Raw Materials, etc : Technical parameters are found by technical experts based upon their study of the company's consumption norms of raw materials, power and fuel, etc. The parameters differ from actual consumption norms because the technical parameters are based on best consumption norms achieved by a unit over a fairly long period. In case of initial commencement of production, sometimes, standard or guaranteed norms of consumption of raw materials are adopted. Then consumption norms would vary from company to company depending upon technology, age of plant, quality of input materials, etc.

Determination of Capital Employed : It is necessary to work out the capital employed before providing for profit margin. The pertinent question is "what would be the capital employed and on what basis the same should be computed".

Capital employed represents the sum total of (i) average net fixed assets after providing depreciation, and (ii) networking capital. Net fixed assets mean gross block *less* cumulative depreciation. Working capital represents the difference between current assets *minus* current liabilities. As the fair price has to be fixed for a particular pricing period which is normally three years, it is necessary to work out the net fixed assets for the pricing period. Additions to the plant and machinery, building or balancing equipment, required during pricing period also form part of net fixed assets. Requirement of working capital may be very high in some companies while in others it may be very low. It is necessary to arrive at normative working capital which should reflect the average requirement of the industry. Working capital is expressed as so many months' cost of sales *minus* (i) depreciation, (ii) commission, and (iii) royalty based on sales. Thus, the capital employed is abase for calculation of return.

Determination of Return on Investment : Up to 1976, the pricing body was allowing return on capital employed. In most cases 15% return on capital employed was allowed by the Tariff Commission.

However, in exceptional cases return was allowed on cost of sales. In 1976 post-tax return on networth concept was introduced by Government. The main reason for the change from the capital employed concept was that it tended to create a bias in favour of borrowed capital. Since the return was normally higher than the market rate of interest, industry was resorting to finance their requirement with borrowed capital. Under the post-tax return on networth concept, the ultimate return would vary depending upon the debt-equity ratio of each unit. It is necessary to find out the rate of return on investment desired. Obviously the rate should cover:

(i) Interest on borrowings

(ii) Dividend to shareholders

(iii) Bonus to employees

(iv) Taxation

(v) Ploughing back of funds into business for normal growth.

Networth Concept : Networth concept referred to above is very simple. Capital employed is calculated by adding the net fixed assets and working capital. The capital employed so worked out is segregated into networth and borrowings on the basis of debt-equity ratio of the company as per the latest year's balance sheet. The return is calculated on networth after providing for corporate tax. Interest is also allowed on borrowing at the average rate of interest of the company for the latest year. The mechanism of return on networth is made clear in the following examples:

Cost Escalations : When conditions of the economy are reasonably stable, there is no need for cost escalation clause. Price increase in the input factors is unavoidable due to constant inflationary trends. The increase in the price of inputs may be due to Government action, that is, increase in the basic price of coal, power or furnace oil, etc., or increase in the price of basic input raw materials. To take care of such upheavals, the price fixing body normally recommends in each case an escalation clause to the Government. Such clause permits under specified conditions adjustment of price for variations in cost. The very basic purpose of providing an escalation clause is defeated, if the company does not get the price increase in time.

Mathematical Approach to Optimal Pricing (Using Calculus): If the average revenue (demand curve), marginal revenue and marginal cost functions are assumed to be linear over the range of output considered, it is possible to determine the optimal price and output mathematically.

Transfer Pricing

A transfer price is the notional value placed on goods and services transferred from one division to another division within a large business organisation. Some companies have the problem of pricing goods and services which are transferred to other divisions/units of the same company, such pricing is referred to as 'intracompany', 'intradivisional' or 'transfer pricing'. The term 'intracompany transfer' is used to include any transfer of products between divisions, plants or units. Products transferred may include partly finished goods or finished goods transferred for use. The value at which goods or services are transferred from one unit to another unit is called intracompany transfer price. A well-established method of measuring the efficiency of the company is decentralisation, which usually involves the setting up of a number of separate profit centres. When each decentralised unit of an organisation is deemed as a profit centre and transfer of goods and services amongst the independent profit centres take place, the problem of intracompany transfer pricing arises. Geographically dispersed or international companies often face the problem of pricing goods and services, which are transferred to other divisions or units of the same company.

Objectives of Transfer Pricing: It is most essential to specify the overall company's objectives before decision is taken to adopt a particular transfer pricing method. The main objectives of intracompany transfer pricing are summarised below:

(i) To foster a commercial attitude in those who are responsible for the performance of profit centres. The main emphasis here is on profitability. This objective forces the units to improve their profit position.

(ii) To optimise the profit of the company over a given short period of time. Here the stress is on maximum utilisation of plant capacity.

(iii) To optimise the allocation of companies' financial resources. This is a long-term objective. The allocation of resources is based on relative performance of various profit centres, which in turn are influenced by transfer pricing policies.

(iv) To enable the performance (profitability) of a division to be evaluated by compensating it for benefits provided for other divisions and charging it for benefits received.

(v) To motivate managers for maximising the profitability of their divisions acting in the best interest of the organisation as a whole.

(vi) International groups may try to manipulate transfer prices between countries in order to minimise overall tax burden.

Importance of Transfer Pricing System : For the following reasons a transfer pricing system is of particular importance to an organisation:

(a) An inefficient transfer pricing system can lead to sub-optional decisions, which may lead to inherent losses of significant propositions.

(b) An error in transfer pricing may have considerable impact on divisional profits and morale of the concerned divisional manager and his staff.

(c) Behavioural problems are the major problems arising out of transfer pricing system. An imposed transfer price, which is unfair either to purchasing division or the supplying division, can lead to considerable resentment, hostility and loss of motivation. This could easily counter any of the benefits claimed for a divisionalised type structure. Effort should be made to avoid behavioural problem by use of system, which lends sufficient opportunity for fair arguments leading to acceptable decision in the available framework.

(d) The transfer price must represent a fair value of service of goods being provided, as it will underlie segments's performance evaluation.

(e) A bad transfer pricing policy can give rise to interdivisional conflicts, which can be expensive in terms of resentment, loss of resources, and time taken in arbitration between centres. The problem can be mitigated by including through foresightedness, clear instructions in the system relating to different situations, which may arise between the transferor and the transferee division.

Criteria for judging a Transfer Pricing System : Transfer pricing is of particular importance in an organisation as it improves decision-making in a decentralised organisation conforming to three basic objectives of decentralisation, *i.e.,* goal congruence, performance evaluation and autonomy. The criteria for judging a good transfer pricing includes:

(i) It should provide adequate measures of profit for the division to ensure motivation for the divisional head and his team.

(ii) The transfer pricing should be goal congruent. Dysfunctional decision-making should be avoided as a result of transfer pricing system. At times divisional interests are sacrificed for overall company interests without completely ignoring the interest of the concerned division.

(iii) It should provide adequate information to senior management for use in company decision-making and evaluation of divisional performance.

(iv) It should promise fairness in treatment and due share both to purchasing and supplying divisions.

To sum up, a good transfer pricing system should foster a healthy inter-departmental competitive spirit without needless arguments. There should be a well-laid down system to resolve the differences instead having the need to seek the intervention of higher management time and again involving wastage of resources.

Transfer Pricing Methods : If there are many independent units of an organisation, pricing is influenced by the following two systems:

Laissez Faire, i.e.,: the system under which each independent unit has full freedom to negotiate the prices of its goods and services.

Centrally Imposed System: Under this system, the pricing by independent units is regulated by guidelines laid down by the top management.

Transfer pricing methods arcbroadly classified into the following three categories:

(a) Cost-based transfer pricing;

(b) Market prices; and

(c) Bargained or negotiated prices.

Cost-based Transfer Pricing : The various methods of cost-based transfer pricing are discussed below :

Actual Cost of Production : This is the simplest method of transfer pricing. Under this method, it is difficult to measure the performance of each profit centre. The purpose of adopting this method of transfer pricing is to meet the demand of user unit. This method is used where the responsibility for profit performance is centralised.

Variable Cost : The price equal to variable cost will be very attractive to the buying unit but not to the selling unit. When it is not the purpose to measure the profit performance of each unit, but overall profitability of the company is the main objective, this method is used. This method is particularly useful when the capacity of the selling unit is idle. The adoption of variable cost in transfer pricing will lead to full utilisation of capacity. This method is seldom used in practice.

Standard Cost : Under this method, all transfers are valued at standard cost. The variances from standard cost are normally absorbed by the supplying unit. In certain cases, variances from standard cost are transferred to the user unit and, therefore, inventories are carried both by the selling unit and user unit at standard cost. Once the standards are properly set, operation of this system is simple. Here again, the responsibility of profit performance is centralised. Profit performance of each unit cannot be measured.

Cost of Sales : This is also known as full cost method. Under this method, in addition to actual cost of production, expenses like selling and distribution and administration are also allowed to be recovered from user division. The managers of supplying divisions are responsible for profit for outside sales but supplying divisions are not permitted to make profit on goods transferred to other divisions. This method is better than the previous method. At least the supplying divisions are allowed to recover full cost of goods transferred. Under this method, measurement of divisional profit performance is not possible.

Cost of Sales Plus : It is assumed that the supplying division is selling to outside parties as well as transferring the goods to other divisions of the company. Under these circumstances, the user division is allowed to recover full cost of sales plus some mark-up or an allowance for profit. This allowance is either expressed as a percentage of capital employed or cost of sales. The fallacy of this method of transfer pricing is that selling divisions are allowed to recover selling expenses from the user divisions even though no selling expenses are incurred on inter-division transfers. To meet this objective, standard cost or actual cost plus profit margin is used for transfer pricing. This method will suit those cases where there is no outside buyer of the product. Sometimes budgeted cost plus a specified return on capital employed is also used. Once the method to be adopted is decided by the top management and accepted by both divisions, it is easy to operate this method of transfer pricing. Under this method, profit performance of each unit is measurable and efficiency or otherwise can be reasonably determined.

Opportunity Cost-based Transfer Pricing: Horngren has advised that for decision-making purposes a transfer price should be one which is based on marginal (incremental) costs of goods plus any opportunity cost to the firm as a whole (for not being able to use them in best possible way). The effect of this will be different in different situations:

In perfectly competitive market, i.e.,: all products sold internally can be sold externally, transfer pricing technique will be:

where $SVC + LCM$ = Prevailing market price

SVC = Standard variable cost

LCM = Lost contribution margin

In Slightly Imperfect Competitive Market, Technique will be: SVC+ LCM = Adjusted market price, *i.e.*, prevailing market price *less* economies achieved by selling internally.

***In Perfectly Competitive or Slightly Imperfect Market, i.e., most products sold externally* :** Products sold internally do not have a market price. Production capacity used to produce internally sold products can be used to produce externally sold products. Transfer price technique: *SVC* + *LCM* = Phantom market price. This reflects the opportunity cost of producing the product for the internal user.

Prorating-based Transfer Pricing: Prorating-based transfer pricing is used in special situations where the group as a whole benefits from doing the work internally rather than accepting external quotation. In such cases best course is to share group contribution advantage on some equitable way between divisions involved through negotiation.

Market Prices : Under the cost-based methods of transfer pricing, it was assumed that departments or units of a company would not be treated as a separate profit centre for efficiency measurement. Under market price method, the transfer prices to other divisions are based on market prices. A competitive market implies the existence of buyers and sellers. Such a market provides an incentive to efficient production because excessive costs cannot be passed on to buyers. Since market prices will, by and large, be determined by demand and supply in the long run, it is claimed that profits, which result under this method, will provide a good indicator of the overall efficiency of the various units.

In certain cases, the division may not be trading externally. In the circumstances, the market price is determined on the market reports, which maybe an inaccurate guide to the actual prices. In view of this, the measure of efficiency generated may be distorted. There are circumstances when the actual costs will be more than the market prices. Selling division will thus be inefficient and user division will be treated as efficient one. Competitive market prices, thus, provide reliable measure of divisional income because these prices are established independently.

The limitations of market price method are summarised below:

(i) Collection of market prices presents a lot of difficulty. There may not be any market price at all when the goods are manufactured for captive consumption only.

(ii) In the spell of rising prices, market price method is very difficult to be used because prices become obsolete in short space of time.

(iii) The use of market price method demands the company should attempt inter-unit elimination of profits. This exercise may be easy to look at but it is very difficult to operate in practice.

(iv) Market price consists of cost elements like packing, selling and distribution expenses. The selling unit does not incur all these expenses. As such adoption of market price may not be a satisfactory process.

(v) When this method is used, stock is valued at market price and, therefore, elimination of unearned profit relating to closing stock becomes necessary.

Negotiated Transfer Prices : Here each decentralised unit is considered as an independent unit and competitive price is arrived at by negotiation or bargaining. Divisional managers have full freedom to go for outside purchases if the prices quoted by other divisions are not acceptable to them. A system of negotiated prices will foster the commercial attitude amongst divisions of the company. However, the cost of freedom may be that the profit of one division is earned at the expense of other divisions. The buying division may be tempted to purchase from outside source if the outside prices are lower than the internal division's price. In order to avoid the danger of overall profits, which may be reduced in this way, the top management may impose constraints on external trading. In order to have an effective system of intracompany transfer pricing, the following points should be kept in view:

(1) Prices of all inter-division transfers should be determined by negotiation between buyers and sellers.

(2) Negotiators should have access to full data on alternative sources or markets.

(3) Buyers and sellers should be completely free to purchase from outside the company.

The administration of intra-company transfer pricing is the sole responsibility of top management. All pricing disputes which are not settled at divisional level will have to be referred to the top management for decision. Management by exception will have to be followed in such cases. Overhead company's objective should be kept in view while regulating such prices.

Negotiated vs. Imposed transfer prices : Transfer prices should preferably be negotiated between vending and purchasing division. At times situation arises, where central management has to impose a verdict on one of the divisions. In general, negotiated prices are preferred due to the following reasons:

(i) Negotiated prices reflect a fair method of establishing a contract price between a buyer and a seller.

(ii) Negotiated price means implicit acceptance of fairness on the part of vending and purchasing division.

(iii) Negotiated price gives rise to perceived autonomy in decision-making, which is very important, if benefits of divisionalisation are to be achieved.

(iv) Negotiated price leads to better communications between buying and selling division, which is vital, if the dysfunctional decisions are to be avoided.

Dual Transfer Pricing: Due to conflicting interests of buying profit centre and selling profit centre, it is just not possible to have a single transfer price. The buying profit centre and selling profit centre have different interests in the transfer price. In one case, the price is used to make a decision and in other case, the price is an important factor in evaluating the performance of the selling profit centre. For this reason, it is suggested by some authors that there is no need to have a single transfer price. Even in dual price, differing approaches have been suggested, as is clear from the subsequent discussion:

Charge the Receiving Division with Variable Cost and Credit the Supplying Division with an Amount in Excess of Variable Cost: This can be illustrated based on hypothetical data given below:

(a) Units transferred—1,00,000 units.

(b) Final product is sold at Rs. 10 per unit.

(c) Variable cost of Supplying Division is Rs. 2 per unit.

(d) Conversion cost of Receiving Division is Rs. 6 per unit.

(e) It is assumed that inter-divisional transfers are made at standard variable cost plus 50% to Supplying Division. Receiving Division is charged with standard variable cost.

The results of each division now will be as follows:

Supplying *Division*		*Receiving Division*	
Transfer to Supplying Division at Rs. 3		Sales of finished product	
(1,00,000 units at Rs. 2		at Rs. 10	10,00,000
plus 50%)	Rs. 3 ,00,000		
Less: Variable Cost:			
Less: Variable cost		Supplying Division Rs. 2,00,000	
(1,00,000 x Rs. 2)	2 00,000	(Rs. 1,00,000 x Rs. 2)	
		Conversion cost	
		(Rs. 10,000 x Rs. 6)	
		6,00,000	8,00,000
Contribution	1 ,00,000	Contribution	2,00,000

The logic for this approach is simple. If the Receiving Division is charged with standard variable cost per unit, the manager will be induced to take the correct decisions for the organisation as whole. The performance of the manager of the Supplying Division would also be enhanced by supplying sufficient goods to meet the requirements of the Receiving Division, because each unit transferred will be at a price of Rs. 3 providing a contribution towards the total fixed costs.

The two-part Tariff System, i.e., Allowing a Fixed Make-up on Variable Cost and Fixed Cost of the Supplying Division : At times the buying division negotiates to buy a portion of the 'capacity of the vending division at an agreed price'. In doing so, it is charged by a two-part pricing mechanism, namely, the proportion of the fixed costs (*plus* a profit margin, if appropriate) and the variable costs *plus* a mark-up per unit purchased. The portion of the fixed cost should be at budgeted cost and not at actual cost. Suppose following information is given:

Division X purchases product Alpha from Division *Y*. Product Alpha is not sold externally and a comparable product cannot be found in the market. Alpha represents 40% of Division *Ys* capacity.

Division Y's fixed overheads are budgeted to be Rs. 5,00,000 per annum. The standard variable cost is Rs. 5 per unit. The profit mark-up has been agreed at 5% on variable costs and 10% on fixed costs.

Division X will, therefore, pay capacity charge of 40% x Rs. 5,00,000 = Rs. 2,00,000 *plus* a 10% mark-up making it Rs. 2,20,000.

Division X will also pay a unit price of Rs. 5 + 5% = Rs. 5.25.

Charging the Buying Centre with Synthetic Market Price and Crediting Supplying Centre with Standard Variable Cost Plus Mark-up or Full Cost Plus A Normal Mark-up: The synthetic market price represents variable cost of the selling responsibility centre *plus* the opportunity cost to the company as a whole. In this situation, the income for the company as a whole will be less than the total profit of responsibility centres. In preparation of financial statements, exercise is attempted to eliminate unearned profit on intra-company transactions. Any amount transferred in excess of company costs would have to be eliminated.

It is clear from the above that there can be different interpretations of "dual transfer price" but it is widely recognised that it is just not possible to have a single transfer price due to conflicting interests of buying and selling profit centres. Dual transfer price has not been in common use due to practical difficulties, but it is obvious only that dual transfer pricing system is capable of promoting goal congruence, motivation, autonomy and performance evaluation under all conditions.

International Transfer Pricing : The correct transfer price for decision-making may conflict with the price which is used to determine profits for the assessment. This conflict may arise when the supplying and the receiving divisions are located in different countries with different taxation rates. If the taxation rates in one country are much lower than those in the other country, it could be in the interest of the company, if most of the profits were allocated to the division, which operates in the low taxation country. It is pertinent to mention here that transfer price can have an impact on import duties and dividend repatriation. Import duties can be minimized by transferring products at lower prices to a division located in a country with high import duties. Some countries also restrict the repatriation of income and dividends. By increasing the transfer prices of goods transferred into divisions operating with these restrictions, it is possible to increase the funds repatriated without violating dividend restrictions. These points are of great value in determining the transfer price between subsidiaries of multinational companies.

The Chartered Institute of Management Accountants, London, (CIMA) Proposals to be Observed in Setting Transfer Pricing : The *CIMA* published Management Accounting Guidelines: Inter-unit Transfer Pricing in October 1981, which gave the following list of points to be observed in transfer pricing system:

1. The opportunity to submit a quotation should always be made available to an internal supplying division, when its management believe that they can produce the required product.
2. Opportunities to re-quote should be made available to the supplying division when its original quotation exceeds the external quotation. It should be recognised that external supplier will cease to submit competitive quotations, if their bids are always unsuccessful.
3. Transfer prices should always be agreed in advance of work commencement.
4. Whilst a market price should form the basis of the transfer price, allowance should be made for selling expenses not

incurred in an internal sale (credit, advertisement, etc.) and also for possible cost disadvantage operating on decentralised basis.

5. In the absence of a market equivalent price, a negotiating procedure should be adopted by the trading divisions. These negotiations should not be allowed to become unduly protracted. Head Office interference should, however, be kept to the minimum and arbitration should be made available, where both parties request it.

6. Prices based on a total cost incurred should never be employed except in situations where the final contract with the outside customer is on a cost- plus basis.

Readers should realise that transfer pricing is a complex topic. It is extremely difficult to arrive at a transfer price, which satisfied all the relevant criteria of decentralisation. Flexibility is required and the above-mentioned points should be kept in mind for this purpose.

Criteria for transfer pricing :

(i) It should motivate the divisional managers to make sound decisions.

(ii) It should enable a report to be made of divisional profits, that is reasonable measure of the management performance of the division.

(iii) It should ensure that division autonomy is not undermined.

Recommended Procedure for Transfer Pricing :

1. When the market for the intermediate product is perfect, the correct transfer price is the external market price for the product. The supplying and the receiving divisions will themselves determine the optimum output level.

2. The market for the intermediate product may be imperfect or perhaps no market may exist. If the supplying division has no capacity constraints, the correct transfer price is the marginal cost of the supplying division for that output

at which marginal cost equals the sum of the receiving division's net marginal revenue from converting the intermediate product and the marginal revenue from any sale of the intermediate product on the external market. Where unit variable cost is constant and fixed cost remains unchanged, this rule will give a transfer price, which is equal to the supplying division's unit variable cost.

3. Where unit variable cost of the supplying division is not constant, then marginal cost transfer pricing rule requires that Central Headquarters set the transfer pricing by combining cost and revenue information for the supplying and receiving divisions. This will lead to divisional autonomy being undermined. It also leads to a performance measure which does not provide a true reflection of each division's contribution to total company profits.
4. Intra-division transfer price conflicts can reduce, if the receiving divisions agree to make a lump sum payment, which adequately takes care of supplying division's requirements for meeting the receiving division's requirements.
5. Dual transfer price can be introduced. This constitutes determination of the transfer price for decision-making and another transfer price for measuring performance. This method is not widely used for obvious shortcoming.
6. When the divisions are located in different countries, relative taxation rates will also influence transfer pricing.
7. Relationship of transfer transactions with total transactions of supplying division will also influence the transfer pricing, *i.e.,*:
   (i) Transfers of significant amounts occur, but such transfers are not a predominant part of the supplying division's business.
   (ii) Transfers constitute a predominant part of the supplying division's business and it can meet all probable requirements.

(iii) The supplying division does not have the capacity necessary to meet all requirements.

International Transfer Pricing and Income Tax Act—Draft Rules for Transfer Pricing : The Finance Act, 2001 substituted the old Section 92 of the Income Tax Act by Sections 92, 92A, 92B, 92C, 92D, 92E and 92F in which taxing methodology of the connected international transactions has been introduced. These Sections define the meaning of connected parties, nature of international transactions, pricing methodology, etc. New provisions such as "Meaning of international transactions" and "International transactions to be valued at arm's length price" are discussed below:

Meaning of International Transactions. International transactions relate to purchase, sale or lease of tangible or intangible property, provision for services and lending or borrowing money between two parties, either or both whom are non-residents and they are associated enterprises (Section 92D). So if the parties are not associated such transactions do not fall under international transfer pricing mechanism.

A more comprehensive list of connected transactions is available in Accounting Standard-18 issued by the Institute of Chartered Accountants of India that includes :

(a) purchase and sale of goods;

(b) purchases or sale of fixed assets;

(c) rendering services or receiving of services;

(d) agency arrangements;

(e) leasing or hire-purchase arrangements;

(f) transfer of R & D;

(g) licence agreements;

(h) finance (including loans and equity contribution in cash or kind);

(i) guarantees and collaterals; and

(j) management contracts including deputation of employees.

International Transactions to be Valued at Arm's Length Price: Principle of arm's length pricing is applicable for three elements:

(i) income (revenue) of the transactions to be derived applying arm's length price;

(ii) expenses and interest of the transactions to be derived applying arm's length price; and

(iii) any cost allocation or apportionment or any cost distribution arranged or agreed between two parties (who are associated persons and either or both of whom are non-residents) for any service, benefit or facility is to be derived applying arm's length price (Section 92).

Draft Rules for Transfer Pricing : The Central Board of Direct Taxes has formulated draft rules for transfer pricing.

Major Considerations in Passing Accounting Entries Relating to Rransfer Pricing : Most companies, which have a significant volume of intra-company transfers, will make these transfers at some transfer price above the cost. Therefore, some of the portion of intra-company profits will be in inventories at any given time. In accordance with generally accepted accounting principles, profit can be made only on sales outside the company. Therefore, it is necessary to make elimination entries, when financial statements are made. Unless elimination is attempted, there will be overstatement relating to sales, accounts receivables, cost of goods sold, work-in-process inventory and finished goods inventory. Internal reports of responsibility centres are ordinarily designed for performance evaluation and decision-making purpose, while financial accounts are prepared for creditors, investors and other external users. Thus, intra-company profits must be eliminated periodically, when financial statements are made.

Profit centre statements give separate recognition to intra-company sales, cost of goods sold and accounts receivables plus any other related matters such as intra-company loans. Generally, certain reconciliation is again needed when one location has made a transfer and recorded the sale, but buying location has neither received the goods nor recorded the purchase.

The influence of taxation on transfer price : At times taxation influences the transfer price considerably. Some companies with international network seek to minimise its tax burden by adjustment of transfer price. This is done to shift profits between the group companies. This practice may help to increase after-tax profit of a particular Division in the group, but the divisional profits so arrived at cannot be used for measuring performance or efficiency. Besides, result of pricing transfers with a primary interest in tax avoidance may have behavioural repercussions.

Estimated Price

Estimating costing is not a new method of costing. It is a technique generally used for quotations, price fixations, etc. Estimating costing aims at ascertaining cost of products or services for future period. It is very useful for non-standard products and for jobbing work, where standard costing is difficult to apply. Estimating costing, thus, facilitates to find out !what the cost will be in future'. It is based on the average of past actual figures adjusted for anticipated changes in future.

Uses of Estimating Costing : The uses of estimating costing can be summarised as follows:

Predetermination of Cost. The main disadvantage of historical costing is that the cost data are available only after expiry of the period under review. Therefore, no remedial measure can be taken to remove inefficiency. To obviate this difficulty, estimating costing is used. Estimating costing is a pre-determined cost with reference to normal working conditions for a specified future period. It helps management in decision-making.

Pricing for Bidding and Submitting Quotations and Tenders : It is a well-known fact that all companies try to capture Government orders for supply of goods and services. For this purpose, they have to submit quotations for products or services. Estimate for cost of product is very important because there is a time lag between submitting a quotation or signing a contract and actual supply of product.

Pricing Fixation : Estimating costing helps price fixation in those companies which do not maintain elaborate cost accounting records. This situation is very true in Indian context where large number of small-scale industries are coming up. It helps the management to compare actual price with estimated price.

Cash Budgeting : Success of cash budgeting will depend upon estimated sales and estimated costs of products. If costs and prices are not properly estimated, the whole process of cash budgeting is bound to be disturbed. In the present inflationary trends, shortages and uncertainties, estimating costing is the only efficient technique.

Profit Planning: It is necessary to anticipate costs, sales and profit for profit planning. In jobbing industries, where input and output are not standardised, planning of profit assumes significant role. Thus estimating costing facilitates profit planning in such situations.

Cost and Price Estimation for Bidding, Quotations and Conclusion of Agreements : Out of all the uses of estimating costing, it is necessary to discuss cost and price estimation for bidding, quotations and conclusion of agreements. A company is called upon to furnish estimates of costs and prices for its products or services for entering into agreement or for offering quotations of prices in respect of job or service to be undertaken for a customer. Before preparation of cost/price estimate for quotations, it should be borne in mind the price quotation should not be too high because it will lead to loss of business, nor it should be too low because it will lead to loss. It is the duty of cost accountant to prepare the cost estimates on the following lines:

(a) he must consider the market conditions before giving quotation or signing agreement,

(b) consider the cost and volume relationship for the contract to be signed,

(c) nature of products being offered,

(d) duration of the contract,

(e) Wether escalation clause is being appended to the contract,

(f) terms of payment, and

(g) how far idle capacity is being utilised.

After considering all these factors, he must prepare the estimates of cost and prices so that contract is decided in company's favour.

Procedure for Determining Estimated Costs : The necessary prerequisites of cost and price estimation are as follows:

(1) Complete drawings and specifications of the product.

(2) Requirement of tools, jigs and fixtures.

(3) preparation of sequences of products.

(4) Time cycle of production.

(5) Expected production requirements.

(6) Present actual product cost.

(7) How far previous cost estimates deviated from actuals.

(8) Forecasting of raw materials, power and fuel prices.

(9) Impact of future DA increase or new wage agreement.

For estimated costs and prices, following elements of cost/ price should be carefully determined:

(1) Material quantities and prices,

(2) Direct labour hours and hourly wage rate,

(3) Overheads, and

(4) Profit margin.

These are discussed below.

Materials Estimates : Material prices are functions of material quantity, quality and material rates less scrap/solvent recoveries. Material quantity estimates are based on: (i) Engineering specification, (ii) Pilot runs, (iii) Record of past performance, (iv) Measurement of materials in the finished products, and (v) Material yields based on best of consumption norms. Other function of material prices is material rate. Future prices of materials are difficult to be predicted in these inflationary conditions. Therefore, it is advisable to enter into a running contract or supply of materials. In the absence of this arrangement, estimated market prices must be predicted on the basis of analysis of published quotations.

Labour Estimates : Estimated labour cost is usually determined in one of the two ways, *viz.*, (i) piece rate, and (ii) time rate. In the first case, labour cost is determined by multiplying the piece rate with the number of units produced. In the second case, it is arrived at by multiplying labour rate per hour with labour hours required for production. In determining the labour rate, fringe benefits, overtime, production bonus, etc., should also be included. In addition, expected wage revision should also be considered.

Estimating Manufacturing Overheads. First of all, manufacturing overheads should be segregated into fixed and variable. Estimating fixedoverhead is a cumbersome process. Estimation of overhead items like rent, insurance of property tax is quite simple. One of the important factors for determining the overhead rate is the future capacity utilisation. This capacity should not exceed the normal capacity.

Profit Margin : The company is expected to earn a reasonable profit on its investment. On the basis of estimated cost plus an element of profit, estimated price is worked out for quotation or submitting tenders. However, price depends on a large number of factors. Cost estimate is only one factor. The price quoted should not be either too low or to high. It is the duty of the cost accountant to find a cut-off point between these two extremes.

Errors in Estimation : Cost estimates are best possible projected cost. It entails certain judgements, interpretation of past data and as such it is subject to certain amount of errors. These errors may arise due to the following reasons:

(a) *Errors Due to Omissions :* It is common experience that errors due to omission often appear in the cost estimates. For instance, cost of outside jobbing work which is part of the cost of production of stainless steel vessel was not included in the quotation which resulted in the errors in the estimates. Therefore, cost estimates should be thoroughly checked by a senior officer of the estimating department.

(b) *Uses of Averages :* The choice of averages is a matter of compromise between accuracy and effort. Judgement and experience are the only means of making choice. Therefore, cost estimating process is always subject to some errors.

(c) *Inadequate Data:* Errors may also arise due to insufficient data required for cost estimates. Such errors normally arise when preparing an estimate for non-standard, special jobbing work. Therefore, in order to avoid this situation, estimator must be provided with all the relevant data and in the form required by him.

(d) *Substitution of Materials :* Cost estimates are based on standard bill of materials. Circumstances such as shortages or non-availability of a particular raw material may compel the production department to use substitutes. This effects the accuracy of estimates.

(e) *Change in Capacity Utilisation.* This change reflects the fixed cost. But lower capacity utilisation may be due to power cuts, non-availability of materials, go slow, strikes, etc., and other unavoidable factors such as accidents, fire, earthquakes, etc.

Export Pricing

Export pricing is a little technical and is computed differently from the price for domestic sales. Certain elements which enter into internal price do not apply when goods are to be sold abroad. For example, advertising expenses within the country and administrative costs are not fully applicable on export sales and as such do not form part of export pricing.

If the price is quoted *FOB* (Free on board), it includes the following:

(1) Ex-factory price of the product.

(2) Special packing charges.

(3) Inland transportation cost.

(4) Wharfage and port charges.

(5) Export duty, if any.

(6) Other miscellaneous charges.

However, *CIF* price includes *FOB* price plus cost of ocean freight and marine insurance up to the port of destination.

Methods of Export Pricing : Since price for export continues to be an important tool of promoting sales abroad, its calculation will have to be done with utmost care. International market situations vary from country to country and from time to time. Export pricing strategy in terms of cost-plus policy, marginal costing, dual and differential pricing has, therefore, to be adopted according to specific marketing situation. Each of these methods are discussed below:

Cost-plus Method : Under this method, a fixed profit margin is added to total cost for export pricing. This method seems to be most natural to be adopted by the trade. However, price based on this method is cost-oriented rather than market-oriented particularly in case of non-traditional products to be sold in the international market where there is cut-throat competition. While assessing the profitability of export sales, it is necessary to view cost price and sales volume in an integrated manner. Since export normally results in additional sales turnover, export price should comprise only those items of cost which are attributable to export production.

Marginal Cost Method : Under this method, only those costs which are directly relevant to manufacture of export products are taken into account.

The overhead costs which are costs of being in business and not attributable to the product concerned are excluded from the ex-works price of an export product. Ex-works price of export product comprises:

(a) Cost of materials. (b) Labour,

(c) Power and fuel, and (d) Special packing cost for exports.

The export incentives available should be deducted from the amount thus calculated. This pre-supposes that fixed costs are recoverable from domestic sales.

The principle of marginal costing holds good only if:

(i) Surplus capacity is available in the plan.

(ii) The unit is not wholly/largely export oriented, i.e., its total/major share of production is not exported.

(iii) Capacity of its domestic market to bear fixed cost is not limited.

(iv) There is scope for price manoeuvrability in domestic market.

In the absence of the above given factors, fixed cost may be ignored while taking short-term pricing decision.

Dual or Differential Pricing Method. This method is adopted where marginal costing may not be necessary and/or is not possible to be adopted in case of all export products/markets. Depending upon (a) nature of market. *(b)* extent of competition, and (c) export incentives and assistance, marginal costing may not always be necessary. While some products may be priced at full cost, others may be priced at only direct cost in the same market.

Export prices are sometimes quoted much below marginal cost. Such situations are exceptions rather than the rule and may arise on account of

(i) political motivation,

(ii) to clear excessive stocks, and

(iii) to drive the competitors out of market.

For determining the cost of export product, direct export assistance is deducted. This may be in the form of:

(i) Cash assistance,

(ii) Custom duty drawback,

(iii) Refund the excise duty, if paid,

(iv) Refund of octroi, if paid,

(v) Other assistance, if any, and

(vi) Benefits arising out of import replenishment licences.

Cost Accountant's Role in Pricing : A Cost Accountant plays a substantial role in pricing decisions. Following discussion deals in details with this aspect:

1. A Cost Accountant, by virtue of his expertise and by application of integrated approach combining Economics, Cost Accountancy and Management Accountancy plays a

dynamic role in price fixation both in the industry as well as in Government. In industry, he plays a leading role as price fixatioin expert. He presents reliable cost data and analyses it. He also participates effectively as a part of the management team in evolving pricing policies and their implementation.

2. As a Cost Accountant in Government, he plays a very complex role in a team of experts like Economists, Engineers and Cost Accountants. Amongst these professionals, he has to play the role of a leader. On the basis of cost data furnished by the industry and verified from all angles, he works out the actual as well as future cost of a product and estimate fair selling prices which will remain effective for the pricing period. This requires higher degree of specialisation in the subject.

3. Pricing is a profit-planning problem. Management is always in search of alternative courses of actions. In this process, Cost Accountant has an important part to play in assisting management in evaluating the various alternatives. This function is performed by determining anticipated cost to make and sell the company's products and anticipated profit.

4. As a Cost Accountant in the industry, his main role is maintenance of proper cost accounts records, effecting cost control and submission of necessary cost data to price fixing authorities. In addition, he has to focus the attention of Government on the various limiting factors faced by the company in production and sales, procurement of raw materials, etc. He has to present the anticipated picture of the company so that all factors are considered by price fixing authorities while determining fair selling price of a product. If he fails in this direction, the future profitability of the company is bound to dwindle.

5. Cost Accountant has to play his role in formulation of the

objectives, policies and procedures for fixation of product prices. The Cost Accountant plays a strategic rule in determination of pricing policies. He must bring forth all the relevant factors that will affect the pricing policies.

6. Cost Accountant has to perform a leading role in the Cost Reduction Team. Cost reduction helps in improving the profitability of the company. In the cut-throat competition, the existence of a company is jeopardised unless it takes effective cost reduction and cost control measures.
7. He is responsible for the efficient functioning of Costing Department. He must procure timely cost data to management for control purposes. He has to provide the relevant information to Cost Auditor for getting the cost accounts audited. He is an important link between the organisation and the Cost Auditor, Department of Company Affairs and pricing body like Tariff Commission.
8. Cost Accountant's role is more important in presenting to management the profitability of each product or service. He is also required to present a comparative picture of actual profits of each product or service with standard or budgeted profits.

Pareto Analysis (80 : 20 Analysis) and Pricing : It is observed that in practice 20% of the total quantity of stocks may account for about 80% of its value. This principle is known as Pareto Analysis and is based on observation by Pareto. Main point is that a very small proportion of items usually accounts for the majority of value. By concentrating on small proportion of stock items, which jointly account for 80% of the total value, a firm may be able to control most of its monetary investment in stocks. This phenomenon can be observed in many business situations. The management can use this analysis in a number of different circumstances to attract management attention to the key control mechanism. The analysis of the company's estimated total sales revenue might indicate that approximately 80% of its total sales revenue is earned from about 20% of its products. This analysis is based on observations by Pareto that a small proportion of items usually accounts for the majority of value.

Application of Pareto Analysis : Pareto analysis can be applied in suitably presenting the data relating to performance indicators through selection of representative process characteristics that truly determine or conform to the desired quality or outcome. The Pareto Analysis can be applicable to the following business situations:

Pricing a Product: In a multi-products situation, it would not be possible for the company to analyse price-volume relationships for all the products. By adopting some cost-based pricing formulae for the less important revenue earning products, the management may be able to devote more time to establishing cost-price-volume relationships for the more important products. In practice, approximately 20% of the products may account for about 80% of the total sales revenue. Such analysis may help top management to delegate the pricing decisions for approximately 80% of its product to the lower level of management, thus freeing themselves to concentrate on the pricing decisions for those products that are essential for a company's growth. More sophisticated pricing methods should be applied to the small proportion of products that jointly account for 80% of the total sales revenue.

Stock Control : In practice, 20% of the items in stock account for 80% of the total value of purchases. At the other extreme, about 80% of the items in stock account for approximately 20% of the total value. The control of stock levels is eased considerably, it is concentrated on that small proportion of stock items that account for most of the total cost.

Customer Profitability: In a multi-product situation, profitability analysis is attempted for a number of products. However, for optimising the profitability of a company, major customers are treated as profit centres. It is often found that approximately 20% of the customers generate 80% of the revenue/ profit. Some customers are less profitable than others. Marketing efforts are concentrated on those customers who generate high revenues. Such an analysis is a useful tool for evaluation of the portfolio ofcustomer profile.

Application in Activity-based Costing: It is generally observed that in Activity-based Costing, 20% of an organisation's cost drivers are responsible for generating 80% of the total cost. By analysing and concentrating on those cost drivers that generate most cost, a better control of the overheads will be feasible.

Quality Control : Defect reports are analysed in detail to identify the most common cause of customers' complains. Often 80% of the reported problems are usually traced to 20% the various underlying causes. By concentrating one's efforts on rectifying the major 20% defects, product quality can be improved to a great extent. The Pareto Analysis indicates him frequently each type of defect occurs. The purpose of this analysis is to direct management attention to the areas where best return can be achieved by solving most sought- after quality problems with a single corrective action.

Usefulness of Pareto Analysis : Pareto Analysis helps to clearly establish top priorities and to identify both profitable and unprofitable targets. Uses of Pareto Analysis are:

(i) Identify key problems, goals and objectives for directing management action.

(ii) Select and define key quality improvement programmes.

(iii) Select key performance improvement programmes.

(iv) Allocate physical, financial and human resources.

(v) Verifying operating procedures and manufacturing processes.

(vi) Select key customer relations and service programmes.

(vii) Maximise research and product development efforts.

(viii) Products or services sales and distribution network.

8

Control of Budget

For effective running of a business, management must know:

(i) where it intends to go, i.e., organisational objectives,

(ii) how it intends to accomplish its objective, i.e., plans,

(iii) whether individual plans fit in the overall organisational objective, i.e., coordination, and

(iv) whether operations conform to the plan of operations relating to that period, i.e., control.

Budgetary control is the device that a company uses for all these purposes.

Budget : A budget is a quantitative expression of a plan of action relating to the forthcoming budget period. It represents a written operational plan of management for the budget period. It is always expressed in terms of money and quantity. It is the policy to be followed during the budget period for attainment of specified organisational objectives.

The essential features of a budget are: (a) financial and quantitative statement of the action plan, (b) laid down prior to the budget period during which it is followed, (c) based on management's policy, and (d) prepared for specified objective.

In the CIMA terminology, a budget is defined as follows: "A plan expressed in money. It is prepared and approved prior to the budget period and may show income, expenditure, and the capital to be employed. May be drawn up showing incremental effects on former budgeted or actual figures, or be compiled by zero-based budgeting."

Budgetary Control and Budgeting : The terms budgetary control and budgeting are often used interchangeably to refer to a system of managerial control. Budgetary control implies the use of a comprehensive system of budgeting to aid management in carrying out its functions like planning, coordination and control. It is a system which uses budgets for planning and controlling different activities of business. This system involves:

(i) division of organisation on functional basis into different sections (each section is technically known as a budget centre),

(ii) preparation of separate budgets for each "budget centre",

(iii) consolidation of all functional budgets to present overall organisational objectives during the forthcoming budget period,

(iv) comparison of actual level of performance against budgets. Comparison process is stretched far enough to declare either attainment of objective or basis of revision of plan ofaction, and

(v) reporting the variances with proper analysis to provide basis for future course of action.

In the CIMA (London) terminology—

"Budgetary control is the establishment of budgets relating to responsibilities of executives to the requirement of a policy, and the continuous comparison of actual with budgeted results either to secure by individual action the objective of that policy or to provide a basis for revision."

Budgeting is a way of managing business and industry. It emphasises that management should anticipate problems and difficulties. Advance decision should be taken for the course of activities during the forthcoming budget period. Budgetary control denotes a formal system based on the concept of budgeting.

Budgets and Forecasts : A forecast is a prediction of what is going to happen as a result of a given set of circumstances. A budget is an approved plan of action expressed in figures relating to a specified period of time. A forecast is a mere assessment of future events and budget is a plan of action proposed to be adhered to during a specified period. A budget is prepared on the basis of forecast made for the budget period and thus a forecast is not all that a budget is. A forecast can be made just by anybody competent to make judgement. A budget is an approved plan of action that is set only by seasoned executives of an organisation. Forecast can be made for purposes other than budgeting. Economic forecast of general business conditions may not have anything to do with budgeting. Budgets are always made with the objects of planning, communication, coordination and control. Forecasting ends after the assessment of prospective conditions. Budgets start with forecasting and lead to a control process, that continues even after budget preparation. A forecast includes projection of variables both controllable or non-controllable that are used in development of budgets.

Aims and Objectives

Planning : Planning is an important managerial function. It helps to decide in advance, what to do, how to do it, when to do it and who is to do it. Planning, thus, helps the managers to anticipate eventualities, prepare for contingencies for achieving the ultimate goals. Budget preparation drives the managers to plan ahead. Managers express their operational plans for anticipated business conditions. Without a formal procedure of budgetary control, many operating managers will not find the time to plan ahead. Thus, budgeting is an important planning device.

Communication : The employees of an organisation should know organisational aims, objectives of sub-units (budget centres) and the part that they have to play for their attainment. Budgets effectively communicate this information to employees. Besides, budgets keep different sections of the organisation informed about the contribution of different sub-units in the attainment of overall organisational objectives.

Coordination : To coordinate is to harmonise all the activities of a company so as to facilitate its working and its success. Coordination will lead to following results:

(a) each department will work in harmony with others,

(b) each department will know the specific role that it has to play in the accomplishment of overall organisational objectives, and

(c) the sequential arrangement of activities of different departments is so governed that overlapping of activities and wastage of time and labour is avoided.

A comprehensive system of budgeting helps to coordinate different functional budgets. In other words, a budget will preclude the production department from producing more than the sales department can sell.

Motivation : If employees have actively participated in budget preparation and if they are convinced that their personal interests are closely associated with the success of organisational plan, budgets provide motivation in the form of goals to be achieved. Whether the budgets will motivate the workers, depends purely on how the workers have been mentally and physically involved with the process of budgeting.

Control : Under the system of budgetary control, budget forecast is thoroughly discussed and reviewed to be finally approved as functional budgets. Thereafter a lot of'cuts' and "adjustments' are made to make functional budgets fit in the organisational objectives. Then budget formation is followed by a feedback system to pinpoint the extent of variation between actual level of performance and budgeted level of performance. Thus, the inbuilt mechanism of the routine of budgetary control is bound to precipitate to an operational control.

Approved Plan : A master budget provides an approved summary of results to be expected from proposed plan of operations. It concerns all functions of organisation and serves as a guide to executives and departmental heads responsible for various departmental objectives.

Requirements of a Good Budgeting System. Following are the requirements of a good budgeting system :

(i) Budgeting process should be backed and supported by the chief executive of an organisation,

(ii) The organisational goal should be qualified and clearly stated. These goals should be within the framework of organisation's strategic and long-range plans.

(iii) The organisational goals must be divided in functional goals.

(iv) The functional goals should not conflict with overall organisational objectives.

(v) All in the organisation should mentally accept the exercise of budget preparation.

(vi) The persons responsible for execution of budget should participate in budget preparation.

(vii) The budget should be realistic. It should represent goals that are reasonably attainable.

(viii) The budget should cover all phases of the organisation.

(ix) The budgeting should be a continuous exercise.

(x) Periodic reports should be prepared promptly, comparing budget and actual results, *i.e.,* there should be effective follow-up.

(xi) Clear-cut organisational lines should be established with appropriate delegation of responsibilities for effective budget implementation.

(xii) The budgeting system should be based on information, communication and participation.

Advantages of Budgetary Control

1. A budget programme forces the managers to plan ahead.
2. It forces early consideration of basic policies.
3. All members of top management participate in budget committee. For this reason even planning at departmental level gets benefit of experience of seasoned executives.

4. All functional heads are compelled to make plans in harmony with the plans of other departments.
5. Management is forced to put down in cold figures, what it means by satisfactory results.
6. It demands the most economical use of labour, materials, facilities and capital.
7. It inculcates a habit of timely, careful, adequate consideration of all factors before reaching important decisions.
8. The use of budgets removes clouds of uncertainties for lower levels of management regarding basic policies and objectives.
9. The use of budgets promotes understanding of the problems of co- workers.
10. It facilitates periodic self-analysis of the organisation.
11. It aids in obtaining bank credit.
12. Management is forced to give timely and adequate attention to the effect of changing business conditions.

Limitations of Budgetary Control

1. Estimates are used as basis for budget plan and estimates are based mostly on available facts and best managerial judgement. Since a lot of human element is involved in exercising managerial judgement, it is but natural to give some allowance in interpretation and utilisation of estimated results. Budgeting based on inaccurate forecasts is useless as a yardstick for measuring the actual performance.
2. The circumstances are constantly changing and, therefore, budgets and budgetary techniques will not be useful, till they are continually adapted.
3. In order that a system may be successful, adequate budget education should be imparted at least through the formative period. Sufficient training programmes should

be arranged to make employees give positive response to budgetary activities.

4. Execution of budgetary control will not automatically occur. A continuous budget consciousness throughout the organisation is needed for achievement of this objective.

5. Budgetary control cannot reduce the managerial function to a formula. It is only a managerial tool which increases effectiveness of managerial control.

6. The use of budget may lead to restricted use of resources. Budgets are often taken as limits. Efforts may, therefore, not be made to exceed the performance beyond the budgeted targets, even though it may be physically possible.

7. Frequent changes may be called for in budgets due to fast-changing industrial climate. It may be difficult for a company to keep pace with these fast changes, because revision of budget is an expensive exercise.

Preliminaries for Operation of Budgetary Control

Specification of Organisational Objective : Budget presents a view of a plan in figures. It is necessary that broad objectives of organisation are specified before this plan is stated. The statement of broad objectives of organisation will involve expressing mission, vision and ethical tone of organisation. This type of specification will lay down a sort of guide for managers to take corrective decisions and independent decisions within the given framework.

Establishment of Budget Centres : Budget centre is a section of an entity for which control may be exercised and budget prepared. For this reason, an organisation is divided into different segments, which are clearly defined for the purpose of budgetary control according to responsibilities of departmental heads. These segments of organisation defined for the purpose of budgetary control are technically referred to as budget centres. For each budget centre a budget is prepared. Preparation of budget for a budget centre is specifically linked with the responsibility of concerned departmental head. The budget which is prepared for a 'budget centre' is called a departmental budget. With the help of departmental budgets functional budgets are compiled. Functional budgets are integrated to present organisational budget. A machine shop is a 'budget centre'. The budget for a machine shop is a departmental budget. Because 'machine shop' is a department relating to production, the figures must be summarised in production budget, which is a functional budget.

Linking of Budget Requirements with Chart of Accounts : Budgets for different budget centres are prepared on standard forms. If requirements of forms is linked with chart of accounts, information of different budget centres will be consistently compiled involving minimum loss of time. Suppose advertisement budget is being compiled and information for miscellaneous expenditure is to be collected. It will be an easy exercise to gather this information, if code heads to be referred to in this connection are specified in the form on which information for budget is being collected.

Establishment of Budget Committee : In small organisations one executive may handle work relating to preparation of budget, but in big organisations having different units at different places, a budget committee is formed having representation of chief executive, budget officer and heads of all budget centres. Often chief executive of an organisation is the head of this committee, so that decisions of this committee may be binding on others. The budget officer acts as a secretary to chairman. The departmental heads of budget centres form a group that passes judgement over the issues presented to budget committee for deliberation. Following are the main functions of a budget committee:

(i) It reviews the budgets prepared by heads of budget centres.

(ii) Different budgets may not be in harmony with each other and in these cases budget committee (comprising always of seasoned executives) recommends a decision for revision of budget.

(iii) It reviews the revised budget and approves it finally.

(iv) It receives and analyses the periodic performance report from different budget centres in the enterprises.

(v) In a situation involving disputes it considers various alternatives and recommends final decision for corrective action.

(vi) It recommends forms and changes in programme, policy and procedure.

(vii) It recommends action to be taken in special circumstances.

It is an apex body which works for operation of system of budgetary control. The two facets of budgetary control, *i.e.*, planning and control, are executed through the budget committee.

Preparation of Budget Manual : For proper operation of budgetary control, a budget manual is prepared setting out responsibilities of executives involved in the routine of introduction of budgetary control. This manual contains standardised forms which become input resources for compilation of budgets. The procedure and routine of budget preparation is well spelt out in the Budget Manual. It contains a complete programme of activities involved in budget preparation.

Following is the brief summary of the contents of a Budget Manual:

(a) Different terms are clarified.

(b) Objects are clearly defined.

(c) The role of different functional heads is specified.

(d) Procedures of budgetary control are dealt with in detail.

(e) Responsibilities for preparation of different budgets are fixed.

(f) The reports and statements required at different points of time in budget period.

(g) If system of budgetary control is mechanised, it will contain information like account code, budget centre code and other codes relating to item number of different forms, etc.

(h) It will include the statement of sequence in which budgets will be presented and discussed for final approval. It will set out how sessions will be arranged for discussing the different budgets.

(i) Budget manual states dates on which different performance reports and statement of expenditure should be submitted to the budget committee for analysis and review.

Determination of Budget Period : CIMA defines budget period as "the period for which a budget is prepared and used, which may then be sub-divided into control periods." Budgets having short duration are very costly, because revision of budget is an exercise requiring substantial expenditure and labour. During preparation of budget, a sort of budget atmosphere sets in the enterprise and other activities do suffer attention. On the other hand, long-term budgets are difficult to be controlled. With passage of time element of control slackens and it is also difficult to accurately forecast the future. Whether a budget is to be a long-term budget or a short-term budget is to be decided primarily with reference to following two factors: (a) Type of business, and (b) Amount of control required.

Type of business is a decisive factor in determining the budget period. In enterprises requiring huge capital outlay like shipping companies and companies engaged in the manufacture of heavy power generating equipment, budget period may extend from three to five years. Tne budget period should normally coincide with the financial accounting period in order to compare actual results with the budget estimates. It should also be noted that "time period covered" wiltnot be the same for all budgets, yet the budget period must be definitely established.

In industries engaged in motor manufacturing, radio manufacturing and other consumer goods manufacturing, budget period is not very long, because designs change very quickly. Concerns of this type prepare budgets extending from one year to two years. The enterprises engaged in manufacture of goods having seasonal demand may like to extend budget period to six months only. It is difficult to lay down guidelines which should be strictly adhered to for determining the budget period. The following points give a general impression of length of budget period in undertakings carrying on different types of business:

(a) Trading—One year; (b) Capital Expenditure—many years;

(c) Research and Development—many years; and (d) Seasonal Business—six months.

The other factor influencing determination of budget period is control. Element of control slackens in the long-term budget. It is also difficult to accurately forecast for a long time to come. There are conflicting opinions about determining the extent of budget period. Certain managers go to the extent of saying that accuracy in prediction is of secondary importance to benefits that are derived by habit of being forced to look far in future. Keeping all this in view, it can be said that budget period should be only as long as circumstances permit.

Certain enterprises go still far using a system of continuous budgeting. Under this system, budgets are kept under periodic review (say, monthly) and if it is necessary, budgets are modified for following one or two months ahead. This system keeps budgeting alive to new changes and reduces variances to the minimum. Besides the two basic factors (type of business, amount of control required), the other factors that influence determination of budget period are: (i) Type of budget (sales budget, production budget and capital expenditure budget), (ii) General economic conditions, and (iii) Trade cycle of business.

Determination of Key Factors : It is also referred to as 'limiting factor', governing factor and principal factor. Key factor is a factor whose influence must be first ascertained to ensure that function budgets are reasonably capable of fulfilment. Budget factor influences all functional budgets. Often, sales is the key factor, but apart from sales there can be numerous budget factors. Following is the representative list of key factors :

(a) Sales
- (i) Market potential.
- (ii) Consumer demand.
- (iii) Insufficient demand.

(b) Material
- (i) Non-availability of a particular material.
- (ii) Restrictions imposed by local governments due to licensing or quota system.

(c) Labour
- (i) Non-availability of a particular grade of labour.

		(ii)	Change in political conditions.
(d)	Plant	(i)	Limited capacity.
		(ii)	Non-availability of imported plant and equipment due to Government restrictions.
(e)	Management	(i)	Shortage of efficient executives.
		(ii)	Restricted policy due to lack of capital.
(f)	Working capital	(i)	Shortage due to lack of funds.
		(ii)	Inefficient use of working capital.

Consideration of key factor is always the starting point of budgetary activities. Key factor is defined and concerned budget is first of all attempted. For example, if limited sale due to fall in consumer demand is the key factor, first of all, sales budget is prepared. After this budget is prepared, other budgets will be attempted to suit to this budget. If key factor is in operation, efficiency of management lies in directing the budget preparation in such a way that limiting factor is exploited to the maximum limit. Sometimes, there may be two or more key factors in operation. In a situation like this, budget committee will have first of all to determine relative influence of these key factors and thereafter budget preparation will have to be directed to obtain maximum utilisation of available resources in that situation. Services of computer can be utilised for assessing relative influence of key factors using mathematical techniques like linear programming and operational research. Key factor is not a permanent factor and management may overcome its influence by restriction of local authority. It can also be overcome by asking the workers to work overtime or extra shifts. If availability of trained personnel is the key factor, management may arrange for training programmes to overcome the bottlenecks caused due to this reason.

Patronage From Top Management : For the true success of budgetary activities, impetus and direction must come from the top management. If involvement of top management is missing, it will be difficult for budget officer to bring round the reluctant line managers to his way of thinking. Thus, right from the start, activities should be initiated in such a manner that involvement of top management in budgetary activities becomes apparent.

Level of Activity : The proposed level of activity for the budget period will be determined after a considerable progress of budgetary activities, consideration of key factors and relative review of functional budgets. Still, the drill of budget preparation starts with same level of activity in view. This point may range anywhere near the following limits:

(i) activity level based on past performance,

(ii) activity level assuming highest possible level of efficiency, and

(iii) activity level based on normal level of efficiency.

It is not a sound practice to start the budgetary activities with the activity level based on past performance. This approach brings about complacency and disregards the fact that conditions change very fast. Starting with a level of activity which assumes highest possible efficiency is also not a good approach because it is difficult to be achieved. The best approach is to strike a compromise between the above two limits. The drill should be started keeping in view the activity level capable of attainment by efficient working under the existing conditions.

Fixed Budget : A fixed budget is a budget which is used unaltered during the budget period. It is prepared for a particular activity level and it does not change with actual activity level being higher or lower than budgeted activity level. In other words, this budget does not highlight the 'activity variance', i.e., the change accountable for actual activity level being different from budgeted activity level. A budget may be prepared for, say, 1,00,000 units. Actual activity level may be say, 1,20,000 units. If it is a fixed budget, then absolute differences of budgeted figures and actual figures will be found out without any type of adjustment for change in level of activity.

A fixed budget may roughly meet the needs of profit planning, but it is almost completely inadequate as a cost control technique. Following are the *disadvantages* of fixed budget:

(1) It is misleading. A poor performance may remain undetected and a good performance may go unrealised.

(2) It is inadequate for control purposes.

(3) It violates logic. Based on logic, comparison should be made between two things with a like base. When fixed budget is used, budgted costs at budgeted activity are compared with actual costs at actual activity, *i.e.,* two things with two different bases are compared.

There is no criterion to immediately highlight good or bad performance. Still, some companies defend the use of fixed budget maintaining that their operation is very stable and the variation in activity is so slight that activity changes will have little effect on either budget or actual cost. This may be true in exceptional cases, but in general this is difficult to believe. For this reason fixed budget have got only theoretical relevance.

Flexible Budget : "A flexible budget is a budget which, by recognising different cost behaviour patterns, is designed to change as volume of output changes."— CIMA. It is designed to furnish budgeted cost at any level of activity actually attained. Flexible budget is also known as variable or sliding scale budget. The main characteristic of flexible budget is that it shows the expenditure appropriate to various levels of output. If the volume changes, the expenditure appropriate to it can be established from the flexible budget for comparison with actual expenditure as a means of control. The flexible budget provides a logical comparison of budget allowances with actual cost, *i.e.,* a comparison with a like basis. When flexible budget is prepared, actual cost at actual activity is compared with budgeted cost at actual activity, *i.e.,* two things to a like base. Flexible budgeting helps both in profit planning and operating cost control. When flexible budget is prepared, budget cost allowances are adjusted according to actual activity of the operation. Actual activity usually varies from budgeted activity and consequently budgeted cost allowances are adjusted according to actual level of operations. With flexible budget, it is possible to establish budgeted cost for any range of activity. For preparation of flexible budget, items of costs have to be analysed individually to determine how different items of costs behave to changes in volume. Therefore, indepth cost analysis and cost identification is required for preparation of flexible budget. This cost analysis and cost identification will involve categorising the expenses as fixed, variable and semi-variable. Fixed items of expenditure will be the same for all level of activity. For items of variable expenditure, rate per unit of activity is determined and based on this relationship variable expenses for any levels of activity can be found out. Extra efforts are made in analysing semi-variable items of expenditure in fixed and variable elements. Actually a flexible budget constitutes a series of fixed budgets, i.e., one fixed budget for each level of activity.

Budget Cost Allowance/Flexed Budget: "CIMA defines it as the budgeted cost ascribed to the level of activity achieved in a budget centre in a control period. It comprises variable costs in direct proportion to volume achieved and fixed costs as a proportion of the annual budget."

Method of Graphic Presentation : Another method of preparing flexible budget is the graphic method. Under this method, an estimate is made of fixed and variable expenses at various levels of activity. The figures, thus, derived are plotted on a graph paper to get the curves for these levels. It is very easy to find budget cost allowance for a particular level through this method.

Difference between Flexible Budgets and Fixed Budgets : The basic and vital difference between fixed budgets and flexible budgets should be thoroughly understood. Under fixed budgets, budgeted cost as per budgeted activity is compared with actual cost as per actual activity. Under flexible budgets, budgeted cost as per actual activity is compared with actual cost as per actual activity. This point constitutes the most vital difference between flexible budgets and fixed budgets.

Types of Budgets (other than Fixed and Flexible Budgets)

1. *Basic Budgets.* These budgets are made for use unaltered over a long period of time. These budgets are not updated, as the conditions change. Revisions of pay scales or changes in price of material will not lead to changes in these budgets. The main shortcoming of these budgets is that changed conditions give rise to variances, which

obscure operating variances. These budgets are not very good for control purposes.

2. *Current Budgets.* These budgets are established for use over a short period of time and are related to current conditions. These budgets dominantly highlight operating variances. Variances purely due to changed conditions are reduced to the minimum. These budgets can be referred to as effective control devices.

3. *Appropriation Budgets.* These budgets set out a limit for a particular type of expenditure like capital budgeting, advertising and research. Budgeted amount becomes the maximum limit that can be spent for a given item of expenditure. These budgets are used when effectiveness of expenditure is difficult to measure. Government budgets are mostly appropriation budgets. In business and industry capital expenditure budgets are only this type of budgets.

4. *Capital Expenditure Budgets.* It is a plan for proposed outlay on fixed assets like land, building and plant and machinery. These budgets are long-term budgets. Proper care should be taken to bring about harmony between capital expenditure budgets and operational budgets.

5. *Departmental/Functional Budgets.* CIMA defines it as a budget of income and/or expenditure applicable to a particular function. A function may refer to a department or a process. Functional budgets frequently include:

   (a) production cost budget (based on a forecast of production and plant utilisation);

   (b) marketing cost budget, sales budget;

   (c) personnel budget;

   (d) purchasing budget; and

   (e) research and development budget."

6. *Rolling/Continuous Budgets :* According to CIMA it can be defined as a budget continuously updated by adding a

further period, say a month or quarter and deducting the earliest period. Beneficial where future costs and/or activities cannot be forecast reliable. For preparation of these budgets, budgeting is a continuous process. As the month or a quarter passes, forecast for that period is dropped and a forecast for a further month or quarter is added in such a way that always a twelve-month forecast is available. These budgets prove to be very costly, but operational variances are considerably reduced by use of these budgets.

7. *Performance Budgets:* It is an adjusted budget prepared after operations to compare actual results with cost, that should have been incurred at actual level attained.
8. *Line item Budget (Govt.):* The listing of cost by subject, such as salaries, stationery and advertising.
9. *Operating Budget:* Budget of the profit and loss account and its supporting schedules.
10. *Summary Budgets:* A summary budget summarises all functional budgets. The end products of summary budgets are:
    (a) the budgeted profit and loss; and
    (b) the budgeted balance sheet.
11. *Master Budget:* The summary budget is reviewed, readjusted and rebudgeted till a satisfactory budget is drafted. This budget is then accepted by top management and only after receiving acceptance of top management it is called a Master Budget. Master budget is a summary budget, which has been formally accepted by top management. Compromise may be necessary before a summary budget becomes a master budget.
12. *Zero-base/priority-base Budgeting:* A method of budgeting whereby all activities are re-evaluated each time a budget is set. Discrete levels of each activity are valued and a combination chosen to match funds available.

Functional Budget

The discussion under the chapter will deal with establishment of following budgets: (i) Sales Budget, (ii) Production Budget, (iii) Production Cost Budget, (iv) Material Budget, (v) Purchase Budget, (vi) Labour Budget, (vii) Overhead Budget, (viii) Administration Cost Budget, (ix) Research and Development Budget, (x) Capital Expenditure Budget, (xi) Selling and Distribution Cost Budget, (xii) Cash Budget, (xiii) Master Budget.

Sales Budget : The sales budget is the most important functional budget. If sales figure is incorrect, practically all functional budgets and consequently master budget will be affected. It is the keystone of budget structure. The importance of this budget further increases, if sales is the key factor. The sales budget primarily forecasts what the concern can reasonably expect to sell both in quantity and value during the budget period. Sales budget can be prepared showing sales under any one or combination of the following headings:

(1) *Product :* If a company is producing more than one product, then estimates of sales of each product are presented.

(2) *Territory:*Under these headings geographical break-up of sales is given, ie., sales area-wise or country-wise.

(3) *Types of Customers:* A concern may have different types of customers like Government departments, foreign companies and private companies. Sales can be presented customerwise to show how different customers are contributing to total sales of the company.

(4) *Salesmen:* Presenting sales according to salesmen may exhibit a relative view of sales performance of different representatives.

(5) *Month, Quarter or Week:* In order to determine trend, it may be necessary to present sales according to month, quarter or week.

The exercise of preparing sales budget can be broadly divided into two categories:

(a) Sales forecast,

(b) Evaluating sales forecast.

Sales forecast. Sales forecast is the foundation of budget structure. Following methods are used for sales forecasting:

(1) *Salesmen's Estimate:* Under this method, those responsible for sales take active part in sales budget formulation. Estimates are primarily established by salesmen taking into account the current conditions and customers' potential of that area. District sales executives review these estimates and send it to executive committee for final consideration and tentative approval.

(2) *Executive Opinion Method:* This is also referred to as group judgement method. Under this method, all top executives from Production, Purchase, Finance and Administration, jointly use their experience and knowledge to project sales on the basis of group opinion. Under this method, it is not considered appropriate to ask sales force to make estimates. This method is frequently used, because it is simple and economical.

(3) *Statistical Method:* Under this method, technically trained individuals use sophisticated approaches to determine the trends in order to present a realistic approach. Past data is anlysed and index number, etc., are used to measure the fluctuations in business. This anlysis brings to light three types of sales trends, *i.e.,* (i) Long-term trend, (ii) cyclic trend, and (iii) seasonal trend. Long-term trend is highlighted by plotting sales data on a moving average basis. Cyclic trends show the pressure of business cycles on sales. This can be computed by taking percentage of deviation between long-term trend and actual annual sales. The analysis can be plotted on graph paper to present pictorial view. Often all business conditions are subject to seasonal variation in sales. This can be highlighted by plotting sales for several years. Many businesses are subject to seasonal variation in sales. First of all, monthly sales data are plotted for several years. Seasonal variation is highlighted by showing how monthly sales vary from monthly average for the year. Statistical methods should

be used for projecting sales but complete reliance on statistical methods should be avoided. Statistical methods should be used to provide help but not to provide answers.

(4) *Market Analysis Method:* In big organisations, there is a market research group, that is responsible for broad and specialised activities involved in market research. The real purpose of market research is to evaluate customers' motivation. Market research is a very technical function and it is based on study of behavioural sciences particularly psychology and sociology. Market research activities' include consulting journals, publications, surveys and interviewing customers to determine their potential and preferences. Market research activities highlight important facts like state of strata of customers in a particular area, customers' preferences in a particular area, fashion trends and price that customers are likely to pay on the basis of their potential and liking. After collecting primary data in a systematic manner, market research personnel try to project the share of market that a company can reasonably expect. Market research can be conducted for (i) Product research, (ii) Consumer research, (iii) Motivational research, and *(iv)* Promotional research. (This is done to determine the effect of different methods of advertising and publicity.)

Evaluating Sales Forecast: After quantitative sales forecasts have been established, these are evaluated for the purpose of preparing sales budget. Determining selling prices of different products depends, besides management policy, on numerous external factors. Some products may have to be marketed on a non-profit basis as an essential service to customers or for prestige purposes. Management may find it necessary to sell some products at a price lower than normal for promoting their sales in a particular area. With the help of quantitative sales forecast and selling prices of different products, sales budgets are developed projecting sales (in quantities and money) during the budgeted period, following example will give a complete idea of how a sales budget is prepared.

It is very necessary to coordinate Production Budget with Sales Budget to avoid imbalance in production. The sales department disproportionately emphasises only one factor, *i.e.*, volume of sales, they may think of selling what they think are the most profitable lines. They may overlook products that company has facilities to produce. By keeping balance between Sales Budget and Production Budget, a situation that leads to idle capacity should be avoided. Production is an area where scientific management has had its maximum application. Production efficiency leads to increase in earnings. It is an important budget and forms basis for preparation of material, labour and factory overhead budgets. Following example will give a detailed idea of production budget preparation:

Production Cost Budget : Production cost budget expresses the cost of carrying out production plans and programmes set out in production budget. It summarises material cost, labour cost and factory overhead for production. Fixed overhead and variable overheads are shown separately. In brief, this budget summarises material budget, labour budget and factory overhead budget.

Material Budget

Material budget shows estimated quantity as well as the cost of each type of direct material required for producing the number of units in production budget. There are two states of preparing material budget. First, quantities of different types of direct material are estimated. Secondly, price of each kind of direct material and component is found out to obtain cost of different types of materials and components to be consumed in production. It is necessary to know unit material utilisation rate for preparing material budget. The unit material rate is multiplied by number of units to be produced in order to determine the total units of material required for estimated production. It serves the following purposes:

(1) It helps the purchase department to plan purchase schedule to avoid default in delivery of material.

(2) It forms basis for purchase cost budget.

(3) It forms basis for determination of minimum and maximum levels of inventory of material and components.

Purchase Budgets : Purchase budget sets out 'purchase' plan of the company during the budget period. Material budget only gives an idea of the material requirements of the organisation during the budget. For preparing purchase budget, it is also necessary to know the level of inventories to be maintained. The governing points for preparation of purchase budget are:

(1) Opening stocks and closing stocks of different types of materials and components. Care should be taken to maintain inventory sufficient enough to avoid hold-ups in production. (2) Orders already placed. (3) Storage space available. (4) Economic order quantity. (5) Price to be paid. (6) Seasonal discount that can be availed of. (7) Finance available. (8) Policy of management regarding the material that can be manufactured.

The purchase budget shows the purchase plan of an organisation during the budget period and this is prepared giving regard to factors like storage capacity and finance available so that capital tied up in stock is minimum and production programme also continues smoothly. The preparation of purchase budget is the direct responsibility of purchase manager. He should have sound knowledge of different markets for different products. He provides the projected unit cost to be used in preparation of the purchase budget. It is difficult to lay down a proforma for the purchase budget that will suit the requirements of all organisation's. The proforma for the purchase budget should be developed to suit organisations' requirements.

Labour Budget

After production budget is prepared it is easy to prepare labour budget. It contains the estimates relating to number of employees and type of employees required for the budgeted output. Labour required is classified according to grades and thereafter requirement of each grade is specified. After labour requirements relating to different grades are finalised, estimated rate per hour and labour cost per unit is arrived at.

Overhead Budget

Companies divide their overhead costs in two categories for the purpose of control, i.e., fixed overhead and variable overhead. Depreciation, insurance and taxes are the main items that fall within the category of fixed overheads. Variable overheads include indirect material, indirect labour and indirect expenses, which are used according to production. Preparation of overhead budget involves following :

(1) Fixed Overhead Budget. (2) Variable Overhead budget.

Preparation of fixed overhead budget is very easy, because items to be included in the category of fixed overhead can be forecasted with a fair degree of accuracy. Property taxes, fire insurance, rent, salary of manager, foreman, etc., and depreciation are the various items to be included in this budget. Fixed overhead budget is not dependent on sale or production budget. Methodology for preparing fixed overhead budget is also very simple. Usually a separate sheet is used for each item of cost and total is sub-divided by departments or divisions. Each budget for fixed overhead item shows total estimated cost for that item and the share of the total assigned to each service of production department. It is very difficult to estimate variable overhead accurately. Therefore, preparation of variable overhead budget presents considerable amount of difficulty. Variable overhead budget includes indirect material, indirect labour and indirect expenses which vary according to production. The budget is prepared with the cooperation of foreman, departmental heads and other factory executives. Preparation of variable overhead budget is based on scheduled production and operating conditions. Main considerations in preparing variable budgets are past experience, present cost and effect of budgeted production on relative cost items during forthcoming budget period. All variable budgets show total amount of each item of cost and share of total assigned to each service and production department. Cost department renders valuable advisory service in the preparation of these budgets.

Administration Cost Budget

Administration cost is by and large fixed and, therefore, these budgets are prepared for a given capacity on the pattern of fixed cost budgets. Preparation of administration budget involves budgeting for top management functions like legal, finance, accounting, management information services, internal audit and taxation. The main difficulty in preparation of administration budget is the measurement of output, which is vague and ill-defined. For this purpose, administration function is divided in homogeneous activities and a broad unit of measurement is found out for each activity.

Research and Development Budget : Research activities include development of new products, betterment of existing products and improvement of processes. The expenditure of research depends on nature of company's products, economic condition, competition, technological development in related industry and the policy of management. In large multinational companies involved in multiproduct activities, expenditure on research may be significant. It is very difficult to measure the profitability of research and development expenditure. For this reason, research expenditure is often based on an established perceniage of sales or estimated amount expected to be available during the; forthcoming budget period.

This difficulty is experienced because there is no direct relationship between benefits and research and development expenditure. The research and development expenditure is based more on managerial judgement than quantitative data available with the company. Here discussion will be confined to budgetary control of research and development expenditure. Research and development budget is an appropriation type budget. Generally, a total of allowed expenditure provides a base for preparation of this budget. Research Director considers the relevant factors and decides for a research activity likely to take maximum contribution to company's profitability. In a large organisation, there may be several budget centres under the function "research and development". In a situation like this, the preparation of research and development budget should be split up in two phases:

(a) Profit-wise, and

(b) Budget centre-wise.

The consolidation of budgets of all budget centres under research and development activity will give a research and development budget for the company. Project-wise presentation of research and development budget will reveal appropriation of budgeted amount for different projects with other necessary information.

Capital Expenditure Budget : The capital expenditure budget represents the expected expenditure on fixed assets during the period. It relates to projects involving huge capital outlay and long-term commitment. Most of the capital investment decisions affect operations of business over a series of years. Large risks and uncertainties are associated with capital investment decisions. For this reason the task of preparing capital expenditure budget is carefully attempted only by very senior executives of the organisation to ensure that capital outlays: (i) are used only in most profitable alternatives, (ii) do not endanger the financial postion of the company, and (iii) are in conformity with overall organisational objectives. Preparation of capital expenditure budget serves the following purposes:

1. Helps to evaluate capital expenditure proposals.
2. Helps in the coordination of proposed capital expenditure with other operational budgets. The proposed capital investment proposals must fit in with overall organisational plans.
3. Helps to establish priorities so that projects having most to offer are given first consideration.
4. Helps to control capital expenditure. Before the capital investment proposal approved it is screened by senior executives at various levels of management and after the proposal is approved a follow-up system is adopted for comparison of actual performance with original estimates.
5. Helps to plan for financing of capital investment proposal by carrying out suitable adjustment in cash budget of the company.
6. Facilitates a systematic procedure for appraising the profitability performance of these projects. The follow-up system used to analyse past decisions also helps to improve future forecasts.

The projects included in capital expenditure budget may be for any of the following purposes:

(i) Non-profit projects, *i.e.*, the projects to meet legal or safety requirements,

(ii) Non-measurable profit project, i.e., the projects with intangible and long-term advantages.

(iii) Capital replacement project, i.e., the projects undertaken to replace wornout or obsolete equipment.

(iv) Expansion projects, i.e., the projects undertaken to add to the compnay's working capacity.

Preparation of Capital Expenditure Budget : Proposal for Capital expenditure may be initiated by any one form operating level to top level of management. The request is first appraised by the concerned departmental head, who, if project appears to be sound, makes formal request for "capital appropriation" to top management. Engineering department and finance and accounts department may render useful service to the depdartmental heads in making a convincing case for technical and financial strength of proposal. A request for "capital appropriation" for a particular project must contain such information as:

(a) Description of project.

(b) Reasons calling for the proposed change.

(c) Estimates of the cost of proposal.

(d) Estimates about life of the project.

(e) Advantages to be gained by accepting the proposal.

(f) Disadvantages of not accepting the proposal. Demand for putting up 'capital investment proposal' on this pattern is growing in present changing economic environment.

(g) An idea of how the proposal can be financed.

The capital investment proposal should be accompanied by comments from the following:

(i) Production Manager, (ii) Works Manager, (iii) Sales Manager, and (iv) Distribution Manager.

Individual requests from departmental heads are submitted to budget committee for preliminary review, screening, coordination and consolidation. Appraisal procedure and discussion are sometimes repeated for revaluing the competing capital investment proposals. Careful attention is given to ensure that imbalance in capacity is avoided. Only the proposals, that appear to be sound and worthwhile, are sent to top management for final approval. To what level the 'project proposal' goes depends on the amount of expenditure involved. Some projects can be sanctioned by the Chairman of the organisation, but some projects involving capital outlay of more than a particular amount may have to be placed before the Board of Directors. Approval of request means that it fits in the overall organisational objectives. It does not carry authority to immediately start the project. First, capital expenditure budget is coordinated with cash budget and after ensuring that sufficient funds are either available or can be raised, authorisation for an expenditure can be granted. A capital expenditure budget must reveal such information projectwise as: (1) Original appropriation, (2) Cumulative expenditure up-to-date. (3) Unutilised appropriation, (4) Fresh appropriation, and (5) The limit carried over to next period for a particular company.

***Selling and Distribution Cost Budget*:** The discussion on selling and distribution cost budget can be divided in two categories: (0 Discussion on items to be included in selling and distribution cost; and (ii) Methodology of preparing selling and distribution cost budget. A good deal of controversy exists relating to items to be included in category of selling and distribution cost. Thus, before attempting selling and distribution cost budget, a decision should be taken about the items to be included under this budget. After the product has been brought in saleable condition, a lot of cost is incurred on selling and distribution, before the product finally reaches the consumer. According to accepted acccountancy principle, the cost (the cost on selling and distribution for carrying the saleable goods to customer) that falls under the cagtegory of selling and distribution cost budget represents the cost of selling and distribution of quantities shown in sales budget. Following items form part of selling and distribution cost budget:

(1) Cost of demand creation and securing orders. It will include salesmen's salaries, commission and travelling expenses, etc.

(2) Cost of handling orders. It will include the cost of placing order, storage, packing, freight, billing, credit and collection.

(3) Cost of supervision of salesmen. It will include the salary and travelling expenses, etc., of sales manager in district offices and expenses of general sales office.

Preparation of selling and distribution cost budget is based primarily on sales budget, because the selling and distribution cost budget shows the cost of selling and distribution of quantities shown in sales budget. Based on sales budget, estimates regarding each type of selling and distribution cost are initially put up by district staff to zonal sales manager. They review it in the light of anticipated changes in rent, rates and taxes, etc. A lot of review and discussion takes place to incorporate anticipated changes. All these estimates are then consolidated. After consolidation a final selling and distribution cost budget is presented to budget director or budget committee for approval.

Cash Budget : It is a forecast of cash flows, i.e., receipts during the budget period. This is also referred to as ways and means budget. The advantages of anticipating cash position well in advance are too obvious to require discussion. Employees must be paid. Taxation liability must be settled promptly. Failure to meet any of these obligations will lead to irreparable loss to company's reputation. In most cases monthly cash forecasts for the budget period are made, but company can make weekly or even daily forecast according to its business operations. It is necessary to have proper coordination between cash budget and other functional budgets. Preparation of cash budget is based primarily on following information: (i) Detailed estimate of cash receipts, (ii) Detailed estimate of cash disbursements, (iii) Time-lag induced by credit transaction and (iv) Time-lag in items of revenue and expenditure. Following are the main objectives of cash budget:

(1) It ensures whether sufficient cash is available for revenue and capital expenditure.

(2) It shows when additional finance is needed and how much additional finance is needed.

(3) It shows when surplus funds are available in business. These funds can be profitably invested outside business according to prevalent circumstances.

(4) Preparation of cash budget helps the company to plan its cash position in such a way that maximum seasonal discounts are availed of.

Cash budgets are not made for performance evaluation. Keeping company's liquid position sufficiently sound to meet its daily obligation is the main object of preparing these budgets. For this reasons, it will be very good for a company to use idea of continuous/rolling budgeting in preparation of cash budget. Under continuous budgets, when a month or a quarter passes, forecast for the period is dropped and forecast for a further month or quarter is added in such a way that a twelve-month forecast is always available. Preparation of continuous cash budget may be a very costly exercise, but operational variances are considerably reduced by use of these budgets. Cash budget is prepared by any of the following three methods:

Receipt and Payment Method : Under this method, all receipts and payments which are expected during the period, should be considered. Cash requirements of all functional budgets including capital expenditure budgets are taken into account. Accruals and adjustments are excluded while preparing the cash budget by receipt and payment method. All anticipated cash receipts are added to the opening balance of cash. The expected cash payments are deducted from this to arrive at the closing balance of cash for the month. It is a very simple method. An example given below will fully illustrate preparation of cash budget by payment and receipt method.

Adjusted Profit and Loss Account Method : Under this method profit and loss account is used as basis for making the cash forecast. This method is based on the assumption that profit is equivalent to cash. The adjustments made to arrive at the profit will be added back, if these adjustments do not involve cash outflow. For example, depreciation on fixed assets, accrued expenses, etc., will be added back to profit to arrive at the cash balance available at the closing date. These adjustments do not involve cash outlay. This method is less detailed than receipt and payment method. It is used for making long-term cash forecast. The procedure for preparing cash budget from given profit and loss account is detailed below:

(1) Cash balance at the beginning of the period is the starting point.

(2) Net profit shown by forecasted profit and loss account is added to opening cash balance.

(3) Add non-cash items of profit and loss account like:

(a) Depreciation,

(b) Outstanding expenses,

(c) Accruals for warranties,

(d) Accrual for income tax, and

(e) Accrual for dividend.

(4) Capital receipts add to opening balance.

(5) Capital expenditure reduces the balance.

(6) Dividend paid will reduce the balance. (It should be noted that it will exclude provision for dividend.)

(7) Adjustment for changes in current assets should be carried out. Increase in current assets will reduce the balance. Decrease in current assets will increase cash balance.

(8) Adjustments for changes in current liabilities are carried out. Increase in current liabilities will be added to the cash balance and decrease in current liabilities will reduce the cash balance.

Cash Budget

(By Adjusted Profit and Loss Method)

Cash Balance		36,000
Addition to Cash		
1. Net profit for the year	28,200	
2. Adjustment for non-cash items:		
(a) Outstanding salaries and wages (Rs. 1,000 - Rs. 400)	600	
(b) Depreciation on plant and machinery	4,000	
(c) Depreciation on furniture and fixture	2,000	
3. Capital receipts:		
(a) Share capital	20,000	
(b) Debentures	4,000	
4. Decrease in current assets:		
Debtors	12000	
5. Increase in current liablities:		
Creditors	2,400	73,200
Cash available		1,09,200
Deduction from Cash		
1. Dividend	20,000	
2. Increase in current assets: stock	12,000	
3. Capital expenditure—Land and building	20,000	52,000
Cash balance available on 31.3.2004		57,200

Balance Sheet Method : Under this method, a forecast balance sheet is prepared considering changes in all items (except cash) of balance sheet like fixed assets, plant and machinery, furniture and fixtures, debtors, share capital, debentures and creditors, etc. The two sides of balance sheet are balanced and the balancing figure represents closing balance of cash. It may be a balance with back or an overdraft according to the nature of balance being debit or credit. The procedure for preparing a cash budget under balance sheet method is detailed below:

(1) A forecast balance sheet as at the end of next period is prepared. Itemwise figures should be taken from last

balance sheet and according to information given these are adjusted to be presented in forecast balance sheet. For example, the share capital shown in last balance sheet may be Rs.5,00,000. The additional information may highlight that there will be a fresh issue of capital for Rs. 20,000 during the year. The share capital to be shown in forecast balance sheet should be Rs. 5,20,000. like this, all items (except cash) are picked up from last balance sheet to be revised for presentation in forecast balance sheet according to information available.

(2) Profit figure should be taken after allowing for adjustments for even non- cash transactions. These non-cash adjustments become contrary to changes exhibited in forecast balance sheet. For example, depreciation is a non-cash adjustment. When cash budget with balance sheet method is attempted, profit after considering depreciation should be shown in balance sheet, because assets are shown in forecast balance sheet after adjustment of depreciation. (It should be noted here that in profit and loss method of preparing cash budget profit without adjustment of depreciatiori will be considered.)

(3) After all items in previous balance sheet have been presented after revision according to additional information available, difference of assets and liabilities of forecast balance sheet is found out. This balancing figure will represent closing balance of cash.

Advertisement Cost Budget : Since no direct relationship exists between advertisement expenditure and output, it becomes a problem for company's executives to determine the amount to be spent on advertisement. Following problems are faced in preparation of advertisement budget:

(1) Effectiveness of advertisement cost cannot be measured with perfect accuracy.

(2) Time lag exists between incurrence of expenditure and its effects. It disturbs the justification of the amount to be spent on advertisement during budget period.

(3) A particular sale may be the result of contributory factors like availability of buying power, competition and a particular market situation, etc. It is difficult to isolate the effects of advertisement cost from these influences.

(4) Different media of advertisement affect sale to different extent. It is difficult to isolate the effects of different media of advertisement.

It is ideal to say that advertisement cost should be related to incremental income to be derived from the advertisement cost. This holds good only in theory. In practice, only intuitive judgement based on experience determines the appropriation for advertisement cost budget. The preparation of advertisement cost budget can be divided in three parts :

(1) Determining the different media of advertisement to be used like radio, newspaper, TV., cinema slides, gift items, etc.

(2) Determining the budget appropriation.

(3) Allocation of the available budget appropriation in different media of advertisement.

For the first two problems, only experience presents the best answer. For the third problem, *i.e.,* determining the budget apportionment, any of the following basis is used:

(i) *Percentage of Sale.* An established percentage of sale is the most common method of determining budget apportionment for advertisement cost budget. This method is not sound, because it disregards that effectiveness of advertisement cost varies with changes in business cycles, changes in sales volumes, changes in sales regions and intensity of competition.

(ii) *Availability of Funds.* Under this method, budget appropriation for advertisement depends on expected funds to be available. This method is based more on expediency than logic.

(iii) *Competition.* Under this method, budget appropriation for advertisement depends on what the competitors are spending for this purpose. It is not a sound method because it is again difficult to determine, whether competitors are getting best results. Selling conditions of different companies in some industry may not be identical. Therefore, depending on what competitors are spending on advertisement cannot give a rational solution for determining company's advertisement budget appropriation. It should be noted that once approved, advertisement budget consists obviously fixed expenses.

Plant Utilisation Budget : This budget sets out the plant and machinery requirements to meet the budgeted production during the budget period. For preparation of plant utilisation budget, the plant capacity is expressed in terms of convenient units such as working hours, weight or number of units, etc. This budget highlights the budgeted machine load in each department and focuses attention on overloading so that remedial action can be taken in time to explore the alternative like shift-working, purchase of new machinery, overtime working and sub-contracting, etc. When plant utilisation budget highlights underloading, the sales manager can be requested to increase the sales volume of certain products by reduction in prices, discounts, change in terms of payment and advertising, etc.

The plant utilisation budget is prepared as follows:

Plant Utilisation Budget

Deptt.	*Machine*	*No. of hours available*	*Normal time cost*	*Capacity in hours*	*Output per hour*	*Quantity*
A	1					
	2					
	3					
Total						

Personnel Budget

This budget sets out the requirements of direct labour and indirect labour to carry out the budget plan relating to the period. It is based upon the functional budgets like production budget, sales budget, maintenance budget, capital expenditure budget and research and development budgets. These direct and indirect requirements are experessed in personnel budgets in the form of rupee value, number of labour hours, number and grade of workers or any other convenient unit. While preparing personnel budget provision is made for shift and overtime work, implementation of training programmes and new wage agreements.

Master Budget : After all the functional budgets have been prepared, these are summarised in the form of a summary budget. The summary budget gives a forecast profit and loss account and forecast balance sheet for the budget period. The budget committee considers the summary budget and adjudges it as satisfactory or otherwise. If summary budget is not found satisfactory by the budget committee, it issues directions for necessary changes. The proposed changes are incorporated and revised summary budget is prepared. The revised summary budget thus prepared is presented to the Board of Directors for approval. After the Board of Directors approves the summary budget, it is known as master budget. Thus, the master budget is the organisation's formal plan of action for the forthcoming budget period. It is an integrated form of all functional budgets bearing approval of top management.

The master budget is a complete financial presentation of the operating plans of the entire company for the budget period. It is the company's individualised key to successful financial planning and control. It sets out a basis for readily computing costs, profits and financial conditions resulting from any sales volume and product mix. It provides the basis of computing the effect of any changes in any phase of operations, such as sales volume, product mix, prices, labour costs, material costs or change in facilities. It segregates income, costs and profits by areas of responsibility. Master budget presents all this information to the depth appropriate for the top management's action. Any further breakdown than this is available in the detailed budgets and these detailed budgets support the summaries given in the master budget.

In the master budget, costs are classified and summarised by types of expenses as well as by departments. This information extends the range of usefulness of master budget. The master budget has sometimes been called a 'pilot model' of the company. Master budget is the best media of understanding the company's micro-economics relating to the forthcoming budget period.

In final accounts closing, preparation of Balance Sheet and Profit and Loss Account is an event that marks the closure of this activity. Master budget represents the final product of the activities relating to budget preparation. In accounts closing, records of actual happenings are consolidated and summarised, whereas in preparing the master budget the plans or budgets for the coming years are finalised. The typical contents of company's master budget are summarised below:

(i) It contains budgeted profit and loss account for the budget period;

(ii) Abudgeted balance sheet as it will appear at the end of the budget period; and

(iii) In additional, it is supported by each budget, capital expenditure budget, functional budget, etc.

The master budget is not merely a compendium of theoretical calculations. All the figures, that contains, are the reflection of the actual intentions of the company relating to different areas for the forthcoming budget period. The figures in master budget reflect the considered judgement of all the people within the company, who are authorised to spend the company's money and its affairs. Following are the advantages of a master budget:

(1) It is an approved document which shows projected profit position of the organisation.

(2) Preparation of master budget enforces coordination among functional budgets.

(3) Budgeted Balance Sheet shows the projected financial position of an organisation.

The analysis of this financial position by use of different ratios will reveal the extent and reason of different changes.

The difference between master budget and functional budget should be properly understood. Master budget is the master plan which sets out the company's overall plan of action for the budget period. Functional budgets represent sectional goals for the budget period. Preparation of master budget basically starts form last year's profit and loss account, balance sheet and set of information and instructions for the forthcoming budget period. Based on past experience, last year's data are adjusted to incorporate the expected changes. Following steps are usually involved in the development of master budget:

(i) Preparation of functional budget incorporting the expected changes in the forthcoming budget period.

(ii) Up and down adjustments to bring about harmony among different budgets.

(iii) Preparation of summary budget to produce.

(a) Budgeted profit and loss account, and

(b) Budgeted balance sheet.

(vi) Authentication of summary budget by the board of directors so that this can be accepted as master budget indicating the formal plans of action for the forthcoming budget period.

Report Writing : A report is a document, in which a given problem is examined for the purpose of conveying information, putting forward ideas and sometimes making recommendations as the basis for action. A reporting system should be tailored to give management the facts in the form, that will be most readily understood.

Major Considerations in Report Writing

1. Keep the background needs of the readers in mind.
2. Adhere to the time schedule for the report.
3. Make the report as brief and as simple as possible.
4. Include only the information that directly applies to the subject.
5. Verify the accuracy and reliability of all facts used.
6. Utilise a writing style, that is clear in statement and easy to read.
7. Use illustrations and visual displays, whenever possible (charts, diagrams, graphs and pictures).
8. Make the report attractive in appearance and make every effort to avoid crowding.
9. Organise the report carefully, dividing the report into parts, which are logically arranged.
10. Conclude the report with a brief summary of important points covered.
11. Draw conclusions that are soundly based on facts.

12. Make recommendations that are supported by evidence reports.
13. Place the report control number and code on the title base or the first page of the report.
14. Include a contents guide in long reports.
15. State the objectives or purposes of the report.
16. Prepare a summary of long reports at the end. This summary should include the writer's recommendation.
17. Include lengthy exhibits in an appendix at the end of the report in the form of statistcal tabulation, charts, graph, etc., if they are considered essential.

Common Forms of Reports

1. *Narrative Reports* : These are descriptive and verbal reports.
2. *Statistical Reports* : These reports rely on tables, numbers, graphs, charts, etc.
3. *Periodic Reports* : Reports may be issued on regular scheduled basis, for example, daily, weekly, monthly, quarterly and annually.
4. *Progress Reports* : These reports include interim reports between the start and completion of a project. These reports are also called follow-up reports.
5. *Special Reports* : These reports are sent irregularly in response to a specific, non-routine request. In control reports, a subordinate summarises the activities under the jurisdiction and accounts to his superiors for results, that he has previously committed himself to achieve. This practice of'reporting by results' is based on the control aspect of management by objectives.

Cost Reports : Cost accounting reports must be prepared and distributed to three levels of management, *i.e.*, top management, middle management and operating management. The greater is the degree of control required, the shorter should be the period of time covered in the .report. Following is the representative list of cost reports, which is customarily made to different levels of management:

Name of Report	Original copies addressed to	Copies to	Periodicity
For Top Managment			
1. Master Budget	Managing Director	All Functional heads	Yearly/half yearly as per budgeting practice
2. Comparative income statement productwise	Managing Director	All Functional heads	Yearly/half yearly/ monthly
3. Stock turnover	Managing Director	Production Controller	Monthly
4. Differential cost estimates for short-term decisions such as choosing optimum level and product mix	Managing Director	Sales Controller	According to exigency of situation
5. Break-even volume	Managing Director	Production/Sales Manager	As per exigency
6. Stock levels	Managing Director	Production Manager	Monthly
7. Idle capacity	Managing Director	Production/Sales Manager	Monthly
8. Labour cost	Managing Director	Production Manager/ Personnel Manager	Monthly
9. Work order position—Productwise	Managing Director	Sales/Production Manager	Monthly

Contd.

10. Volume Variance Report	Managing Director	Sales/Production Manager	Monthly
11. Profit Variance Report	Managing Director	Production/Sales Manager	Monthly
Middle Management			
12. Sales analysis by product/territories and channels	Sales Manager	Managing Director	Fortnightly
13. Product cost estimate (for price fixation and quotation)	Sales Manager	Production Manager	When required
14. Selling and Distribution cost estimates	Sales Manager	Managing Director	As per exigency
15. Selling and Distribution Cost Analysis-Product wise	Sales Manager	Managing Director	As per exigency
16. Finished stock	Sales Manager	Managing Director/ Production Manager	Fortnightly
Operating Management			
17. Departmental operating statement	Manager in charge of the Department	Production Manager	Monthly
18. Machine utilization	Shop Foreman	Department/Production Manager	Weekly

Cont.

19. Idle Time	Shcp Foreman	Department/Production Manager	Weekly
20. Overtime	Shop Foreman	Departmant/Production Manager	Weekly
21. Scrap and Spoilage	Shop Foreman	Department/Production Manager	Weekly
22. Labour efficiency	Shop Foreman	Department/Production Manager	Weekly
23. Pending shop order	Shop Foreman	Department/Production Manager	Weekly
24. Purchase Price variance	Purchase Officer	Production Manager	Monthly
25. Utilization variance	Shop Foreman	Production Manager/ Chief Inspector	Monthly
26. Efficiency variance	Shop Foreman	Production Manager	Monthly
27. Expense variance	Shop Foreman	Production Manager	Monthly

9

Statements of Finance

The Concept

Business as we know is concerned with the financial activities. In order to ascertain the financial status of the business every enterprise prepares certain statements, known as financial statements. Financial statements at least refer to the two statements which are prepared by a business concern at the end of the financial year. These are : (i) Income statement or Trading and Profit and Loss account which is prepared by a business concern in order to know the profit earned and loss sustained during a specified period; (ii) Position statement or Balance Sheet which is prepared by a business concern on a particular date in order to know its financial position. These statements are added the statement of Retained Earnings and some other statements (such as, fund flow statement, cash flow statements, etc.) and schedules of fixed assets (such as, Investments, Equipments) and Debtors etc. to give a full view of the financial affairs. All these statements are collectively called as package of financial statements.

Definition : A financial statement is a collection of data organised according to logical and consistent accounting procedures. Its purpose is to convey an understanding of some financial aspects of a business concern. In other words, financial statements are the outcome of summarising process of accounting. A financial statement has been defined by some prominent scholars as follows:

1. According to *John N. Myer,* "The financial statements provide a summary of the accounts of a business enterprise, the balance sheet reflecting the assets, liabilities and capital as on a certain date and the income statement showing the results of operation during a certain period."
2. According to *Smith and Asburne,* "Financial statement is the end product of financial accounting in a set of financial statements prepared by the accountant of a business enterprise, that purpose to reveal the financial position of the enterprise, the result of its recent activities, and an analysis of what has been done with earnings."
3. According to *Anthony,* "Financial statements, essentially are interim reports, presented annually and reflects a division of the life of an enterprise into more or less arbitrary accounting period, more frequently a year."

The Nature

The financial statements are prepared on the basis of recorded facts. The recorded facts are those which can be expressed in monetary terms. The statements are prepared for the particular period generally one year. The transactions are recorded in a chronological order as and when the events happen. The accounting records and financial statements prepared from these records are based on historical costs. The financial statements, by nature, are summaries of the items recorded in the business and these statements are prepared periodically, generally for the accounting period.

According to *John N. Myer,* "The financial statements are composed of data which are the result of a combinations of (i) recorded,facts concerning the business transactions (ii) conventions adopted to facilitate the accounting technique (iii) postulates or assumptions made to and (iv) personal judgements used in the application of the conventions and postulates."

The following points of the nature of financial statements are discussed below :

Recorded Facts : The term 'recorded facts' refers to the data taken out from the accounting records. The records are maintained on the basis of actual cost dala. The historical cost is the basis of recording various transactions. The figures of various accounts such as cash in hand, cash at bank, bills receivables, sundry debtors, fixed assets etc. are taken as per the figures recorded in the accounting books. The assets purchased at different times and at different prices are put together and shown at cost prices. As recorded facts are not based on replacement costs, the financial statements do not shown current financial condition of the concern.

Accounting Conventions : Certain accounting conventions are followed while preparing statements. The convention of valuing inventory at cost or market price, whichever is lower, is followed. The valuation of assets at cost less depreciation principle for balance sheet purposes is followed. The convention of materiality is followed in dealing with small items like pencils, pens, postage stamp etc. These items are treated as expenditure in the year in which they are purchased even though they are assets in nature. The stationery is valued at cost and not on the principle of cost or market price whichever is less. The use of accounting conventions makes financial statements comparable, simple and realistic.

Postulates : The accountant makes certain assumptions while making accounting records. One of these assumption is that the enterprise is treated as a going concern. The other alternative to this postulate is that the concern is to be liquidated, this, is untenable if management shows an intention to liquidate the concern. So the assets are shown on a going concern basis. Another important assumption is to presume that the value of money will remain the same in different periods. Though there is a drastic change in purchasing power of money the assets purchased at different times will be shown at the amount paid for them. While preparing Profit and Loss account the revenue is treated in the year which the sale was undertaken even though the sprice may be received in a number of year. The assumption is known as realisation postulate.

Personal Judgements : Even though certain standard accounting conventions are followed in preparing financial statements but still personal judgement of the accountant plays an important part. For example, in applying the cost or market value whichever is less to inventory valuation the accountant will have to use his judgement in computing the cost in particular case. There are a number of methods of valuing stock, *i.e.*, First-in-first out, and last-in-first out, average cost method, standard, cost base stock method, etc. The accountant will use one of these methods for valuing materials. The selection of depreciation method, to use one of the several methods for estimating uncollectable debts, to determine the period for writing off intangible assets are some of the examples where judgement of the accountant will play an important role in choosing the most appropriate course of action.

The Characteristics

The Financial statements are prepared with a view to depict financial position of the business concern. Therefore, the financial statements should be prepared in such a way that they are able to give a clear and orderly picture of the concern. The ideal financial statements should have the following characteristics :

True Financial Position : The information shown by the financial statements should be such that a true and correct idea is taken about the financial position of the concern. No material information should be withhold while preparing these statements.

Effective Presentation : The financial statements should be presented in a simple and lucid form so as to make them easily understandable. A person who is not well versed with accounting terminology should also be able to stand or stand the statements without much difficulty. This characteristic will enhance the utility of these statements.

Brief : So far as possible, the financial statements should be prepared in brief. The reader will be able to form an idea about the figures. On the other hand, if figures are given in details then it will become difficult to judge the working of the concern.

Attractive : The financial statements should be prepared in such a way that important information is underlined so that it attracts the eye of the reader.

Comparability : The results of financial statements should be in a way that it can be compared to the previous years statements. The statement can also be compared with the figures of other concerns of the same nature. Sometimes budgeted figures are given along with the present figures. The comparable figures will make the statements more useful. The Indian Companies Act, 1956 has made it obligatory to give previous year's figures in the balance sheet. The comparison of figures will enable a proper assessment for the working of the concern.

Relevance : Financial statements should be relevant to the objectives of the business concern. This is possible only when the person preparing these statements is able to properly utilize the accounting information. The information which is not relevant to the statements should be avoided, otherwise it will be difficult to make a distinction between relevant and irrelevant information.

Promptness : The financial statements should be prepared and presented at the earliest possible. The statements should be ready, immediately at the close of the financial year.

Easiness : Financial statements should be easily prepared. The balances of different ledger accounts should be easily taken to these statements. The calculation work should be minimum possible while preparing these statements. The size of the statement should not be very large. The columns to be used for giving the information should also be less. This will enable the saving of time in preparing the statements.

Analytical Representations : The information should be analysed in such a way that similar data is presented at the same place. A relationship can be established in similar type of information. This will be helpful in analysis and interpretation of data.

Aims and Objectives

Financial statements are the sources of information on the basis of which conclusions are derived about the profitability and financial position of the business concern. These informations are important for the owners, creditors and the general public. The primary objective of financial statements is to assist in decision-making. The Accounting Principles Board of America states the following objectives of financial statements :

(i) To provide reliable financial information about economic resources and obligations of a business concern,

(ii) To provide other needed information about changes in such economic resources and obligations.

(iii) To provide reliable information about changes in net resources arising out of business activities.

(iv) To provide financial information that assists in estimating the earning potentials of business,

(v) To disclose, to the extent possible, other information related to the financial statements that is relevant to the needs of the users of these statements.

The Importance : The financial statements are mirror which reflects the financial position and operating strength or weaknesses of the concern. The information given in financial statement is very useful to a number of parties. These are the following :

Owners : The owners provide funds for the operation of a business and they want to know whether their funds are being properly utilized or not. The financial statements prepared from time to time satisfy their curiosity.

Management : Management is the art of getting things done through others. This requires that the subordinates are doing work properly. Financial statements are an aid in this respect because they serve the manager in appraising the performance of the subordinates. Actual results achieved by the employees can be measured against the budgeted performance they were expected to achieve and remedial action can be taken if the performance is not up to the mark.

Further, the financial statements are useful for assessing the efficiency for different cost centres. The management is able to exercise cost control through these statements. The efficient and inefficient spots are brought to the notice of the management. The management is able to decide the course of action to be adopted in future with the help of financial statements.

Creditors : Creditors want to know the financial position of a concern before giving loans or granting credit. The financial statements help them in judging such position. The trade creditors are paid in a short period. This liability is paid out of current assets. Hence, they will be interested in current solvency position of the enterprise. The calculation of current ratio and liquid ratio will enable the creditors to assess the current financial position of the concern in relation to their debts and these ratios are calculated with the help of financial statement.

Investors : There are two types of investors — short-term and long-term investors. They are interested in the security of the principal amount of loan and regular interest payment by the concern. The investors will study the long-term solvency of the concern with the help of financial statements. The investors will not only analyse the present financial position but will also study future prospects and expansion plans of the concern. The possibility of paying back the amount of loan in the case of liquidation of the concern is also taken into consideration.

Prospective investors, who want to invest money in an enterprise, would like to make analysis of the financial statements of that enterprise to know how safe the proposed investment will be.

Employees : Employees are interested in the financial position of a concern they serve, particularly when payment of bonus depends upon the size of the profits earned. They would like to know that the bonus being paid to them is correct or not; so they become interested in the preparation of correct Profit and Loss Account. Generally these works are done through trade associations.

Government : Central and state governments are interested in the financial statements because they reflect the earnings of the business for a particular period for the purpose of taxation. Moreover, these financial statements are used for compiling data concerning business which, in turn, help in compiling national accounts. These statements enable the government to find out whether business is following various rules and regulations or not. These statements also become a base for framing and amending various laws for the regulation of business.

Bankers : The banker is interested to see that the amount of loan is secured and the customer is also able to pay the interest regularly. The banker will analyse the balance sheet to determine financial position of the concern and profit and loss account will also be studied to find out the earning position. A banker has a large number of customers and it is not possible to supervise their business activities. It is through the financial statements that a banker can keep a watch on the business plans and performance of its customers. These statements also help the banker to determine the amount of securities it will ask from the customers as a cover for the loan.

Stock Exchange : The stock exchange deals in purchase and sale of securities of different companies. The financial statements enable the stock broker to judge the financial position of different concerns. The fixation of prices for securities, etc. is also based on these statements.

Research Scholars : The financial statements being a minor of the financial position of the concern, are of immense value to the research scholars who want to make a study into financial operations of a particular concern.

Consumers : Consumers are interested in the establishment of good accounting control so that cost of production may be reduced with the resultant reduction of the prices of the goods they buy.

Limitations : There is great importance of financial statements for the concern, but they do not present a final picture of the concern. Their utility depends upon a number of factors. The analysis and interpretation of these statements should be done very carefully otherwise misleading conclusions may be drawn.

Following are the main limitations of financial statements :

Only Interim Reports are Provided : Financial statements do not give a final picture of the concern. The actual position of the business can only be determined when it is sold or liquidated, however, the statements have to be prepared for different accounting periods, generally one year, during the life time of the concern. The allocation of expenses and revenues depend upon the personal judgement of the accountant. The existence of contingent assets and liabilities also makes the statement improvise. Thus, financial statements do not give the final picture and they are at the most interim reports.

Lack of Precision : Financial statements may not be realistic because these are prepared on the basis of certain basic concepts and conventions. For example, going concern gives us an idea that business will continue and assets are to be recorded at cost but the book value at which the asset is shown may not be actually realisable. Similarly, by adopting the principle of conservatism the financial statements will not reflect the true position of the business.

Records only Monetary Facts : Financial statements disclose only monetary facts, *i.e.*, those transactions are recorded in the books of accounts which can be measured in monetary terms. Those transactions which cannot be measured in monetary terms such as, quality of production manager, conflict between production manager and marketing manager, etc. may be very important for a business concern but not recorded in the business book.

Historical in Nature: These statements are prepared after the actual happening of the events. They attempt to present a view of the past performance and have nothing to do with the accounting for the future. Modern management is forward working but these statements do not directly help them in making future estimates and taking decisions for the future.

Inadequate Information : There are many parties who arc interested in the information given in the financial statements but their objectives and requirements differ. The financial statements as prepared under the provisions of the Companies Act, 1956, fail to meet the needs of all. These are mainly prepared to safeguard the interests of shareholders.

Scope of Manipulation : These statements are sometimes prepared according to the needs of the situation or the whims of the management. A highly efficient concern may conceal its real profitability by disclosing loss or minimum profit whereas an inefficient concern may declare dividend by wrongly showing profit in the profit and loss account. For this over or under valuation of inventory, over or under charge of depreciation, excessive or inadequate provision for anticipated losses and oilier such manipulations may be resorted to. Window dressing may also be resorted to in order to show better financial position of a concern than its real position.

Lack of Objective Judgement : Financial statements are influenced by the personal judgement of the accountant. He may select any method for depreciation,valuation of stock, amortisation of fixed assets and goodwill, and treatment of deferred revenue expenditure. Such judgement if based on integrity and competency of the accountant will definitely affect the preparation of the financial statements.

Artificial View : These statements do not give a real and correct report about the worth of the assets and their loss of value as these are shown on historical cost basis. Thus, these statements provide artificial view as market or replacement value and the effect of the changes in the price level are completely ignored.

Types of Financial Statements : Financial statements primarily include two basic statements :

(i) the income statement or the profit and loss account and

(ii) the position statement or the balance sheet.

However, Generally Accepted Accounting Principles (GAAP) specify that a complete set of financial statements must include :

(i) An Income statement

(ii) A balance sheet

(iii) A statement of changes in owners account

(iv) A statement of changes in financial position.

Before we discuss the form and contents of those statements, let us briefly discuss the meaning and significance of each of these statements :

Profit and Loss Account

Trading concerns, whose financial activities are respected to purchases and sales of goods, prepare Trading and Profit and Loss account in order to ascertain their net income or net loss. In other words, Income statement is prepared to determine the operational position of the concern. It is a statement of revenues earned and the expenses incurred for earning that revenue. If there is excess of revenues over expenditure it will show a profit and if the expenditures are more than the income then there will be a loss. The income statement is prepared for a particular period, generally one year. When Income statement is prepared for the year ending 31st March, 2002 then all revenues and expenditures falling due in that year will be taken into account irrespective of their receipt or payment.

Manufacturing concerns require information regarding the cost of production also, so they prepare one more additional account, known as Manufacturing Account. In case of joint stock companies Profit and Loss Appropriation Account is also prepared to show the disposal of profit earned by the company corporation. All these statements constitute income statements.

The Profit and Loss Account may also be called by various names. There is a lack of uniformity in giving a common title to this statement. Ordinarily, any of the following titles may be used : (i) Statement of Profit and Loss (ii) Income Account (iii) Statement of Income (iv) Statement of Earning (v) Statement of Operations (vi) Statement of Income and Surplus (vii) Statement of Income, Profit and Loss (viii) Statement of Income and Expenditure

Definition : 1. According to *Faulke,* "The Income statement is the schedule that shows the Income and Expenditure of a business enterprise over a period of lime and then gives the final figure representing the account of Profit or Loss for the accounting period." 2. According to *John N. Myer,* "The Income statement summarises the operation of a business during a specific period of time and shows the result of such operation in the form of net income and loss."

The Importance : Income statement are prepared to achieve the following purposes :

(i) Ascertaining Cost of Production, Gross Profit/Gross Loss and Net Profit/Net Loss,

(ii) Ascertaining cost of goods sold and establishing its relationship with the sales.

(iii) Establishing relationship of direct expenses with the Gross Profit,

(iv) Ascertaining profitability of the business by establishing relationship of Gross Profit and Net Profit with sales

(v) Determining operating cost and ascertaining operational efficiency of the business by establishing relationship between operating costs and sales,

(vi) Comparing the actual performance of the business with the desired performance, discovering the weaknesses of the business.

Position Statement

Balance Sheet is one of the important statements depicting the financial position of the concern. It shows on the one hand the assets and properties and on the other hand the sources of those assets and properties. The balance sheet shows all the assets owned by the concern and all the liabilities and claims it owes to owners and outsiders. It is prepared oh a particular date. Normally there is no particular sequence for showing various assets and liabilities. The Companies Act, 1956 has prescribed a particular form for showing assets and liabilities in the balance sheet for companies registered under this Act. The companies are also required to give figures for the previous years along with current years figures.

Definitions : 1. According to *Tawe and Paula,* "Balance Sheet is that which describes it broadly as statement showing the financial position of a concern by means of debtors and creditors balance at a given date." 2. According *to A.N. Agrawala, "A* Balance Sheet is not an account but it is a statement of the assets and liabilities of a business at a particular date. A careful study interpretation and critical examination of the asset and liabilities of a company at a particular date gives good idea of its financial position on that date."

Special Features : Balance Sheet is the position statement which shows the position of assets and liabilities. It has got the following special features :

Balance Sheet is a Statement : Though balance sheet is an integral part of double entry system, but it is not an account. It has got the balances of certain ledger accounts. The balance of all ledger accounts are not shown in it.

Prepared on a Specified Date : Balance sheet is prepared on a specific date, *i.e.,* at the end of financial year (31st March). It is common practice and also legal requirement to prepare balance sheet together with Trading and Profit and Loss Account at the end of the accounting year. It may be prepared after every six months if the proprietor so desires. Accounting year may consist of calendar year or assessment year or its own accounting year. Companies are required to adopt assessment year (April, 1 to 31st March) as per legal requirement. Sole proprietorship and partnership can adopt accounting year which suits them.

It is a Statement of Assets and Liabilities : Though the balance sheet has debit and credit balance but its sides are named as assets and liabilities. The left hand side is a liability representing credit balance. Right hand side is assets representing debit balances.

Knowledge about the Nature of Assets and Liabilities : Balance sheet categorises assets as liquid assets, current assets, fixed assets and fictitious assets. Knowledge of liabilities as current liabilities, fixed liabilities and reserve and funds can be gained from balance sheet.

Knowledge of Financial Position: Balance sheet depicts true financial position of the business. The position can be ascertained by the study of the balance sheet. We can calculate short term and long-term financial ratios, proprietory and other ratios to have a knowledge of the financial standards of the business.

Assets and Liabilities Tally Each Other : The total of assets must be equal to liabilities. According to accounting equation, assets are always equal to liabilities. If the total of assets and liabilities are not equal, there is likely to be certain mistake.

The Importance : Balance sheet is a vital part of final account. It has to be compulsorily prepared as per legal provision. Objects of balance sheet have been summarised as under : (i) Main objects of balance sheet (ii) Subsidiary objects of balance sheet

Main Objects of Balance Sheet : The main object of balance sheet is to assess the financial position of the enterprise. It is the list of assets and liabilities of the enterprise on a specific date. The short-term and long-term financial position of the firm can be obtained from the analysis of the balance sheet. Keeping in view this fact it is said that balance sheet is a mirror reflecting the true value of assets and liabilities on a particular date.

Subsidiary Objects of Balance Sheet : The preparation of balance sheet has the following subsidiary objects :

Knowledge of Proprietory Ratio: Balance sheet provides requisite information to ascertain proprietor's funds and the capital employed by him. Capital, reserves, retained earnings and accumulated profits form proprietor's fund. Proprietor's claim against business is said to be proprietor's fund. Proprietory ratio shows the relationship between proprietor's funds and total assets.

Protection Against Possible Losses : The balance sheet throws light on the current liability and current assets. The ideal ratio between current assets and current liabilities is 2 : 1. If it is lesser than that the short-term financial position of the firm cannot be said to be healthy. In such case, firm will adopt suitable measures to protect itself from possible misfortune.

Calculation of Financial Ratios : Balance Sheet provides sufficient information for calculation of short-term and long-term financial ratios. These ratios indicate the present and prospective financial position of the firm.

Calculation of Working Capital : Working capital is the excess of current assets over current liabilities. Information regarding current assets and current liabilities is available from the Balance Sheet. Working capital should be sufficient to meet relative requirement of the business.

Ascertaining Funds from Operation : Balance sheet helps in ascertaining the funds from operation. It shows the operational efficiency of the firm.

Knowledge Regarding Sources and Application of Funds : Balance Sheet helps in ascertaining sources from where additional funds have been obtained and where they have been applied. For this purpose funds flow statement is prepared. The total of inflow and outflow of funds is always equal.

Retained Earnings

The term 'Owners Equity" refers to the claims of the owners of the business (shareholders) against the assets of the firm. It consists of two elements—(i) Paid-up share capital and (ii) retained earnings. A statement of retained earnings is also known as Profit and Loss Appropriation Account. As the name suggests it shows appropriation of earnings. Under this statement, the previous year's balance is first brought forward. The net profit during the current year is added to this balance. On the debit side, appropriation like interim dividend paid, proposed dividend on Preference & Equity Share Capital, amounts transferred to debenture redemption funds, general reserve, etc. are shown. The balance in this account will show the amount of profit retained in hand and carried forward. The appropriations cannot be more than the profits, so this account will not have a debit balance. There cannot be appropriation without profits.

Statement of Changes in Financial Position **:** The basic financial statements, such as the Balance Sheet and Profit and Loss Account a business reveal the net effect of the various transactions on the operational and financial position of the company. But there are many transactions that do not operate through Profit and Loss Account. Thus, for a better understanding another statement called statement of changes in financial position has to be prepared to show the changes in assets and liabilities from the end of one period to the another point of time. The objective of this statement is to show the movement of funds (working capital) during a particular period. The statement of changes in financial position may take the form of fund flow statement or cash flow statement.

Form and Contents of Profit and Loss Account **:** The Profit and Loss Accpunt or Income statement is prepared according to the nature of business. A trading concern will prepare Trading and Profit ami Loss Account for finding out Gross Profit and Net Profit respectively. In case of Sole Proprietory and Partnership concerns there are no prescribed forms for income statement. The preparation of this statement is not compulsory but desirable. In case of Joint Stock Company the preparation of Income Statement for every financial year is compulsory. Though Companies Act does not prescribe any form for Income Statement. The Profit and Loss Account, like balance sheet, can be prepared cither in 'T' form or Account form or in statement form. From the point of view of analysis and interpretation, the statement form is always preferred. Again, the Profit and Loss Account in the statement form can be prepared in two ways :

Single-step Income Statement **:** Under this method all expenses (operating or non-operating) are substracted from all revenues (operating and non-operating) and the balance so obtained is net income. Under this method items of revenues and expenses are not grouped into distinct heads or sub-heads.

Multi-step Income Statement **:** Under this method sales minus returns and cost of goods sold ajre considered first, which gives Gross Profit. Secondly all operating expenses are substracted from

Gross Profit and the balance is known as operating profit. Thirdly, all non-operating incomes are added in all, non-operatiag expenses are subtracted and thus, Profit before tax is obtained which is known as Net Profit. Lastly, provision for tax is deducted from net profit and the balance, is known as Net Profit after tax. Thereafter, dividend on preference and equity shares, transfer to general reserves, etc. are deducted from net profit after tax and thus we get retained surplus.

Explanation of the Contents Used in Profit and Loss Account

Cost of Goods Sold : It is also known as cost of sales. It represents the costs incurred in manufacturing or purchasing the goods that have been sold to customers. The method of determining the cost of goods, sold differs from concern to concern depending upon the nature of the business in which the concern is engaged:

Determination of cost of goods sold in respect of a Trading Concern :

	Rs.
Opening Stock of Finished goods	—
+ Purchases *less* returns	—
+ Carriage on purchases	—
- Closing stock of finished goods Cost of Goods Sold	—

Determination of cost of goods sold in respect of a manufacturing concern :

		Rs.
Raw Materials		—
Wages	—	
	Prime Cost	—
Factory Overhead	=	
	Works Cost	—
Office Overhead	—	
	Cost of Production	—
+ Opening Stock of Finished Goods	—	
- Closing Stock of Finished Goods		
	Cost of Goods Sold	

Cost of goods sold may also be ascertained with the following formula :

Cost of goods sold = Sales - Gross Profit

Sometimes, the amount of gross profit is not given, instead its percentage to sales is known in that case :

$$\text{Cost of Goods Sold} = \text{Sales} - \frac{(\text{Sales} \times \text{G.P. \%})}{100}$$

Operating Expenses : Operating expenses are those, which are directly related with the business operation. Administrative Expenses, Finance Expenses, Selling and Distribution Expenses are the example of Operating Expenses. When operating expenses are deducted from Gross Profit, we get operating profit. Thus, the amount of operating expenses may also be ascertained by the following equation :

Operating Expenses = Gross Profit - Operating Profit

OR

Operating Expenses = Gross Profit + Operating Loss

Net Operating Profit : This is ascertained by deducting operating expenses from gross profit. This is an important item of Profit and Loss Account for the purpose of management planning and control, because it does not consider those activities and their results which are hot related to the main operations of the concern. This may be ascertained with the help of following equations :

Net Operating Profit = Sales - Cost of Sales - Operating Exp.

OR

Net Operating Profit == Gross Profit - Operating Exp.

Form of Profit and Loss Appropriation

Account (a) T 'Form'(*For the year ending 31st March*)

	Rs.		Rs.
To Transfer to General Reserve	—	By Balance b/d	—
To Transfer to Sinking Fund	—	(Balance of Profit	
To Interim Dividend	—	from Previous Year)	
To Proposed Dividend	—	By Net Profit	—
To Balance c/d	—	(For the current year)	
(Retained Surplus)	—-		—
	—		—

Form and Contents of Balance Sheet : Traditionally, a Balance Sheet is prepared by diving it into two parts. Assets are shown on the right hand side and Liabilities and owners' Fund are shown on the left hand side of the Balance Sheet. Just an opposite practice is followed in America. This form of Balance Sheet is called 'Account type' or' T' Form Balance Sheet. This form of Balance Sheet has been recognised by the law in India. However, emphasis has recently been laid down on the 'statement form' of the balance sheet in place of'T' form of balance sheet by the accountants for the purpose of its analysis and interpretation. This statement form of Balance Sheet is also known as 'Single Column Balance Sheet'.

Balance Sheet is a statement showing the total values of assets owned and total liabilities owed by a company on a particular date. Section 211 of the Companies Act provides that the Balance Sheet shall give a true and fair' view of the slate of affairs of the company as at the end of the financial year (31st March) and shall be in the prescribed form set out in Part I of Schedule VI or as near thereto as circumstances admit. Schedule VI prescribes two alternative formats of Balance Sheet namely Horizontal and Vertical Form. A company is free to select cither of the form.

Horizontal Form of Balance Sheet : Horizontal form of Balance Sheet is an orthodox method of Balance Sheet. It is 'T' shaped. It has two sides—the assets being stated on the right hand side and liabilities on the left hand side. All assets and liabilities are classified into homogeneous categories in order of permanence.

Vertical Form of Balance Sheet :Vertical form of Balance Sheet is a modern practice. It is a single column Balance Sheet divided into two sections. The first section shows the sources of funds like share capital reserves and surplus, secured loans and unsecured loans. The second section consists of application of funds in the form of Fixed assets, investments, net current assets (current assets less current liabilities). It is an improvement over the horizontal form because it highlights the manner in which the funds employed by a company are represented by the assets of the company. The relationship between the different components of the Balance Sheet can be easily understood even by a layman.

Explanation of Balance Sheet Items

Liability Side

Share Capital : The heading 'share capital' should disclose authorised, issued and subscribed share capital stating the number and the nominal value "of the shares.

If preference shares have been issued, share capital will also disclose the relevant information. Calls-in-arrear, is to be shown as a deduction from the called up amount; the amount due from directors is to be stated separately. Calls-in-advance is to be shown as a separate item. Forfeited share account must be shown as an addition to subscribed capital. Shares allotted for consideration other than cash, *e.g.* shares issued to vendors and shares issued as bonus shares, must be separately stated.

Reserves and Surplus : Under this heading all those reserves which have been created out of undistributed profits are shown. Here these items will be shown separately :

(i) Capital Reserve

(ii) Capital Redemption Reserve

(iii) Securities (shares) Premium

(iv) Sinking Fund

(v) Other Reserves

(vi) Balance of Profit and Loss Account (Cr.)

Secured Loads : Secured loans are the loans which are secured against tangible assets. Debentures are always secured either on fixed charge or floating charge. Loans from banks, subsidiaries etc. are also shown under this heading, if they are secured. Interest accrued and due on secured loans is also shown under this heading.

Unsecured Loans : Unsecured loans do not carry any charge on the assets and include fixed deposits and loans and advances from bank etc. Unsecured loans are classified into short-term loans and advances and other loans and advances. Short-term loans and advances are the loans and advances which become due for payment within one year from the date of Balance Sheet.

Current Liabilities and Provisions : This heading has two sub-headings :

Current Liabilities : (Current liabilities include sundry creditors, bills payable, advance payments, unclaimed dividends and acceptances, etc.

Provisions : Provisions include provision for taxation, proposed dividend, provision for contingencies etc. Provision for depreciation and provision for doubtful debts may be shown as deductions from the amounts of concerned assets.

Contingent Liabilities : A contingent liability is a liability which comes into existence on the happening of an uncertain event. For example, liability on account of bills discounted with the bank is a contingent liability. If contingent liabilities are not provided for in the books, they will appear below the balance sheet by way of foot notes under the heading contingent liabilities. It includes the following :

(i) Claim against the company not acknowledged as debts.

(ii) Uncalled liability on shares partly paid.

(iii) Arrears of fixed cumulative dividends.

(iv) Estimated amount of contracts remaining to be executed on capital account and not provided for.

(v) Other moneys for which the company is contingently liable.

Items of Assets Side of the Balance Sheet

Fixed Assets : Fixed assets are the assets which are acquired and hold permanently in the business and are not meant for resale. Fixed assets are presented in the order of permanence. Goodwill is written at the top followed by other intangible and tangible assets. The original cost and the addition thereto and deductions therefrom during the year and the total depreciation written off upto the end of the year are to be stated.

Investments : The statement of investments is annexed with the balance sheet. The statement should classify trade investments and other investments. Trade investments, are made for the purpose of trade. Investment can also be classified as short-term and long-term investments. The nature of investments and their mode of valuation should also be revealed.

Current Assets : According to *Alexander wall,* "Current assets are such assets as in the ordinary and natural course of business move onward through the various processes of production, distribution and payment of goods until they become cash or its equivalent by which debts may be readily and immediately paid." Current assets are either cash in hand and at Bank or shortly convertible into cash like debtors and bills receivable are one step away from cash. The stock-in-trade is considered to be two steps away from cash because first sales will be made and then collection will be undertaken. The commonly used method for the valuation of stock is, cost price or market price whichever is less. This is do not avoid losses, if there is a fall in the prices of stocks. The debtors are shown after making a provision for bad and doubtful debts. The debtors, if more than six months old, are separately shown. The amounts owed by directors, etc. if included in debtors, are separately mentioned.

Loans and Advances : Loans and advances are classified on the basis of security, age and readability. Other relevant details should also be given in the balance sheet.

Miscellaneous Expenditure : This heading includes the items of certain expenditures to the extent not written of or adjusted. Miscellaneous expenditures are generally deferred revenue expenditure like preliminary expenses, discount on issue of shares or debentures etc.

Profit and Loss Account : The debit balance of Profit and Loss Account is shown on the assets side of Balance Sheet because it has to be written off gradually.

Some Important 'Terms' Used in the Analysis and Based on Division of Balance Sheet

Liquid Assets or Quick Assets : Liquid assets are those assets which may be converted into cash as and when desired or required without any material capital loss. As discussed earlier, all current assets are expected to be converted into cash within the normal operating cycle of the business. Excluding stocks and prepaid expenses all other current assets are likely to be converted into cash as and When required and desired without any loss. Hence all current assets minus stocks and prepaid expenses are said to have an element of liquidity and, therefore, they are known as liquid or quick assets, with the help of accounting equation liquid asset can be ascertained as follows:

Liquid Assets = Current assets - Stock of all types and prepaid expenses

Working Capital/Net Current Assets : This is an important term for the purpose of analysis. From the accounting point of view, excess of current assets over current liabilities is known as working capital. Since capital employed is equal to fixed assets plus current assets minus current liabilities, hence, working capital is also equal to capital employed minus fixed assets. We can put it in an equation form as follows :

Working Capital = Current Assets - Current Liabilities

OR

Working Capital = Capital Employed - Fixed Assets

Capital Employed : The concept of capital employed is used in many senses serving in each case different purposes. Following are the different concepts of capital employed :

Gross Capital Employed : Gross capital employed is also known as total resources, which is equal to total actual assets of a concern.

Net Capital Employed : Net capital employed is equal to total real assets minus current liabilities. Alternatively, Fixed Assets + Working capital is equal to capital employed. We can express in equation form as follows :

Capital Employed = Total real assets - Current Liabilities

OR

Capital Employed = Fixed Assets + Current Assets - Current Liabilities

OR

Capital Employed = Fixed Assets + Working Capital

Proprietor's Net Capital Employed : It is also known as net worth, owners equity, shareholders' funds. It is equal to total assets minus total liabilities.

Average Stock or Average Inventory : If opening slock plus closing slock is divided by two then we get average stock. But, if opening stock is not given then, value of closing stock is considered as average stock.

10

Linear Programming

Linear programming is a mathematical technique to optimise the allocation of scarce resources. Most ol the management decisions are essentially resource allocation decisions. In these problems, management is faced with a situation, that involves allocating labour, material, capital etc. in such a way that will maximise profit or minimise costs. Linear programming is a technique for solving problems of this type. A linear programming model can be constructed and solved to determine the best course cf action within the restrictions or constraints that exist. The linear programming model consists of:

(a)an objective function, and

(b)certain constraints.

The Requirements

Linear programming can be used to solve the problems which have the following characteristics:

(a) The problem can be stated in numeric terms.

(b) All factors given have linear relationship, *le.,* if one unit requires 5 man- hours, 2 units require 10 man-hours, and so on.

This is called additive assumption. Every relationship must be linear or every relationship should be able to be linearly approximated.

(c) Problem must involve choice among the alternatives.

(d) There must be restrictions or constraints on the factors involved. There may be restrictions on the availability of resources. For example, it may be given that there are only 3,000 machine hours available in a week. Constraint may relate to a particular characteristics. For example, a fertilizer mix may contain a minimum of 15% phosphate and 25% nitrogen.

(e) Linear programming approach is based on divisibility assumption. It is the assumption that the total" resources required are directly proportional to the volume of output (or other activity). If one unit of Product P needs 2 labour hours and earns contribution of Rs. 6 and one unit of 0 needs 3 hours and earns a contribution of Rs. 8, then 12 unitsof Pand 5 units of ©in total will need (12 x 2 hrs) + (5x3 hrs) = 39 labour- hours and will earn a contribution amounting to (12 x Rs. 6) + (5 x Rs. 8) = Rs. 112. This divisibility assumption of'direct proportions' explains the meaning of linear' in the title 'linear programming.

Aims and Objectives

Every linear programming model must have an objective function. This is quantified statement of what the best results are or what the best advantage is, which is being aimed for as the objective of the resource allocation decision. Following points should be kept in mind:

(i) The objective function will be either:

(a) to maximise a value *(i.e.,* contribution and profit), or

(b) to minimise a value *(i.e.,* costs)

(ii) The objective function is expressed in terms of the 'decision variables' in the model. Suppose a company makes three products*X, Yand* Zand wishes to maximise the contribution, the objective function will be expressed in terms of quantities of X, *Yand* Zthat are made and sold. If the contribution of X, *Yand* Zare Rs. 5, Rs. 4 and Rs. 3 respectively, the objective function will be to maximise 5X+ 4Y+ 3Z, where X, *Yand* Z are the decision variables, *i.e.*, the quantity of each product, that should be made and sold.

(iii) The contribution or cost of items are directly proportional to the level of activity. It, therefore, follows that the objective function can always be stated as:

maximise (or minimise) $a_1 x_{1,+} a_2 x_2 + a_3 x_3 + \ldots a_n x_n$ where x_1, x_3, x_3............ x_n are the decision variables a_1, a_2, a_3, ... a_n are the constant for each variable *(le.,* contribution per unit of product or cost per item).

The Constraints : A constraint is simply an algebraic statement of the limits of a resource or input. Since the resources are scarce, there are limitations on what can be achieved. For example, if material and machines are in restricted supply, output will be limited by the availability of these resources. In a linear programming model, these restrictions are a set of conditions, which the optimal solution must satisfy and these are known as constraints.

(i) It should be possible to express the constraints mathematically. For this purpose, it is essential to understand the meaning of certain mathematical signs.

(a) the expression $a > b$ means a is greater than or equal to b.

(b) the expression $a < b$ means a is less than or equal to b.

(ii) There are three basic types of constraints:

(a) $a_1 x_1 + a_2 x_2, \ldots a_n x_n < b_1$

(b) $b_1 x_{1\,+}\, b_2 x_2 \ldots b_n x_n \geq b_2$

(c) $y_1 x_1 + y_2 x_2 \ldots y_n x_n = b_3$

The third type of constraint is equality constraint. It is rare, while types (a) and (b) constraints are common.

(iii) This can be explained by an example. Suppose a company makes 3 products X, *Yand* Z, which require 2 hours, 5 hours and 1½ hours of machine tfme respectively on tne same type oi machine, which has been imported from U.K.' recently. The capacity of machine in the next month will be restricted to 400 hours. The company is committed to supply one particular customer with atleast 50 units in total of X and although customer will accept any combination of X and F in this total order. Now, the problem of management is to decide how many units of X *Yand* Z should be made next month. There are two conditions, which must be satisfied. These relate to machine hour capacity and sales order.

If x = the number of units of Xto be made,

y = the number of units of *Yto* be made, and

z = the number of units of Z to be made;

the constraint could be written as follows:

$2x+ 5y+ 1.5z < 400$ (machine-hour)

$x + y > 50$ (sales order)

Non-negativity Constraint : The variables in linear programming model should be non-negative in value, *i.e.,* 0 or a positive value. Therefore, additional constraint in the above example will be:

$x>0; y\geq0; z\geq0$

One should not forget this constraint in formulating a linear programming problem.

Considerations of Constant Factors Like 'Fixed Costs' in the LP Formulations : LP is concerned with changes in costs and revenues. Therefore, such factors as fixed costs, which would be unchanged over the range of output being considered should not be considered in the LP Formulating. To eliminate the effect of fixed costs and to maintain linear relationships it <s usual to use

contribution *(le.* sales less marginal cost) rather than profit in the objective functions.

The Formulation

Two points should be. remembered:

(i) Framework of linear programming problem is to optimise (maximise or minimise) an objective function, subject to a set of conditions or constraints. Variables whose quantity or value are to be found by solving a linear programming problem are called decision variables. The first step is to identify and express objective function in the linear programming format.

(ii) Identify the constraint and express them as:

$a_1x_1+a_2x_2+...+a_nx_n \leq C_1$

$b_1x_1+b_2x_2+...+b_nx_n \geq C_2$

This format has been discussed already.

A linear programming problem can be solved by any of the following methods: (i) Graphical Method, and (ii) Simplex Method.

When the problem has been expressed in standard format, it can be solved by either of the two methods. If there are only TWO unknowns on decision variable, then the problem can be solved by graphical methods. If there are *THREE* or more unknown variables, then the usual solution technique is the simplex method. Both these methods are dealt with in detail in the following discussions:

Graphical Method : This method is very simple and it should be employed wherever possible. Following are the important points relating to graphical method:

(i) It can be used only when there are two constraints (or unknowns).

(ii) Graphical method can deal with any number of limitations. Each limitation is expressed as a line on the graph paper. If there are a large number of lines, it may make the graph difficult to read. This is not a problem in examination question.

(iii) Both the maximising and minimising problems can be dealt with graphically.

(iv) This method can deal with following types of constraints:

(a) Greater than or equal to (>) type, and

(b) Less than or equal to (<) type.

(v) The areas of the graph represent the unknowns,

(vi) Each constraint is drawn as a straight line on the graph paper.

(vii) The area on the graph paper which does not contravene any of the constraints is known as the feasible region.

(viii) The solution point is always at a vertex of the constraints on the edge of the feasible region.

(ix) If a line is drawn representing the objective function, the solution point for maximising problem is the corner of the feasible region farthest to the right.

(x) If a line is drawn representing objective function, the solution point for minimising problem is the corresponding point farthest to the left of the feasible region.

(xi) When the solution point is found, the values of the decision variables can be read directly from the axes of the graph.

Summary : It involves: (i) formulating the linear programming problem, *i.e.*, expressing the objective function and constraints in the standardised format. (ii) Plotting the capacity constraints on graph paper. For this purpose normally two terminal points are required. This is done by presuming simultaneously that one of the constraint is zero. When constraint concerns only one factor, then line will have only one origin point and it will run parallel to the other axis. (iii) Identifying feasible region and coordinates of corner points. Mostly it is done by reading the graph, but a point can be identified by solving simultaneous equation relating to two lines which intersect to form a point on graph. (iv) Testing the corner point which gives maximum profit. For this purpose the coordinates relating to the corner point should put in objective function and the optimal point should be ascertained. (v) For decision-making purpose, sometimes, it is required to know whether optimal point leaves some resource unutilized. For this purpose value of coordinates at the optimal point should be put with constraint to find out which constraints are not fully utilized.

Shadow Prices : The dual price (or shadow price) of a resource, which is a limiting factor on production is the amount by which: (a) total contribution would fall, if company were deprived of one unit of the scarce resource and also, (b) total contribution would rise, if the company were able to obtain one extra unit of the scarce resource, provided that the resource remains an effective constraint on production and provided also that the extra unit of resource can be obtained at its normal variable cost.

The dual prices calculated on the assumption that there is a marginal increase or decrease in the availability of one scarce resource, but with the availability of other resources and demand constraint being held constant. The dual price or shadow price is used to carry out sensitivity analysis on the availability of a scarce resource, ie., on the constraints in the model).

Simplex Method : This method offers a means of solving the more complicated programming problems. This method was developed by *G.B. Dantzig.* It can be used with any number ol unknowns and any number of constraints. Following two points are important relating to Simplex Method:

(i) The computational routine is an iterative process. To iterate means repeat in working towards, the optimum solution. The computational routine is repeated over and over following a standard form. Successive solutions are developed in a systematic pattern until the best solution is reached.

(ii) Each new solution will yield as larger as or larger than the previous solution. This important feature assures us that we are moving close to the optimum solution. The main practical involvement of management accountants with LP is calculating contributions, establishing constraints, expressing the problem in the standardised manner and interpreting the result especially when computer has been used. Since this method involves lengthy and tedious calculations, computers are extensively used for simplex method. The simplex method can be used for both minimising and maximising problems.

The Application

Linear programming is being increasingly used in regard tojthe problems of allocation, assignment 'transportation' etc. The greatest "use of linear programming is in allocation of scarce resources for optimum utilisation. It is an important practical technique»with a wide variety of applications. Some of these applications are summarised below:

Production Planning and Product Mix Problems : *A* factory has a certain production capacity, certain processes to manufacture various products. It may have different types of products to manufacture under certain constraints. Different products may use different facilities in different measures. Different products may have different selling prices and stipulations on maximum and or minimum production levels. In this situation, there may also be a problem of devising a production schedule, that could satisfy future demands (seasonal and otherwise) for the firm's product and at the same time minimising production cost or maximisation of profit. Application of linear programming helps to develop right production schedule/product mix to maximise profit/ minimise cost, etc.

Blending Problems : Sometimes a product can be made from a variety of available materials of various compositions and prices. The problem constitutes of blending some of these materials to make a product, that conforms to laid down specifications. Supply of materials, prices of materials, and other specifications serve as constraints in obtaining the minimum cost material blend. The solution provides the number of units of each raw material to be blended to make one unit of product.

Diet Problems : Sometimes problem is to determine optimal quantities of different foods so that the daily vitamin requirements are met and simultaneously, the cost of buying the food is minimised. In this situation, minimum requirements of nutrients, availability of food and prices become the constraints. The problem constitutes minimising cost subject to given constraints.

Yim-loss Problem : In paper industry, paper of standard width has to be cut into smaller width as per customer requirements with the objective of minimising the waste produced. The use of |LP| immensely minimises the waste generated due to trim-loss. In this situation objective is to minimise waste, subject to demand requirements of rolls of different widths.

Distribution Problem : Sometimes problem constitutes of determining the distribution system, that will minimise the transportation cost from normal warehouses to various markets. For example, a company may have a number of bags of a particular food to be shipped to different warehouses. The demands of warehouses, supplies available at different factories become the constraints and in this situation LP model can be used to minimise cost.

Advertising Mix : Sometimes a media specialist plans to allocate the advertising expenditure in different media (say T.V., Radio, Magazine). The unit cost of message in different media may be different. Then there may be restrictions relating different media. For example, there may be such restrictions as appearance of a particular number of advertisements in a particular medium as effective audience relating to different media. The problem constitutes of finding optimum allocation of advertisements in different media to maximise total effective audience. LP model provides the optimum solution in a situation where an advertising company wishes to plan its advertising strategy in different media.

Manufacturing Problem : A manufacturing environment provides excellent ground for application of linear programming. The key decision is always to determine the number of units of different products to be manufactured to maximise profit subject to given constraints such as ratio in which the products are to be produced, maximum production of a particular product, demand relating to different products, etc. The constraints and even objective may change but manufacturing environment provides maximum situations for application of linear programming.

Assembling Problems : Sometimes an organisation faces the problem of selecting a best combination of basic components to produce such as per laid down specifications. A firm may use different assemblies of different types using different resources. In this situation also optimum solution (maximisation or profit/ optimum utilisation of capacity) is found out subject to given constraints, which may be different in different situations.

Investment Problems : An investor may often face a problem of investing in shares or debentures in order to maximise profit. The return from different modes of investments (Govt. securities, company deposits, equity shares, time deposits, national saving certificates, real estate) may be different. Risk factor relating to different investments may also be different. Time span relevant to different modes of investment may also be different. There may also be such considerations as risk factor may not be more than 4 or funds should not be locked-up for more than 15 years or 30% must be invested in real estate. In this situation, LP model is really helpful.

Agricultural Applications : In this situation also objective normally remains to maximise profit from allocation of activities or minimise cost. A farmer may have available land in which he may grow different crops such as corn, wheat or soyabeans. Each crop may require different man-days and farmer may also have limitations of money to be spent for preparation of land for a crop. Optimum solution is found out subject to laid down conditions after formulation of LP model.

Bibliography

Andriew, B. : *Cost Management*, Sherlock Publication, N.J., 2004.

Anderson, N. : *Work and Leisure*, Routledge and Kegan Faul, London, 1961.

Bhatia, A. K. : *Tourism Management and Marketing*, Sterling, New Delhi, 1997.

Bull, A. : *The Economics of Travel and Tourism*, Pitman, London, 1991.

Burkart, A.J. : *The Management of Tourism*, Heinemann, London, 1975.

Clare, Gunn : *Tourism Planning*, Taylor and Francis, New York, 1988.

Colley, G. : *International Tourism Today*, Lloyds Bank Review, London, 1967.

Crampon, L.T. : *An Analysis of Tourist Markets*, University of Colorado Press, Colorado, 1963.

Dale, E. : *Management Theory and Practice*, McGraw-Hill, New York, 1973.

Donald, E. Hawking : *Tourism Planning and Development Issues*, George Washington University, Washington, 1980.

_______, *Tourism Marketing and Management Issues*, George Washington University, Washington, 1980.

Engel, James F. : *Market Segmentation: Concepts and Applications*, Holt, Rinehart and Winston, New York, 1962.

Foster, D. : *Travel and Tourism Management,* MacMillan, London, 1985.

Inskeep, E. : *Tourism Planning,* Van Nostrand Reinhold, New York, 1991.

Jenkins, J. R. Zif, J.J. : *Planning the Advertising Campaign,* MacMillan, New York, 1973.

Katler, P. : *Introduction to Marketing Management, Analysis, Planning and Control*, Prentice-Hall, London, 1975.

Laws, E.C. : *Tourist Destination Management: Issues, Analysis and Policies,* Routledge, London, 1995.

Mathieson, A : *Tourism: Economic, Physical and Social Impacts,* Longman, London, 1982.

Ogilvie, F.W. : *The Tourist Movement: An Economic Study,* Staples Press, London, 1933.

Pigram, J. : *Outdoor Recreation and Resource Management,* Croom Helm, London, 1993.

Raymond, R. : *Ecological Principles for Economic Development,* John Wiley, London, 1978.

Richards, G. : *Tourism and the Economy,* University of Surrey, Surrey, 1972.

Schmoll, G.A. : *Tourism Promotion,* Tourism International Press, London, 1977.

Seth, P.N. : *Successful Tourism Planning and Management,* Cross Section Publications, New Delhi, 1978.

Tull, D. S. : *Marketing Research: Measurements and Methods,* Prentice-Hall, London, 1993.

Wahab, Salah : *Tourism Management,* Tourism International Press, London, 1975.

Zeithaml, V.A. : *Services Marketing,* McGraw-Hill, London, 1996.

Zoya Khan : *Cost Management in India*, Prime Publications, Pondicherry, 2003.